SAN FRANCISCO, YOU'RE HISTORY!

A Chronicle of the Politicians, Proselytizers, Paramours, and Performers
Who Helped Create California's Wildest City

To Roberta —
Kingston Pierce

J. KINGSTON PIERCE

SASQUATCH BOOKS
SEATTLE

Printed in the United States of America.

Cover design: Betty Watson
Interior design and composition: Lynne Faulk
Credits: **Front cover:** *far left:* suspension of the Bank of California, courtesy of the California State Library, Sacramento, California; *left:* Lillie Hitchcock Coit; *middle:* scene from a Portsmouth Square brothel during an 1865 earthquake, *California Police Gazette; right:* San Francisco opium den, from etching by Paul Frenzeny, *Harper's Weekly; far right:* Stock Broker's Row. **Back cover:** hook-and-ladder fire engine, Bancroft Library. **Interior:** *p. 1,* San Francisco opium den, courtesy of San Francisco Public Library; *p. 63,* Portsmouth Square, courtesy of San Francisco Public Library; *p. 111,* assasination of James King, courtesy of Bancroft Library; *p. 151,* the *City of Tokio; p. 187,* Cliff House, courtesy of San Francisco Public Library; *p. 227,* Joshua Norton, courtesy of San Francisco Public Library; *p. 261,* Lola Montez, courtesy of San Francisco Public Library.

Library of Congress Cataloging in Publication Data
Pierce, J. Kingston, 1957-
       San Francisco, you're history : a chronicle of the politicians, proselytizers, paramours, and performers who helped create California's wildest city / J. Kingston Pierce.
                 p.   cm.
          Includes bibliographical references and index.
          ISBN 1-57061-007-X
          1. San Francisco (Calif.) — History. 2. Celebrities — California — San Francisco — History.
I. Title.
F869.S357P54   1995
979.4'0099 — dc20
[B]   94-37903

Sasquatch Books
1008 Western Avenue
Seattle, Washington 98104
(206)467-4300

In Memory of My Mother,
Daphne Gwendolyn
Sprinkling Pierce

Even when I wasn't sure
that I could succeed as a writer,
she knew that I would.

If only she could know that
her dreams for me came true...

CONTENTS

CREDIT WHERE CREDIT IS DUE

Writers who claim exclusive responsibility for works of this size and scope are fooling themselves but hardly anybody else. My own list of debts begins with those owed to Herbert Asbury, whose exceptional 1933 book, *The Barbary Coast*, introduced me to the seamier side of San Francisco's heritage. If my writing here can stimulate the curiosity of just one young history enthusiast in the same way that Asbury's study sparked my curiosity many years ago, I would surely die a satisfied man.

A number of other people have given me advice on the writing of this volume or have encouraged me to pursue stories that I'd only been vaguely aware of when I began my researches. Special thanks go to Amy Rennert, editor of *San Francisco Focus* magazine, for her interest and support, and to those good folks at the San Francisco Public Library's local history room for their tireless pursuit of answers to my most esoteric questions. I am also indebted to Dick Pintarich, a criminally underappreciated Portland writer who helped teach me that popular history can be marketable; to Byron Rice, a former San Franciscan who served as my advisor on sports subjects; to June Franchebois, for correcting my early twentieth-century terminology; to Karl Petersen and Charles Smyth, who accepted the daunting task of getting me out of the office and onto the running track during my months of writing; and to Stephanie Irving, an old friend and my editor at Sasquatch Books, who fought to get this work published in a form close to what I had envisioned.

Finally, two members of my family deserve extraordinary gratitude because they put up with my long working hours and forgave me the self-indulgence that was necessary to complete this work. My daughter, Cassandra Pierce-Raglione, had to sit with me through many afternoons while I poured over microfilmed newspapers, and she only rarely complained. My wife Jodi—certainly my foremost fan—stuck with me through some rough and frustrating moments, and I owe her a lifetime's debt for her faith in my efforts.

"Nothing ever happened in the past, only in the present. The difference is it was somebody else's present, not ours." — David McCullough

PREFACE

Not long ago I heard a Republican candidate for governor of California tell an audience that he considered it his mission to restore the sanity and wholesomeness that have always been important aspects of this state's heritage. I was amazed. How could somebody who is charged with directing the thirty-first state know so little about its history as to suggest that "sanity and wholesomeness" are anything but recent virtues?

California's roots are, in fact, plagued with prostitution, mayhem, crooked politicos, assassinations, and a lot of good old-fashioned white-collar crime. Despite the continuing lunacy of rampant legal gun sales in our cities, you're probably safer here now than you would have been 100 years ago. That's especially true if you live in San Francisco. Los Angeles might have had its government perfidies, Portland may have the sin of shanghaiing in its past, and the carcasses of once-bustling brothels still skirt some Seattle streets. But San Francisco has all of those vivid vices in its annals, plus it lays title to vigilante killings, religious confidence games, Byzantine crimes of passion, and a diamond mine-salting scheme that ranks right up there with the world's most outrageous hoaxes.

Unlike other places, which matured ploddingly and with at least a modicum of plotting, San Francisco was thrust headlong into its future. Will Rogers was right when he called San Francisco "the city that was never a town." There was a here, here before most of the world even noticed. Or cared. Within a mere three years of its baptism as an American village, San Francisco was careening into an unsteady adolescence during the Gold Rush, and before another fifty years had passed, most of this place was a smoldering, stinking corpse awaiting rebirth and reentry into the race to catch up with its potential.

The idea that great advances could be made here in record time drew a cast of ambitious characters and ne'er-do-wells that can't be equaled in the history of any other town west of Denver. People such as scandalous "spider dancer" Lola Montez; professional stage robber and amateur poet Black Bart; and Joshua Norton, who after going banko in a rice-buying conspiracy, settled into twenty years of insanity as the self-proclaimed Emperor of North America and Protector of Mexico. This was where business monopolists like Charles Crocker and James

Flood made a money mountain out of Nob Hill. Where Andrew Hallidie introduced cable cars. Where a contentious Scottish landscaper named John McLaren made his career building Golden Gate Park and Samuel Clemens rode a jumping frog to international acclaim as "Mark Twain." This is where "urban guerilla" Patty Hearst made her stand; where gangster Al Capone served prison time for tax evasion; where one U.S. senator was gunned down in a duel and another was sued for bigamy—even though he wasn't married.

There's not room in this book to explore all of the city's heritage or the people who shaped it. So instead, I've followed the example given by a favorite Middle East history professor of mine from college (who reveled in tales about Egyptian King Farouk's backroom dalliances): I have told only what I consider some of "the best parts." This means that, while I've sought to bring many recognizable or forgotten individuals alive in these pages, I have limited my comments about others, such as stage rage Adah Isaacs Menken and jeans creator Levi Strauss, and some— notably tragic poet George Sterling, whoremaster Jerome Bassity, dancer Isadora Duncan, and "Sugar King" Claus Spreckels—will just have to wait for attention in a sequel volume.

Rather than arrange this entire book chronologically, I've broken it down into six sections, each covering a different type of story. Within each section, however, the tales are arranged in approximate order of when they happened. One other thing you'll note is that most of my accounts come from the period of 1849 to 1939. It was then that San Francisco firmly established its eccentric uniqueness. Little excitement happened here before the Gold Rush of 1849, and since the Second World War, there's been an homogenization of American metropolises that has had a sadly subduing effect even upon a lunatic place such as this one.

If the truth be told, I've fallen a bit in love with some of the characters in this book, folks like Lotta Crabtree, Lucky Baldwin, Belle Cora, Emperor Norton, and even bitter Ambrose Bierce. Those people made this city the bizarre, insane, and—yes, at times— unwholesome place that it has been. I've merely tried to record their escapades with a minimum of error.

To all those dead who gave this city its life, I say thanks.

—J. Kingston Pierce

THAT CHANGES EVERYTHING

"Of all the marvellous phases of the history of the Present, the growth of San Francisco is the one which will most tax the belief of the Future. Its parallel was never known, and shall never be beheld again."

—Bayard Taylor, journalist and Gold Rush observer

THE FUGITIVE BAY

UNNATURAL BEAUTY

Nearly 10,000 natives were living around San Francisco Bay when Franciscan missionaries arrived to begin their missionary work in the late 1700s. However, those natives tended to live anywhere except on the site of present-day San Francisco. While the Berkeley Hills were lush and the southern peninsula was well wooded, the northern end of the peninsula was windy, sandy, and rather bleak. In fact, there are more trees and probably a greater abundance of animal life in the city of San Francisco today than ever existed on this same land 200 years ago.

O nly by sailing in or out through the vigorous chop of the Golden Gate do you get a clear picture of just how narrow it is—a little over a mile wide, 335 feet deep at the center of the channel. You can't acquire this same sense by driving across the Golden Gate Bridge, for except in the densest of fog, that graceful span manages to add at least some visual breadth to the natural gorge. Photographs are equally notorious for dramatizing this waterway's width. No, you must ride the outflow of seven different rivers through this mighty gap in a mountain range if you are to understand how it was that two separate expeditions, representing two competing countries, could have navigated along the California coast in the middle of the 16th century and completely missed seeing the entrance to San Francisco Bay.

The first of these investigations was captained by Juan Rodriguez Cabrillo, a Portuguese explorer who had been with Hernando Cortés at the capture of Mexico City in 1521. Sailing under the Spanish flag in 1542, Cabrillo and his crew headed their ship, the *San Salvador*, north along the West Coast from Mexico. They hugged the shoreline as much as possible, naming geographical features as they went and presumably trying to match what they saw with what their maps told them they should see. (This might have been a very disorienting experience, since cartographers of that time often depicted California as an island.) The *San Salvador* is supposed to have gotten as far as what's now Point Arena, north of the Golden Gate, before being turned back by rough winds and cantankerous seas. During the return voyage, Cabrillo broke his arm— a wound that would ultimately prove fatal. Though the entrance to San Francisco Bay eluded him, he did discover the harbors at Monterey and San Diego before dying in 1543.

IT WASN'T UNTIL June of 1579 that another brace of European sails was spied off the northern California coast. The ship was the *Golden Hind*, and its commander an ambitious braggart and English filibuster named Francis Drake. He and his crew were coming off a successful campaign of sacking Spanish ports and plundering treasure from Spanish galleons along the west coast of South America. The *Hind*'s hold swelled with gold, and Drake was looking to get back to the Atlantic Ocean and home without losing any of it. That was easier said than done, however. Although Drake's crew was made up of square-rigger seamen who, as Joseph Conrad later put it, "gave back yell for yell to a westerly gale," any route home would severely test their stamina—and maybe also their skill with sword and cannon.

Heading south around Cape Horn, from whence they'd come, would mean braving the hazards of Tierra del Fuego, where Drake had already lost two ships in rough weather. It might also mean running a gauntlet of Spanish privateers hungry for revenge against the thieving Englishmen. The captain considered searching instead for the legendary Strait of Anian, otherwise known as the Northwest Passage, which was supposed to allow ship trade east and west across the breast of North America. But maps were maddeningly imprecise as to where this useful passage began (since, as any schoolkid now knows, it doesn't actually exist). And the farther north the *Hind* sailed, the colder it became, until the meat froze, ropes on the masts grew stiff, and Drake's breath turned to ice upon his dashing mustache.

In the end, Queen Elizabeth I's future champion chose his third alternative: To set off southwest across the Pacific, make for the East Indies, and then complete a circumnavigation of the globe similar to what Ferdinand Magellan had done more than half a century before. As such a maritime marathon promised to put tremendous strain on the

NOT A COMPLETE LOSS

After the death of the Portuguese explorer Juan Cabrillo, Bartolomé Ferrelo, the pilot of Cabrillo's ship, the San Salvador, *decided to take one more shot at the northern California coast. This time, the ship reached a spot near today's California-Oregon border. But again, as Cabrillo had before him, Ferrelo apparently sailed right by the Golden Gate twice without seeing it. His charts show, however, that the crew did observe the Farralones, an inhospitable chain of islands located only 32 miles out from Point Lobos—well within viewing distance of Marin County.*

Golden Hind, Captain Drake determined to first put in at some "convenient and fit harborough" along the coast where his flagship could be repaired, cleaned, and retallowed.

MORE THAN FOUR centuries have passed since Drake's round-the-world voyage, yet speculation as to precisely where the *Golden Hind* anchored in preparation for its Pacific sojourn is as lively now as it has ever been. Authorities seem to agree that landfall took place somewhere near latitude 38 degrees, in northern California, probably in present-day Marin or Sonoma counties. This is backed up by expedition records that describe the Native Americans encountered by the *Hind*'s crew—friendly "Indians" whose language and culture sound similar to those of the coastal Miwok people, who did roam Marin and Sonoma 400 years ago. But three different locations vie for recognition as the spot where Francis Drake left his bootprints on California soil: Drakes Estero, in Drakes Bay, about 25 miles north of San Francisco and in the lee of Point Reyes; Bolinas Lagoon, just off Bolinas Bay; and somewhere inside ample San Francisco Bay, perhaps at San Quentin Cove.

The vicinity of Drakes Bay probably holds the strongest claim. More than 800 artifacts from 16th-century European ships have been dug up there, including a variety of Chinese porcelain left over from the wreck of the Spanish *San Augustin* in 1595. The wind-ravaged white cliffs at Drakes Bay also seem to correspond with Captain Drake's musings about rock faces near his landing that reminded him of England's white cliffs of Dover. "Still," explained British maritime historian John Sugden, in his lively biography *Sir Francis Drake*, "nothing that can positively be linked to Drake has been unearthed" at Drakes Bay.

Most historians now dismiss claims that the *Golden Hind* actually sailed through the Golden Gate. Drake complained during his stopover here of overcast skies and cold mists that made it hard for him to measure the altitude of the sun and stars. This same fog probably hid the entrance to San Francisco Bay. If it hadn't, and the *Hind* had indeed cruised into the Bay, wouldn't it seem logical that the English would have explored it? They should have been excited at such a find, given both the size of this bight and the fact that they had been looking for an inlet leading to the elusive Strait of Anian. Yet accounts of Drake's California reconnaissance make the waters surrounding their anchorage sound much less interesting than the deer, ground squirrels, and native villages occupying the surrounding land.

FOR A FEW DECADES in the mid-20th century, though, it did seem that proof had finally been found of Drake's having discovered San Francisco Bay. In February 1937, a store clerk named Beryle Shinn came forward with a brass plaque that he had allegedly found on a ridge above Point San Quentin. It carried the date June 17, 1579, along with a proclamation describing how the land had been claimed "in the name of Herr Majesty Queen Elizabeth of England and Herr successors forever," and it was signed "Francis Drake." In the lower right-hand corner was a ragged hole that might have accommodated an Elizabethan sixpence. Shinn's find caused an immediate sensation in the historical community, because it was already known that, at the end of his six-week visit to the West Coast, Drake had claimed this part of California—which he christened "New Albion"—on behalf of imperial England. To prove his claim, the captain had posted a plate bearing his moniker, the date, and a sixpence coin showing "her highnesse picture and arms."

While many Drakeophiles decried Shinn's find as a sham, metallurgical tests seemed to support its authenticity. The California Historical Society was satisfied enough that it paid Shinn $3,500 for his artifact, and the question of where Francis Drake had come ashore in northern California seemed resolved—at least until another man, a

WHODUNIT?

Left unresolved by the revelation that Francis Drake's plaque was a hoax is the mystery of who created that fake. One theory asserts that British Captain George Vancouver, who visited this area in 1792, knew of Drake's fabled plaque and, disappointed that he himself did not find it, may have had his men create a substitute. Others believe the deception was perpetrated by a local history professor.

If you'd like to study the controversial artifact yourself, it's still on view in the waiting area just outside the reading room of the Bancroft Library, on Berkeley's University of California campus.

☞

THE MAPMAKER

The Golden Gate's first seafaring explorers arrived in August 1775 aboard the Spanish supply ship San Carlos, *under the command of Lieutenant Juan Manuel de Ayala. After anchoring at present-day Fort Point, Ayala—who had suffered an accidental gunshot wound to the foot some weeks earlier—sent two of his officers to explore the Bay's edges, while he gave names to many of the Bay's physical features, including Sausalito* (saucelito *means "little willow" in Spanish) and round-backed Angel Island (originally* La Isla de Nuestra Señora de los Angeles, *"the Island of Our Lady of the Angels"). He christened another island* La Isla de los

chauffeur named William Caldeira, proclaimed that *he* was the original finder of Drake's plaque. He said that he'd happened upon it in 1933 near Drakes Bay, had toted it around for some time, and after determining that it was really a worthless piece of junk, had pitched it a couple of miles from where Shinn picked it up.

Controversy over the plate's origin raged until 1977, when new handwriting and chemical analyses made questions about the plate's true discoverer insignificant. Scholars determined that the metal not only differed from other extant examples of 16th-century brass, but that it had been machine-rolled, rather than flattened and shaped by a hammer, as was the practice in Drake's era. The plaque was a forgery, "America's counterpart of the Piltdown Man," as Sugden put it, "a cunning hoax that outfoxed the experts of the day to be exposed by the technology of a later age."

FRANCIS DRAKE LEFT the California coast on July 23, 1579. Just over 14 months later, the *Golden Hind* crossed the English Channel and entered Plymouth Sound. In honor of his exploits, and despite protestations from the poor-sport Spanish, Queen Elizabeth knighted Drake. He would become the queen's foremost admiral and help defeat King Philip II of Spain's "Invincible Armada" in 1588, before dying in 1595.

But Sir Francis was never famous for encountering the Golden Gate or the future site of San Francisco. And it would have irked that partisan old sea dog no end to know that it took a contingent of the Spanish army, working its way north from Mexico and following the Golden Gate's cliffs inland, to discover San Francisco Bay in 1769.

FATHER OF
THE MOTHER LODE

It is one of the great ironies of American history that John Augustus Sutter, on whose property the California Gold Rush began in 1848, failed to become wealthy from the whole adventure. Other men walked away from Sutter's land with full purses and glossy new dreams. But Sutter, plagued by debts and fearing that the short-term rush for riches might doom a longer-term dream of building his namesake town in central California, chose not to participate in all the excitement. He was sure that his forbearance and single-mindedness would be rewarded. He was wrong.

Sutter was a fugitive from justice when he sailed into Yerba Buena Cove in July 1839. Far behind him, in Switzerland, were angry debtors, a domineering wife and five children, and police warrants that called for his immediate arrest.

He was born in 1803 at Kandern, a hamlet in southern Germany that sits about 13 miles north of Basel, Switzerland. After moving to Switzerland in his early twenties, he married (in a "shotgun wedding" held one day ahead of the birth of his first son) and entered into a promising dry goods and drapery enterprise. However, Sutter lived chronically beyond his means, splurging on clothes and handsomely bound books. When his business partner suddenly absconded one day with a substantial chunk of their inventory, Sutter's fiscal forecast grew particularly gloomy. For a time, he was willing to borrow money from his well-off mother-in-law, but that situation only depressed his ambitious wife and angered her mother.

In May 1834, Sutter decided he'd had enough. He fled west to France and eventually

Alcatraces, *or the Island of the Pelicans—although it's not the one you think it is. According to* Streets of San Francisco, *by Louis K. Loewenstein, Ayala's original Alcatraz is now Yerba Buena Island, through which the Bay Bridge tunnels at its western end. Fifty-one years later, an English sea captain who was mapping the Bay misapplied the Alcatraz name to that small rocky protuberance of land on which the infamous federal penitentiary now stands. Ayala hoisted sail out of the Bay once his crew's reconnoitering was done and returned to Baja California. But his map proved conclusively that Drakes Bay and San Francisco Bay were separate bodies of water.*

❧❧❧

THE ROYAL ROAD

Famous El Camino Real — *"The King's Highway, which eventually stretched from San Diego into northern California, with a "feeder" route from Mexico — had its beginnings in 1769. That's when Spanish King Charles III's ruthless Visitador General in New Spain (Mexico), José de Gálvez, worried by reports of Russian incursion along the coast, sent an expedition north into California to clear a primitive highway for use by the king's forces. On March 9, a party of 60 soldiers, Franciscan priests, and mostly Christianized Indians left Baja*

☞

to New York City, leaving his wife and family behind. That may not have been a gentlemanly thing to do, especially for one whom historian Hubert Howe Bancroft later called "an inborn gentleman." But as Richard Dillon pointed out in his superb Sutter biography, *Fool's Gold*, the so-called Father of California was always "a man of paradox—at once opportunist and philanthropist; one year largely a conniver, the next, an open-hearted host. He was a soldier of fortune but a picaresque one, his adventuring modified by a prudence which some call a lack of common courage. If a scoundrel at all, he was too lazy or busy to be a thorough-going one. . . . " Sutter was, in short, just the sort of imperfect but passionate individualist who gravitated toward northern California in the days immediately preceding the discovery of gold in the Sacramento Valley.

SUTTER HAD HEARD old Spanish tales of California being a land of profuse wealth, but he hadn't come to find treasure. "Gold digging is a lottery; among hundreds, maybe one or two get rich from it," he once said. "Most people prefer a safe investment; farming is the best of all." His idea was instead to found an agrarian colony in Mexican California that would be suitable for Swiss immigrants. Within a year of his arrival in the territory, he had applied for Mexican citizenship, negotiated for stock with Mexican cattle barons in the area—the so-called *Californios*—and had been granted close to 50,000 acres in two sections to the east of San Francisco, one along the Feather River and another at the intersection of the Sacramento and American rivers. He constructed an adobe fort on a high, flood-free breast of land overlooking the American River and began ringing that with other adobe structures—the nut of his colony, New Helvetia (New Switzerland). A road was cut from this fort to an embarcadero beside the deep Sacramento, and wheat was planted nearby. He set up Hock Farm, his own ranch-estate adjacent to the fort, and employed Indians and some Hawaiians (*Kanakas*) who had been among the passengers on board the ship Sutter rode into San Francisco Bay.

The aspiring grandee was appointed a captain in the local Mexican militia, and in his uniform, with his lengthy sideburns and neatly clipped mustache, he looked rather like the dashing Peruvian liberator Simon Bolívar. Sutter lived the high life, throwing banquets to celebrate his exalted position in valley life, taking mistresses from among his workers, and perhaps indulging a bit too enthusiastically in liquid intoxicants.

Outside of the fact that some of the area's wealthier *Californios* were starting to feel threatened by Sutter's colonial buildup, things seemed to be going along smoothly at New Helvetia.

By late 1847, Sutter's Fort and its community could boast of some 290 white inhabitants, mostly from the eastern United States. There were also the handful of *Kanakas* and about 450 Native Americans who cultivated New Helvetia's fields. A dozen cannon could be found at the fort. An inn, a granary, and other businesses had sprung up in the vicinity. San Francisco entrepreneur Samuel Brannan brought some of his fellow Mormons to the South Fork of the American River, and there they built a flour mill. New Helvetia was becoming a commercial nexus for the valley, and Sutter envisioned the growth of a larger town, which he liked to call Sutterville.

ONE OF THE MOST significant elements of Sutter's expanding baronry, however, was the sawmill that he had under construction on the South Fork, about 45 miles northeast of his fort in a valley occupied by the Indian village of Cullomah (later Coloma). Tall pine trees cut from the Sierra foothills would be processed into lumber at this mill, and then shipped to burgeoning San Francisco, for use in building homes and other structures. The money returned from this enterprise would further build both the profile and prestige of New Helvetia.

California for Monterey under the leadership of Gaspar de Portolá, the new governor of Spanish California. Not recognizing Monterey Bay, Portolá's troops kept marching north, until by late October, they'd reached present-day San Mateo County, about 15 miles south of the Golden Gate. Portolá, critically ill and depressed that he'd overshot his destination, decided to send his sergeant, José Francisco Ortega, ahead with a scouting party. In the first week of November, Ortega's men became the first known European land travelers to sight San Francisco Bay.

MORE EL CAMINO REAL

The expedition mounted by Captain Juan Bautista de Anza in 1775 did the most to extend El Camino Real from Mexico (New Spain) to what is now San Francisco Bay. In late 1775, he set out from the old Mexican town of Tubac, near present-day Tucson, Arizona, with over 200 Mexican pioneers. They reached Monterey 130 days later. De Anza, a few of his lieutenants, and a Franciscan priest, Father Pedro Font, pressed on still farther, arriving at the peninsula's very northern end (now Fort Point) on March 28, 1776. There de Anza planted a cross that he hoped would mark the site of a future presidio, or military outpost.

Work on the sawmill was well under way by New Year's Day of 1848. Foundations were in place, and a tailrace (to send the water that powered the mill wheel back into the river) was taking shape. James W. Marshall, a carpenter who was in charge of the project, had asked that this ditch be deepened. He was busy inspecting the results on the morning of January 24 when something caught his eye. It was "shining in the bottom of the ditch . . . ," he recalled later. "I reached my hand down and picked it up; it made my heart thump, for I was certain it was gold."

Marshall rushed back to Sutter's Fort, arriving in a downpour four days later, his white linen trousers caked with mud, his moccasins squishing water everywhere. Pigeoning the townmaker in his office, Marshall withdrew a rag from his pocket. Inside was a vial containing "what might have been an ounce and a half of gold dust—dust, flakes, and grains," explained Sutter. "The biggest piece was not as large as a pea, and it varied from that down to less than a pinhead in size." Though the find wasn't much physically, Sutter was convinced that it spelled disaster for his dreams, so he made Marshall swear not to tell anyone about the gold.

Sutter went out to Coloma to test for himself the veracity of Marshall's gold claims. Not only was he able to wash bits of the precious metal out of his raceway, but when he and Marshall journeyed upstream, they found even better "color." At the same time, the South Fork Mormons had happened upon traces of gold near their flour mill. They, too, abided by Sutter's prohibition against discussing the metal finds—at least for a while.

Why was Sutter so concerned that these hints of a gold strike be kept hush-hush? Because he believed the future of his commercial enterprises and his vision for Sutterville depended upon hard work. Easy wealth would be a tremendous distraction, one that could ruin his development plans. There was a part of Sutter that craved the fortune which might be panned out of the handsome Sierra foothills. But another part of him desperately wanted the glitter of gold to fade. Pronto.

It didn't fade, though. Almost every day following Marshall's original find, more gold was spotted in the American River. Sutter finally broke his own silence about the potential millions to be found on his land. It sounded too good to be true; previous tales of California gold had been inflated or completely bogus. But when newspapers started announcing "GOLD! GOLD!" men could restrain their greed no longer. Come the end of May 1848, perhaps 150 San Franciscans (out of a total population of 800 or so) had embarked east to the site of Sutter's Mill. They were joined by lucre hunters from all over California—including Sutter's own workers, who'd abandoned the mill to buy gold pans.

JOHN SUTTER HAD BEEN right to worry about the fate of his dreams in any rampage for riches. With most able-bodied males off at the "diggin's," there was hardly anybody left to build New Helvetia up into Sutterville. The poseur baron's debts mounted again—a painful reminder of what he'd gone through so many years before in Switzerland. Beyond selling some of his land, he had few means by which to keep his head above the rising tide of red ink. With law-enforcement types seriously outnumbered by gold-seeking "argonauts" in the Sacramento Valley, looting was common. Rustlers made off with Sutter's cattle and horses. Meanwhile, squatters took over large swaths of his property and told Sutter that they'd leave only under the duress of law. "The squatters are loose in my fields; all is squatted over," he lamented to a friend in 1853. "So long as it [his land claims] is not decided, I am in debt and cannot sell a foot of land at present. Our government did not act right with us Californians."

The old Swiss visionary sought to maintain his stature and influence. He ran for governor of California in 1849, but came in a poor third on election day. The U.S.

secretary of the interior offered Sutter the job of Indian sub-agent for the Sacramento Valley, but he declined, citing deteriorating health and being unhappy with the low wages that post promised. In 1850, 16 years after he left Europe, Sutter's family joined him in California. But his oldest son, John A. Sutter, Jr.—or "August," as he was called—also handed Sutter *père* one of his worst disappointments. Having begun to manage his father's business affairs, August was convinced by wily Sam Brannan that the high townsite of New Helvetia was inferior to something closer by the Sacramento River. If that wasn't bad enough, August also agreed that the town should be called Sacramento City, rather than Sutter's City—a painful thing to August's father, who once declared in his cups that "I strive to be honored. I will do anything for honor."

In the last years of his life, John Sutter tried to strike back at the injustices he felt had been dealt him. But the Sutter of the 1870s was not the Sutter of the 1840s. "The genial, expansive but unscrupulous Sutter of youth was transformed by relative prosperity and genuine prestige into a respectable and fairly honest man—and it proved his undoing," Dillon wrote. "When he acquired scruples and lost the need to live by the sharpness of his wits, he also lost his toughness of character."

Sutter did prosecute an intensive campaign in Congress to win $50,000 to redress the damage that thieves and trespassers had done to his domain. His cause even won endorsements from General William T. Sherman, who as a lieutenant in 1847 had been posted to Monterey (the capital of territorial California), where he'd met with Sutter on several occasions. "It was the common belief," Sherman wrote in support of Sutter, "that had it not been for your fort, and your herds of cattle, sheep, etc., the immigrants arriving in California during the years 1847, 8 and 9 would have suffered for food. It was owing to your efforts to develop the country, more especially in your building of the grist mill and the sawmill at Coloma, that the world was indebted for the discovery of the gold mines."

Lawmakers, however, were less accommodating with their purse strings than Sherman had been with his praise. The Sutter relief bill was tucked away in 1880 with no action taken. Weary of the fight, Sutter turned to the twin succubi of his decline—drink and despair—and before the next session of Congress could again consider his claim, he died.

PREJUDICE AND PRIDE

Slavery was a fact of life in California during its more than a century of loose Spanish administration. But after Mexico won independence from Spain in 1821, slavery was outlawed in both Mexico and Mexican California. Blacks from the Caribbean, Africa, and the spreading United States were invited to settle around the old Spanish coastal missions. However, not many accepted this invitation, and those blacks who did arrive in California—primarily escapees from ships captained by whites—usually retreated to the backcountry, where they could feel safe from retribution or incarceration.

ONE OF THE FEW men with a black heritage to remain in early San Francisco was William Alexander Leidesdorff, a mulatto ship's captain born in 1810 in the Danish West Indies (now the U.S. Virgin Islands) to a peripatetic Dane and a striking native woman. Young Leidesdorff was taken under the wing of a British planter, who sent him to work at a large cotton company in New Orleans with the advice that he should keep his mixed heritage (hidden by his fair skin) a secret.

DOLORES' DOLDRUMS

Although the original church at Mission Dolores has remained intact through the years, its history has been rocky. When, in the early 1800s, the Spanish empire began to founder and the Mexico revolution began, missions such as this one were cut off from the financial support they'd once enjoyed. On top of that, diseases such as measles decimated the flocks of Native American neophytes and weakened the Franciscans' influence over Alta California. Mexico's Secularization Act of 1834 finally stripped the

☞

Franciscan missions of their expansive real estate holdings and sent Mission Dolores into a tailspin. For a quarter century, the church was operated as a dance hall and drinking place, and fights between bulls and bears were sometimes staged on its grounds. In 1859 Mission Dolores was restored as a Catholic church. In 1952 Pope Pius XII came to San Francisco to dedicate the church as a basilica, an honorary church of the Holy Father himself. (Look around the altar for the partially opened umbrella of red and gold, as well as a papal coat of arms, both of which are the marks of a basilica.)

꧁꧂

He sailed around Cape Horn and through the Golden Gate in 1841, his pockets full of money he had made trading cotton throughout the Western Hemisphere. A stocky, rather vain gent with long, dark sideburns and a bushy mustache, Leidesdorff was well trained in both languages and commercial strategies. He quickly made contacts among the Mexicans, Europeans, and Americans who were also seeking to scratch a living from the sandy districts of Yerba Buena. Venturing initially into dry goods trading, he bartered groceries and hardware for potentially more valuable animal hides. From there, he expanded into real estate, buying up as much of the aborning town as he could afford and building one of its first local hotels, the City Hotel, a two-story adobe at the corner of Clay and Kearny streets. Leidesdorff also acquired a substantial warehouse and smaller wharf on what was then the waterfront (and is now the corner of California and Leidesdorff streets), and he erected a good-sized home for himself nearby. In 1847, he purchased a 37-foot, steam-driven side-wheeler that could carry people and supplies around the Bay or up the river to Sacramento.

His stature as a businessman invited Leidesdorff's entry into politics. He served on the town's first six-man municipal council and first school board, did a stint as city treasurer, and was named by President James Polk as vice-consul to the Mexican authorities at San Francisco. Always a rather lonely looking man, he became a fixture on the city streets, hobbling about with a cane, dressed in the brass-buttoned and gold-laced uniform that came with his consular role. But his influence was all too brief. He died of "brain fever" at the age of 38, in 1848.

"It is no injustice to the living, or unmeaning praise for the dead," remarked *The California Star*, "to say that the town has lost its most valuable resident . . . ." Despite his energetic enterprising and the fact that he'd become the town's principal landowner,

Leidesdorff left behind substantial debts—something between $50,000 and $60,000. He hadn't survived quite long enough to benefit from the inflation that accompanied the Gold Rush and pushed the value of his properties up to at least $1 million.

Of course, he also didn't suffer the racial prejudice that followed the 1848 annexation of California by the United States. The ensuing tide of bigotry would probably have denied Leidesdorff the successes and political clout that he won during his San Francisco years.

IN 1849, SAN FRANCISCANS agreed to deny blacks the right to vote in municipal elections or for delegates to California's first constitutional convention. Strenuous efforts by abolitionist speakers kept conventioneers from barring blacks entry into the state altogether, but laws restricting the rights of black Americans did make it onto the books. Not only were they disenfranchised from the democratic process, but blacks were forbidden to homestead here, to serve on juries, or to attend schools with white children. Until 1864, blacks weren't even permitted to ride on San Francisco streetcars. *The Annals of San Francisco*, written in 1854, makes a telling allusion to the status of blacks in the course of explaining anti-Chinese prejudice: "The Chinaman is looked upon by some as only a little superior to the negro, and by others as somewhat inferior . . . " And it certainly didn't help relations among black and white residents that the city's first major fire, in 1849, was blamed on an African-American man, who—in defiance of a rule that allowed blacks only one drink in a saloon, never two—demanded a second libation. For his trouble, the patron was stabbed, and as he toppled to the floor, he knocked over a lighted lantern.

While bigoted views were difficult to take, they didn't stop blacks from moving into the Bay Area. Many African-Americans came with the early Gold Rush hordes, most of them free men from the North and upper South, but some arrived with their Southern masters and later bought their freedom. They settled primarily in the six counties

HEARTBREAKER

The young William Leidesdorff was quite a hit during the time he lived in Louisiana, and it's said that he fell in love there with a golden-headed girl named Hortense, the descendant of distinguished French stock. The pair were scheduled to be married, but on their eve of their nuptials he confessed to her the facts of his parentage. His fiancée wept uncontrollably. She told Leidesdorff that she couldn't keep this story from her father, and that he would never

☞

surrounding the goldfields. Those who came instead to San Francisco were attracted by the high wages being paid to cooks, hotel porters, and other workers in the service trades. Of 459 citizens in 1847, there were only nine black men and one black woman. By 1852, the town's black population numbered 464; eight years later, it had grown to 1,176 in a city of 56,800 people. The majority lived north of Jackson Street and west of Montgomery, but over the years the black community spread west toward Larkin Street and out toward the Bay. It was a vital enclave, supported by its churches, driven by opposition to racism and by the wish to exercise a hand in California's political process. Black cultural organizations, libraries, and newspapers appeared in order to give San Francisco's African-American population hope.

ONE OF THE EARLY black newspapermen was a former Philadelphian named Mifflin Wistar Gibbs, who had relocated to San Francisco as a free black man in 1850. He was then 22 years old and a follower of abolitionist Frederick Douglass.

Gibbs had come to the West Coast looking for opportunity. Shortly after arriving at San Francisco, he was offered work as a carpenter, but other whites on the job told their employer that they'd quit if a black man was hired. And so, instead, Gibbs began a rather lucrative shoeshine business in front of the major hotels, and then partnered up with a fellow black Philadelphian, Peter Lester, to operate the city's only boot store, on Clay Street. In 1855 the politically astute Gibbs founded this state's first African-American newspaper, *Mirror of the Times*. He actively protested—in person, as well as in print—the discriminatory laws being considered by legislators in Sacramento. He campaigned against an anti-black immigration bill in 1858 and saw it defeated in the California State Senate, though it had previously been endorsed by the House. Writing afterward in San Francisco's *Evening Bulletin*, Gibbs eloquently defended the prerogative of free blacks to remain in the United States: "I admit the right of a family or a nation to say who, from without, shall be a component part of its household or community; but the application of this principle should work no hardship to a colored man, for he was born in the great American family, and is your black brother—and is interested in its weal or woe, is taxed to support it, and having made up his mind to stay with the family, his right to the benefit of just government is as good as that of his pale face brother who clamors for his expatriation."

Gibbs went on in 1858 to help lead a contingent of Bay Area blacks north to Victoria, British Columbia, where they helped fill a labor vacuum left from the exodus of Canadian men for the California Gold Rush, as well as the subsequent Fraser River gold rush. He returned to the States to become the nation's first black judge, elected in 1873.

IN THE YEARS leading up to the Civil War, the slavery issue and Abraham Lincoln's divisive presidential campaign of 1860 threatened to abrogate even the limited rights that blacks in California enjoyed. Segregationists hoped desperately to take this state into the war on the side of the Confederacy, and there was a great upswelling of pro-Southern sympathies here. But wiser heads prevailed, and California remained in the Union camp. By the end of the 1860s, there were more than 30 black businessmen in San Francisco. They operated small manufacturing plants, engaged in shipping, or worked in law and medicine. Hundreds of thousands of dollars in personal and real property were in the hands of this town's blacks.

The black population would continue growing over the years, but it would be another century before African-Americans could again claim the rights and privileges that William Leidesdorff took for granted at the very outset of San Francisco's history.

YERBA WHAT?

San Francisco used to be known as "Yerba Buena," thanks to British seaman William Anthony Richardson. He came to the peninsula in 1822. In 1835 he built a primitive residence on the banks of the cove that used to begin just east of today's Montgomery Street. As other settlers joined Richardson he decided that their community needed a name.

He didn't think to choose San Francisco, which had already been applied to the mammoth Bay. Instead, he chose Yerba Buena, (meaning "good herb") a reference to a local mint-flavored plant from which both the Indians and Spanish brewed tea.

THE PROPHET OF PROFITS

San Francisco's first public planner was Jean-Jacques Vioget, a Swiss grocer and tavern keeper who arrived in Yerba Buena during its Mexican port days. Although his principal qualification as an urban strategist may have been that he was the only one here who owned surveying instruments, in 1839 Mexican authorities asked him to draw the rudiments of a village scheme. Vioget, who was familiar with the Spanish Pueblo model, gave the town its own central plaza—the future Portsmouth Square—plus a rectangular arrangement of surrounding streets.

Had it been up to Samuel Brannan, the center of American Mormonism would have been San Francisco, not Salt Lake City. But luck had a habit of deserting this big, broad-shouldered, loud-mouthed promoter at the worst possible moments. The first notable occasion was on July 31, 1846, when Brannan, leading a contingent of 238 Latter-Day Saints, swept through the Golden Gate aboard the sailing ship *Brooklyn*. Elder Brannan had charged his supplicants a pretty penny to make this voyage from New York, around Cape Horn, with the idea that they'd set up a Mormon empire on what was still thought to be virgin Mexican soil. So imagine their shock and disappointment when, approaching the tiny cluster of buildings that made up San Francisco—or, as it was known until 1847, Yerba Buena—they spotted an American flag whipping in the wind above the town's central plaza.

As one story goes, Brannan, standing sternly upon the *Brooklyn*'s deck, saw the flag and, realizing that his imperial dreams had come to an abrupt end, exclaimed in disgust, "There's that damned rag again."

It seems that, during the *Brooklyn*'s lengthy voyage, Mexico had ended its two-year war with the United States and ceded its claim to most of what is now the southwestern United States. Captain John B. Montgomery and his sloop of war, the *Portsmouth*, had arrived at Yerba Buena only 22 days earlier than Brannan's party to officially claim California on the authority of President James Knox Polk.

A year after Brannan's arrival in California, Brigham Young, shepherding a flock of Mormons, crossed the Rocky Mountains and came upon the Great Salt Lake. There

Young proclaimed, "*This* is the place!" Ever since, Utah, rather than California, has been the homeland of the Latter-Day Saints.

But by then, Sam Brannan's conception of what sort of empire he might build on the West Coast had expanded dramatically . . . and had been seriously corrupted by capitalism.

USING MONEY TITHED faithfully to him by his fellow Mormons (money that he subsequently withheld from the collectors sent out by Brigham Young from Salt Lake City), this natural-born dealmaker fired up an antiquated printing press that he'd brought with him on the *Brooklyn*, and in January 1847 he founded San Francisco's first newspaper, *The California Star*. That was only the start of Brannan's pioneering. He also established California's first flour mill, delivered the territory's first non-Catholic sermon and the first in English, performed its first non-Catholic wedding ceremony, and is even supposed to have been the first Californian who had to defend himself in a court of law under the American flag. The case arose from complaints that Elder Brannan had misused Mormon funds. A hung jury left Brannan free, but it marked the end of his power in the Church of Jesus Christ of Latter-day Saints.

Such a turn only allowed Brannan more time to pursue his other interests. Father of four children, he recognized the value of education and employed the *Star*'s leverage in creating the town's first public school. Not satisfied with commanding the press in San Francisco, Brannan traveled east to open a store at Sutter's Fort (now part of Sacramento) and construct a flour mill on the American River.

The timing of Brannan's interest in Sutter and the Sacramento Valley couldn't have been more propitious. Gold was discovered on January 24, 1848, at Sutter's sawmill, also on the shores of the American. A month later, the Mormons whom Brannan had convinced to come work at his flour mill found gold in their own riverbeds. The *Star*

TAKING SHAPE II

The city's next evolutionary step came in 1847, when a 30-year-old Irish engineer and surveyor named Jaspar O'Farrell was asked to extend the Vioget plan. He took to his new task with verve, but with perhaps too much imagination. Businessmen rejected some of his early schemes, which included a 120-foot-wide boulevard across Vioget's old grid. Market Street solved what could have been major property disputes in the town's southeast corner, but it upset landowners who thought that it was a waste of valuable property. After O'Farrell's plan was published, his life was threatened, and he had to escape to Sausalito until passions cooled.

BIGGER IS BETTER

The San Francisco landscape 150 years ago was much different than it is today. Essentially, everything south of Telegraph Hill, east of Montgomery Street, and north of today's Interstate 80 was underwater. San Francisco's commercial district was crowded against the beach at Yerba Buena Cove, so city builders initially sought to level some of the lower hills immediately to the west of town. But the decision was made instead to expand east and fill in Yerba Buena Cove, burying and building over the windjammers that had been abandoned there by men headed for the gold fields. The reclamation began in 1849 and took more than 60 years to complete.

mentioned these mineral findings with little fanfare at first. But after Brannan himself found gold in the area in April, his newspaper filled with reports about how diligent river panning could harvest easy money.

Returning to San Francisco on May 12, Brannan carried with him all the proof that was necessary to convert even pessimists into treasure seekers: a bottle of gold dust. "Gold! Gold!" he declared, brandishing the bottle before crowds at Portsmouth Square (on Kearny Street between Clay and Washington streets) and exciting the populace with his booming preacher's delivery. "Gold from the American River!"

"The man's enthusiasm, the electrifying words, the sight of gold, the accumulated force of rumor and expectation now released, all combined to create a contagion of belief and of impatience to get to the American River," wrote J. S. Holliday in his seminal study of California gold fever, *The World Rushed In*. Within a month of Brannan's display, the normally active streets of San Francisco were quiet as a Sunday service. Almost everybody had left, hoping to get their shot at the millions of dollars that might lie buried beneath the Sierra foothills.

BRANNAN, THOUGH, HAD his own money-making schemes in mind—and they didn't involve getting his fingernails dirty. He knew that all of those would-be miners would need provisions. *Lots of them.* And he was ready to supply the goods. Calico, coffee, sugar, shovels, beans, blankets—Brannan's Sacramento store peddled them all, and often at great profit, since no man was about to let a few extra coins stand between him and a future fortune. Business grew even brisker in 1849, after news of the gold strike had made its way to New York and New England. Sam Brannan was ready for the crowds when they sailed into San Francisco Bay; he sold them everything they needed to work the diggings, plus copies of *The California Star*, which fueled their desperation for better and, naturally, more expensive mining equipment (again available through Brannan).

And when some of those same men returned from the diggings with wealth sparkling in their palms, the entrepreneurial elder was there again—only this time he was selling and renting real estate to everybody who wished to put down roots in California. By 1851, Brannan owned one-fifth of San Francisco and one-fourth of Sacramento. Revenue from his rentals alone helped him become one of San Francisco's first millionaires.

Along with settlers and fortune seekers, the Gold Rush attracted thieves, burglars, assassins, and other less desirable citizens to the city. Like San Francisco's other burghers, Brannan was distressed by the rising criminal tide and ineffective law enforcement. In 1851 he organized the First Committee of Vigilance, a group of men who took the law into their own hands for the stated protection of people and their property. He remained as the committee's president until later that year, when his interest flagged and his hesitation in the midst of emergencies was perceived as a liability.

This initial period of vigilante rule—lasting 100 days—was a sad and violent one, resulting in public hangings and beatings. Those men who signed on with Brannan and other citizen battalions could never again claim to be wholly law-abiding, for they had exercised lawlessness contradictorily in pursuit of justice. But they did achieve at least a temporary reduction in criminal activity within the city, and Brannan was subsequently exalted as something of a civic champion.

In the wake of the Vigilance Committee's work, San Franciscans felt safe to venture again onto their sidewalks and Brannan got right back to business. He exhausted some of his fortune trying to develop trade with China, but had more than enough left over to loan the Mexican government money when it needed some. It's said that Brannan entertained royally, often inviting such notables as the dancer Lola

CHANGING LANDSCAPE

The task of filling in Yerba Buena Cove was monumental, for that bight measured about a mile across and covered approximately 336 acres. Though shallow inshore, its bottom sloped out to a depth of 18 feet where it met the Bay. Using material harvested from the sandy hillocks along Market Street, filling began in 1849 at a pear-shaped lagoon located where today's Jackson and Montgomery streets now intersect. Although the new land gave the

☞

appearance of solidity, some of the first buildings erected atop it listed or sank as water seeping from the Bay undermined their foundations. To keep the water back, the city built a seawall along what it expected would be the far edge of its fill project (essentially, today's Embarcadero) and then stuffed up the cove with dirt and refuse. Most of the material that went into this seawall was quarried down from Telegraph Hill. Construction of the wall began in 1867 but wasn't completed until October 13, 1910.

Montez to his soirees, and that he took mistresses, for whom he built lavish homes.

BUT THEN LADY LUCK suddenly turned her back to Brannan again, kicked up her heels, and was *gone*.

His fondness for drink, particularly champagne—a part of the good life he had so enjoyed—started to overwhelm him. He seemed to lose his magic touch for investments, which only caused him to drink more. After hot springs were discovered at the foot of Saint Helena, at the northern end of the Napa Valley, he snapped up vast amounts of the surrounding acreage and announced his intention to build a resort there. This would be his crowning commercial achievement, a project that he intended to name Saratoga, after the popular spa in New York state. But according to one oft-repeated anecdote, Brannan showed up at the dedication well lubricated, and in delivering his speech he inadvertently gave his resort a name that it could never shake. "I'll make this place," he announced, "the Calistoga of Sarafornia."

Sam Brannan poured not only his money but his heart into Calistoga Springs, hoping to disprove those critics who said he didn't have the stuff of a great man anymore. He raised an ornate, begabled hotel at the hot springs, built a distillery nearby, and promoted the hell out of his venture. For a while, Calistoga was *the* chic vacation spot for Bay Area residents, but its attractions waned and so did Brannan's reputation. His wife divorced him, and their settlement awarded her Brannan's hard-won San Francisco holdings, while he kept the limping resort. She subsequently returned to her native Germany with their children. He returned to the bottle.

After that, there were brief sparks of the old Brannan in San Francisco. He had a stake in building the first Cliff House and fought to keep California from joining the Confederacy during the Civil War. Nothing else, though, seemed to go right. Walking the grounds at Calistoga one day, he was shot eight times by a surprised group of trespassers, but recovered. When his wealth was spent, he drifted south to San Diego County, where he supposedly married a Mexican woman and settled on a ranch near the border.

Only in Brannan's last year of life did luck finally swing back his way, when the Mexican government suddenly paid him almost $50,000 in interest on the money he had loaned it so many years before. That was just enough for Sam Brannan to finally settle all his debts. He died penniless in San Diego in 1889, at the age of 70.

"YOUR STREAMS HAVE MINNOWS AND OURS ARE PAVED WITH GOLD"

Some of the most bizarre photographs from the Gold Rush era are those showing the San Francisco waterfront, crowded with the masts and listing hulks of vessels that had carried men west around Cape Horn or north from the overland passage across Panama, and then had been abandoned. By 1851, about 775 ships had been deserted in the Bay. Observed from a distance, this armada resembled nothing so much as a small forest, its naked, weathered trunks having somehow become entangled with ropes and tipsy cross beams. Up close, the constant creaking and bumping of hulls in Yerba Buena Cove was a white noise behind the town's daily commerce.

"These ships," wrote an argonaut by the name of J. Lamson, who sailed here in 1852, "had a very old, ruinous, antiquated appearance, and at first sight, gave me an impression, that this newborn city had been inhabited for ages, and was now going to ruin. Most of them have their masts standing, and supported by a few ropes and chains."

Lamson noted that ever-resourceful San Franciscans had converted some members of this ghost fleet for temporary use by the community, mostly as storeships, but also as public buildings and offices. The town's first bank even held forth from a scow beached at what is now the intersection of California and Battery streets. "Some of [the vessels] had holes cut in their sides, with short flights of stairs from the water," Lamson explained. "Some were run aground near the shore, and wharves and streets were built around them, where, with houses erected on them, they could scarcely be distinguished from the surrounding shores."

Few of the men who arrived at San Francisco in the opening days of the Gold Rush looked back to wonder what might become of the windjammers that had carried them to this place. All anybody had in mind up front was getting properly outfitted and then getting out of town to the Sierra foothills before the Mother Lode was completely tapped out. *The Mother Lode.* That's what they were calling the mining acreage that reached from about Downieville in the north to Mariposa at the south, and between New Helvetia (Sacramento) and the Nevada border. Some people claimed this was the last great wellspring of the world's wealth. Only millionaires and morons refused to find out for themselves. "The whole country from San Francisco to Los Angeles and from the seashore to the base of the Sierra Nevada resounds to the sordid cry of gold, gold! GOLD! while the field is left half planted, the house half built and everything neglected but the manufacture of shovels and pick-axes," exclaimed *The Californian* in May 1848. That paper's editor understood just how infectious gold fever could be: Shortly after this commentary, he had to suspend publication because his employees had deserted him for the goldfields.

CALAFIA'S COME-ON

Gold in California? The Spanish had long believed that such wealth existed here. A romantic tale published in Seville in 1510 described "an island called California very close to the Terrestrial Paradise" that was ruled by a benevolent Amazon matriarch named Calafia. The best thing about this North American El Dorado, according to the author, was that "everywhere [it] abounds with gold and precious stones and upon it no other metal is found." Following his crushing blow against the Aztecs in Mexico in 1521, Cortés described a large island located just to the northwest of the Aztec kingdom, which he called California.

By the end of 1848, 8,000 to 10,000 miners were reportedly roaming the districts around Sutter's outposts, looking for that Big Strike. One man was said to have walked away from a day's panning with $148 worth of gold. And that was piddling compared with later boasts: that $800 in gold was being hauled from the American River's Middle Fork every day; that two men working the same waterway's North Fork had accumulated $17,000 worth of gold in a week; that a cadre of gents drew $75,000 out of a Yuba River sandbar in just three months. These successes were rare, however. Many of the men who came to pick merrily from California's money tree went away little richer than they had been before, and the longer the search for gold went on, the less there was to go around. But even the early average of $15 to $20 per diem was phenomenal at a time when the daily earnings of a working stiff in the United States was around $3, and a loaf of bread cost a nickel or less.

All this sounds even more remarkable when you consider what meager equipment was used by the first gold seekers. They needed only a pan or a shallow bowl. Into this they would wash dirt and gravel scooped up from mountain streams cold enough to numb their bones. If they were lucky, when they tipped their pans back and forth, water and lighter substances would be sluiced out, leaving only heavier particles of gold behind. The technology didn't become too much more sophisticated even as more miners showed up to tap diminishing resources. Pans were replaced with larger variations on the same system, including wooden cradles and "long toms," both of which could run greater volumes of dirt and gravel through at a time, and catch what gold there was in rails that lined their bottoms. (Not until the 1860s did the ease of surface mining start giving way to the heavy-equipment operations necessary to extract gold from tunnels, shafts, and quartz veins.)

Back East, letters featured in the broadsheets of New York City, New Orleans,

"A walk in San Francisco . . . is a real penance . . . . You can hardly make your way through for the throngs of carts, carriages, horsemen, and pedestrians; and where the streets are not paved with boards, you have to wade through sand a foot deep; and all the while you have no better prospect before your eyes than the naked, monotonous sand hills. Truly it is only those who place all happiness in money who could submit, for the sake of gain, to live in such a place, and forget at last that there are such things as trees, or a green carpet lovelier than that which covers the gold-laden gaming tables."

—Ida Pfeiffer, "A Lady's Visit to California, 1853"

and other metropolises hinted that "a Peruvian harvest of precious metals" was spilling from the Sierra Nevada. The *North American* of Philadelphia quoted the *alcalde* (mayor) of Monterey as boasting, "Your streams have minnows, and ours are paved with gold."

Such rife enthusiasm was met at first with much skepticism. James Gordon Bennett, the earnest and abstemious editor of the *New York Herald*, recognized that "the golden tales of these golden streams will excite the imaginations of many ardent and sanguine minds. . . . " Yet he cautioned people against "packing up and removing off to regions where they may hope to become rich thus rapidly. . . . Be assured that all the gold in the world will not make you happy; pursue, quietly and steadily, the sober path of regular industry; be thankful, contented, and act with honor and honesty, and then you will be happier in the enjoyment of a peaceful conscience and a peaceful life than all the gold of California can make its possessors."

But then President James K. Polk, having received a full briefing on the California diggings (along with a sample of the mineral in question), gave what amounted to a sales pitch for the Gold Rush in his final State of the Union message to Congress, in 1848: "The accounts of the abundance of gold in that territory are of such extraordinary character as would scarcely command belief were they not corroborated by authentic reports of officers in the public service."

THOSE WORDS SEEMED to throw open a human floodgate. Anybody who'd considered going west, but had been restrained by doubts about the Gold Rush's veracity, felt reassured and released. The president himself had sanctified the impossible dream of improbable wealth for anyone daring enough and able enough to go find it! Men quickly booked passage on square-riggers headed around Cape Horn, a perilous voyage of 18,000 miles and five months. Or they sailed to the Caribbean coast of Panama or Nicaragua, and from there hiked cross-country through cholera-choked wallows merely in hopes of catching another ship headed up the Pacific Coast to San Francisco. They wagon-trained across the United States (there was no transcontinental rail link with San Francisco until 1869). Or they caught a ride to Veracruz, Mexico, and then trudged overland to El Camino Real and north to the Sacramento Valley. In short, they did whatever was necessary to "see the elephant"—the popular term for visiting California's gilded placers.

Never in modern history had a peacetime migration of people reached such proportions. In 1849 alone, almost 800 ships departed the harbor at Manhattan, bound for the Golden Gate. By 1851, 100,000 "forty-niners," as the gold seekers were called, had braved overland routes to reach California. San Francisco was positively stampeded, and it would be permanently changed by the Gold Rush diaspora. Streets that had been enlivened during Mexican times by ambitious newcomers, and then drained of almost every living soul by news of the Mother Lode, were suddenly awash in tide after tide of migrants. Businesses boomed in every quarter to service the influx. Sharp-minded shopkeepers who owned scales for weighing out flour, beans, and other commodities began to spend as much time now testing the heft of gold dust, and some of them re-created themselves as bankers. Newspapers sprang up to satisfy the need for news from the outside world and also to promote the city's future development. In 1855, San Francisco published more newspapers than were available in London, England.

Intense demand for food, housing, and clothing, coupled with the ready availability of gold, sent prices spiraling upward. Apples were shipped to the mines and sold for $1.50 apiece. One woman said that she'd earned $18,000 just by hawking pies to miners. It wasn't uncommon for restaurants to charge $6 or more for a simple breakfast. Miners often paid out two-thirds of an ounce of gold *every day* just for food. Fleabag lodgings

NO JOY IN MUDVILLE

San Francisco streets were in sorry shape when Gold Rush prospectors first trod their lengths. Ungraded and unpaved, they were susceptible to the thrashings of rain and wagon wheels. During the winter of 1849–50, when 41 days of rain poured on northern California, stories circulated about carts and mules becoming trapped and horses drowning in the filthy mire. Woe be to the miner who, deep into his cups, should have fallen into the thick mud. Conditions were so bad at the corner of Clay and Kearny streets that somebody put up a warning:

"This Street is Impassable;
Not even Jackassable."

sprang up all over to accommodate the thousands who were willing to pay top dollar for the privilege of rest. And almost everyone lucky enough to have invested in real estate before the Gold Rush found themselves sitting on their own sort of gold mines, as property values shot up five- or tenfold. Large landowners like James Lick, the misanthropic millionaire and soon-to-be-builder of the Lick House hotel, had to pay knuckle-busters as much as $20 a night just to keep "squatters" off their property.

ALMOST ALL OF THE people who shipped west to California in the late 1840s were men. Men outnumbered women 6,000 to 1. Even the mere rustle of skirts outside a watering hole could cause hormone-charged males to stampede for the door. Refinements that might have been called for in a dual-sex environment were in short supply around northern California. What the men created at the gold camps and in San Francisco was "a wild, free, disorderly, grotesque society," as Mark Twain remembered in *Roughing It*. Plain-faced saloons opened to quench the thirsts of the new El Dorado millionaires, serving the most rotgut liquor—pure alcohol diluted in various proportions with water, plug tobacco, and cinnamon root. Gamblers came to town to release miners from the weight of their treasure bags. Prospectors who had struck it rich were often so careless with their mineral wealth that keepers of bars, gambling dens, and brothels learned to be fastidious, knowing that just sweeping the floor after a night's bacchanalia might harvest a few ounces of gold. Although it would be another 10 years before San Francisco's parlor house trade heated up, even by 1850 (when women still made up only 8 percent of California's population), Chilean, Peruvian, and Mexican prostitutes had found a place in the local business hierarchy.

Beginning in 1850, though, manifests for the ships arriving in town started to show significant numbers of female passengers. Many of these women were the so-called

INSANE EXPANSION

San Francisco experienced a growth during the Gold Rush that had no adequate comparison in American history. Some people reveled in all the attendant excitement, but others, like a correspondent on assignment here in 1849 for New York's Evening Post, *were dumbfounded by the torrents of lucre and humanity that poured through the boggy boulevards. As that journalist saw it, "the people of San Francisco are mad, stark mad."*

Gold Rush widows who, having waited for their husbands to return from the far-off Sierras, finally gave up and decided to bring their families to California instead. Others were younger ladies from the East Coast, venturing to California because this was where so many of North America's eligible bachelors had gone.

Foreign travelers added to the social complexity of the Bay's boomtown. During the 1850s, upwards of 30,000 men and several thousand women came here from Great Britain, France, and Germany. Another 25,000 Chinese had put into dock here by the close of 1852. By 1860, 39 percent of Californians came from foreign lands. Not only did these people help create a wonderfully polyglot sidewalk scene in the state, but those who stayed behind in San Francisco infiltrated the local culture with unique approaches to entertainment, trade, and the restaurant business. It is partly thanks to the Gold Rush, for instance, that San Francisco today enjoys its great diversity of ethnic eateries.

WHETHER BECAUSE THEY had struck it rich, or because they didn't see a hope of doing so in their lifetime, within a few years prospectors started pulling up stakes and heading home. In 1853, 31,000 migrants left the Bay Area, to be followed by 22,800 in 1855, 27,900 in 1858, and another 14,500 in 1860. Many of these sods never made it home. They turned up instead in southern Oregon, where gold was discovered in 1852; or in British Columbia, where strikes were made along the Fraser River in 1858; or in Colorado, where the individual gold discoveries along Cripple Creek were harder to find, but sometimes even richer than those in California. Silver unearthed from the eastern slopes of the Sierra Nevada—site of the fabled Comstock Lode—vacuumed off many prospectors who had missed out on the roughly $500 million in placer and lode gold that came from California diggings between 1848 and 1857.

Not everybody left northern California, however—not by a long shot. The Bear

SPICY LITTLE CHILE

There was nothing pampered and pretty about the prostitutes who serviced San Francisco's forty-niners, but they apparently served their purpose, operating primarily on the southern slopes of Alta Loma (Telegraph Hill), in an area called "Little Chile." Frank Soulé, whose observations in The Annals of San Francisco *help form one of the clearest early images of this boomtown, wrote that "Both sexes lived almost promiscuously in large tents, scattered irregularly upon the hillsides. Their dwellings were dens of infamy, where drunkenness and whoredom, gambling, swindling, cursing and brawling were constantly going on . . ."*

SEAT-OF-THE-PANTS SUCCESS

If not for the Gold Rush, the world today might be lacking one of its signature fashion statements: blue jeans. In 1847, their originator, Levi Strauss (born Loeb Strauss in 1829), followed his Jewish family out of Bavaria. He arrived in New York City, where Strauss went to work with two older brothers peddling buttons, combs, scissors, and other dry goods to families living in the countryside. But with the discovery of gold in California, the Strauss brothers decided that the real future for ambitious men lay in the West. So they boarded a clipper ship 'round Cape Horn, carrying essentials of all sorts, especially tent canvas to help house the forty-niners.

State's population climbed 2,500 percent from 1848 to 1852. It went up about another 50 percent from 1860 to 1870. Some of the men who'd departed eventually returned with their families. Some of them told stories about the West that convinced their friends to leave the civil constancy of Philadelphia or Boston or Richmond and follow the siren call to San Francisco.

"The rush to California . . . ," Henry David Thoreau insisted in the last year of his life, 1862, "reflects the greatest disgrace of mankind. That so many are ready to live by luck and so get the means of commanding the labor of others less lucky, without contributing any value to society—and that's called enterprise!"

This New England naturalist and writer was certainly not alone in criticizing the Gold Rush. But he failed to recognize the magic that California and its message of easy riches offered a country where wealth had always been maintained by a select few. No longer did one have to be *born* into economic good fortune, it seemed; one might leap from poverty to prosperity with a minimum of effort but a maximum of daring. Several generations of dreamers, both in San Francisco and elsewhere, were emboldened by that single revelation.

KING OF THE HILLS

No student of American history can fail to be moved by the cool bronze and marble figures that encircle Statuary Hall, the vast former House of Representatives chamber at the U.S. Capitol in Washington, D.C. Most of the 92 figures honored there are immediately familiar, from Generals Ulysses S. Grant and Robert E.

Lee to Senator Henry Clay, Mormon leader Brigham Young, and President John Quincy Adams. But every once in a while you'll find yourself standing quizzically before the representation of a person whose notoriety has somehow been displaced by successive waves of the more recently famous.

Who, for instance, was Thomas Starr King?

In mid-19th-century California, few would have had to ask that question. After all, had it not been for "Starr King," as he was best known, this state might have thrown its lot in with the Confederacy during the Civil War and might later have lost Yosemite to private exploiters.

IT'S SURPRISING HOW much influence King exerted in San Francisco and California, given how little of his life was actually spent there. He was born in New York in 1824; educated himself in history, languages, classical literature, and theology; and was a grammar school teacher and a bookkeeper before serving as pastor at Boston's Hollis Street Unitarian Church.

King was a slight man with a weak chin and thin straight blond hair, and in photos he has the sort of tightly controlled features and intense eyes that are common to old-time undertakers. But his *voice*. . . . his voice was the kind that could silence a fidgety crowd, quiet even an unruly mob. Its strong, confident timbre was nearly powerful enough to embed itself in church walls. People would come faithfully before his rostrum on Sundays not only to hear what he said, but to enjoy his electric delivery. As his friend, the antislavery advocate and Unitarian minister Theodore Parker phrased it, King had "the grace of God in his heart and the gift of tongues." It wasn't long before he ranked among Boston's most popular preachers.

However, King was omnivorous in his interests. In 1860 he published a lovingly

Unfortunately, by the time they arrived at San Francisco Bay in 1853, the rush was over. There was no longer a housing shortage. However, Levi Strauss discovered, there was a pressing need here for pants that could withstand the abuse of mining. And so Strauss, a natural-born marketer if ever there was one, began to make his fabric instead into what he called "waist overalls." The pants were an immediate success. But by 1860 Strauss's supply of the brown tent fabric had run dry, and he resorted instead to importing a blue serge material from Nîmes, a town in southern France. (He later commissioned a New England factory to supply him with the 10-ounce denim.) The rest, as they say, is history.

detailed appreciation of New Hampshire called *The White Hills: Their Legends, Landscapes, and Poetry*. He also joined the Lyceum circuit, rivaling Henry Ward Beecher as a lecturer on various topics of the times.

Like many other well-read people in pre–Civil War America, King was concerned that trouble would arise from the 1860 presidential race—an election that would help decide whether the United States should remain whole or be cleaved asunder by the poised ax of slavery. The Democratic Party's hesitation to nominate Senator Stephen A. Douglas of Illinois, "the only Democrat who could have reached out beyond the slaveholding South and gathered up enough votes from the border states to win," according to *American Heritage* magazine, and the subsequent formation of a Democratic splinter group called the Constitutional Union party, almost assured lawyer Abe Lincoln's election on behalf of the new Republican Party. If that happened, King knew, the South was likely to choose secession over governance by a president who, despite some wishy-washiness on the issue, had been firmly cast in the public's mind as an abolitionist.

Unwilling to sit out the coming conflict in the socially stratified seclusion of Beantown, King took up an invitation in 1860 to lead a struggling flock of Unitarians in faraway and still small San Francisco. Accompanied by his wife Julia, he booked ship passage to the Bay Area via Panama, explaining to a friend, "I do think we are unfaithful in huddling so closely around the cozy stove of civilization in this blessed Boston, and I, for one, am ready to go into the cold, and see if I am good for anything."

AT THE TIME, California was busily charting its political course. Historians disagree, but something between 7 and 40 percent of the state's 380,000 inhabitants had come from slaveholding areas. Only 7 of California's 53 newspapers endorsed Lincoln as president, and after the election was decided in the old rail-splitter's favor, more than a few of

---

GOOD COMPANY

Thomas Starr King is one of only two men selected to represent California in Statuary Hall, at the U.S. Capitol. The other is Franciscan mission founder Father Junípero Serra.

---

those papers that had opposed him called on the state to splinter from the Union and hook up with Oregon as an independent Republic of the Pacific. Back in what was then called Washington City, California Representative John C. Burch called on this state to "raise aloft" the Bear Flag that had flown above the short-lived California Republic in 1846.

After the Confederate siege of Fort Sumter in Charleston, South Carolina, in April 1861, "anti-Union plots and rumors of plots proliferated" in both Oregon and California, Alvin M. Josephy, Jr. writes in *The Civil War in the American West*. "Pro-Southern organizations, including the conspiratorial Knights of the Golden Circle, spread through the two states, the Bear Flag, as well as palmetto flags honoring South Carolina, flew in a number of California towns, and Unionists' fears of a secessionist coup mounted."

There had also been fears concerning the loyalty of federal forces on the West Coast, headed as they were by Brigadier General Albert Sidney Johnston, a Texan with Southern sympathies who had been appointed during the last days of James Buchanan's presidency to supervise Union armies in not only California, but also Oregon and Washington Territory. The justification for those fears came immediately prior to the Fort Sumter engagement, when Johnston suddenly lit out East to offer his services to the Confederacy.

King had little patience with secessionists. His voice rang out from San Francisco: "Our city turns her face persistently towards the East—signifying that California has no insane vision of independence; that she desires no isolated sway over the Pacific, but is bound by loyalty to the empire whose flag she plants on Mendocino, the Hatteras of the West." King's physical health "was not good," explained B. E. Lloyd in *Lights and Shades in San Francisco*. "An affection of the throat frequently gave him trouble." Yet he traveled the state, from cities to dreary mining camps, employing biblical themes

CHIC CHEEKS

Levis pants have changed some over the years. In 1872, at the suggestion of Jacob Davis, a Latvian tailor from Reno, Nevada, inventor Strauss added metal rivets to the stress points around pocket seams and elsewhere. The now-familiar leather label (showing two horses testing the strength of Strauss's pants by trying to pull them apart) made its debut in 1886. The term "jeans" is derived from the French word Gênes, *referring to Genoa, the Italian town where sailors had worn trousers similar to those of Strauss's manufacture. Surprisingly, it wasn't until the 1930s (long after Strauss's death in 1902) that the nickname "blue jeans" came into regular use.*

San Francisco's competition with communities east of San Francisco Bay goes all the way back to the city's very naming.

In 1847, a pair of distinguished settlers named Robert Semple and Thomas O. Larkin decided that Yerba Buena was in entirely the wrong place to become significant. They reasoned that something closer to John Sutter's prospering New Helvetia Colony (Sacramento) would stand a better chance at prosperity. So they asked Mariano de Guadalupe Vallejo, one of the area's principal Californios), to grant them land on Carquinez Strait, in the north Bay region.

☞

and his powerful oratorical presence on behalf of Lincoln and California's essential obeisance to the Union. In one of King's most oft-quoted speeches, he demanded that "the doctrine of secession be stabbed with two hundred thousand bayonet wounds, and trampled to rise no more."

SUCH PATRIOTIC FERVOR weighed mightily on legislators as they met in Sacramento, and much to the surprise of California's all-Democratic and anti-Lincoln delegation in the nation's capital, on May 17, 1861, a joint-house resolution was released, declaring that the 31st state would remain firmly in the Union fold. Confirming California's position were the state elections of that same year, which listed in favor of Republicans and Unionist Democrats, and resulted in sending railroader Leland Stanford to Sacramento for two years as the state's first Republican governor.

But the clergyman's energies weren't exhausted completely by politics. He sought to enhance San Francisco's literary reputation, making friends with writers such as Bret Harte and, through him, becoming acquainted with such recipients of later fame as Mark Twain and the stripling poet Charles Warren Stoddard. He took the opportunity as well to appreciate California's natural bounty. An early environmentalist, King had a poet's ability to describe the state's mountains, rivers, and deserts to San Francisco audiences that had seen very little of their huge, still-unfettered homeland. As he had earlier sat down to honor New Hampshire in print with *The White Hills*, so he planned to champion the Bear State's more rugged landscape, with special emphasis given to the waterfalls, forests, and cliff faces of the Yosemite Valley. "Great is granite," King proclaimed, sharing a passion he'd gained from years of mountain climbing, "and Yosemite is its prophet."

It was partly through King's efforts that Yosemite—which he had visited for the first time shortly after his arrival in California in 1860—survived to be written about in 1912 by Scottish philosopher and scientist John Muir. During the decade following Yosemite's "discovery" in 1851, the U.S. Cavalry had herded the Ahwahneechee Indians away from their sacred valley, and it was rapidly being fenced, farmed, and otherwise homesteaded. Travelers who visited the area, hoping to enjoy wilderness delights that they had read about in newspaper descriptions, were disappointed to see alpine valleys given over to the pleasure of cud-sucking cattle.

Powerful Easterners who read King's dispatches about Yosemite's slow destruction were finally moved to action. In 1864, Frederick Law Olmsted, superintendent of New York's Central Park and the country's most respected landscape architect, encouraged President Lincoln and Congress to preserve Yosemite Valley and the Mariposa Grove of Big Trees as a natural scenic area safe from construction. This was the nation's first such experiment in environmental protection, and it set the stage for many more preservation actions in the future.

At the same time, King didn't ignore his primary responsibility to his religion. Indeed, on January 10, 1864, just two months before his career came to an unexpectedly early close, he dedicated the First Unitarian Church of San Francisco, a stirring $90,000 Gothic edifice, with seating for 1,500 God-fearing souls, that still stands at Franklin and Geary streets, in Japantown.

THE CAUSE OF KING'S DEATH on March 4, 1864, when he was just 39 years old, was ascribed to the one-two punch of diptheria and pneumonia. The *San Francisco Bulletin* made room for Bret Harte's final poetic panegyric to the city's most outspoken humanitarian. The *Alta California* gave over most of its front page to King's passing, noting sadly that the preacher's book on Yosemite had never been finished. The United States

Vallejo agreed, and the two entrepreneurs announced plans to create the town of Francisca, an appellation that affirmed its physical relationship to San Francisco Bay.

Getting wind of this plan, other Yerba Buenans decided that their settlement was more deserving of association with the Bay. Washington A. Bartlett, the first local alcalde (mayor) serving under American rule, proclaimed that as of January 30, 1847, "the name of San Francisco shall hereafter be used in all official communications and public documents or records appertaining to the town." Larkin and Semple had to come up with another designation for their new community. They selected Benecia.

❧

Starr King had a fervent interest in literature and writers. In Bay Window Bohemia, historian Oscar Lewis relates the charming tale of Starr King dropping into a bookstore where Charles Warren Stoddard, then a frequent contributor to The Golden Era *magazine, was employed. King, writes Lewis, "produced a poem clipped from the* Era *and, having praised it highly, asked the youth if by any chance he was its author. Stoddard, vastly flattered, admitted the charge, and King, after further compliments, took his departure, having first presented the budding author with a season ticket to a lecture series he was currently delivering on the American poets."*

Mint in San Francisco closed in his memory, along with other government offices, courts, and businesses. In Sacramento, legislators had the pastor's portrait mounted in the statehouse, and they credited him officially as "the man whose matchless oratory saved California for the Union."

King's deathbed request had been to "keep my memory green." But beyond the memories of his loyal followers, little in the way of a lasting tribute was made until 1892, when a statue was raised on the pastor's behalf in Golden Gate Park. His portrayal in bronze at Statuary Hall in Washington, D.C., was unveiled in 1931. The remembrance that might have stirred Thomas Starr King's heart most, though, is not a thing of artificial beauty, but of natural eminence—a literal way of keeping King's memory "green." After Yosemite won national park status in 1890, one of its mountains and a redwood in the Mariposa Grove were named for the man whose eloquence had helped save them.

THE MAGICIAN OF SAN FRANCISCO

If any single person symbolized San Francisco's boomtown, nothing-is-impossible attitude of the late 19th century, it was banker William Chapman Ralston. Brimming with self-confidence, energy, and the splendid madness of optimism, Ralston never attempted anything on a small scale when doing it up grandly could fetch him substantially greater profits—or win his beloved city some greater prestige.

Ralston dreamed of transforming San Francisco into one of the world's corporate and cultural capitals. Toward this end, and using the seemingly unlimited resources available through his Bank of California, he charged boldly into the maw of financial risk, building factories and mammoth hotels in the city, investing in steamship and telegraph companies, speculating in the Alaska fur trade and plotting for supreme control over the silver hidden in Nevada's Comstock Lode. There were times when it seemed that nothing happened in the Bay Area without Ralston's involvement.

Some people today would say that Ralston behaved rashly, that he was too quick to gamble with his investors' money and too slow to protect against economic disaster. Heck, many of his fellow millionaires said something just like that way back in Ralston's heyday, during the 1860s and 1870s.

But Ralston lived in a naive and hopeful era. With the Nevada silver boom practically tumbling in succession over the Gold Rush, railroads finally connecting the Atlantic Ocean with the Pacific, and Americans flooding recklessly into the West, Californians didn't hesitate to dream. And their dreams could be as oversized as the landscape they found here. Anything seemed possible, from bridging the Pacific with trade, to irrigating the state's driest valleys for agriculture, to flattening Rincon Hill and creating a new commercial zone. All that was needed was money. And visionaries like Billy Ralston.

WHEN HE TOOK HIS FIRST breath, in January 1826, it was of air sweetened by the farmlands of eastern Ohio. "Chap," as he was known in his boyhood, grew up beside the Ohio River, listening to steamboat whistles and watching barges chug along the shore. Similar experiences filled other boys (notably the slightly younger Samuel Clemens) with romantic notions of one day piloting riverboats. But Chap was interested in commerce. When he finally did move to New Orleans and work on Mississippi River paddle wheelers, it was as a clerk.

OUT OF SIGHT . . .
Starr King's body was laid to rest beside the First Unitarian Church. You'll find his stone sarcophagus today inside a shadowy copse of trees at the corner of O'Farrell and Franklin streets, right next to the modern Unitarian Center.

Ralston was 22 years old when news spread that gold had been discovered in California. It took Chap another year (and the burning of his ship) before he was ready to join the human stream west. He got hung up for two years at Panama City, Panama, where he threw in with two friends—Cornelius K. Garrison and Ralph Fretz—who were developing a bank and charter steamship business.

Ralston visited California in 1851, but returned to Panama. Three years later, after his most able partner, Garrison, moved to the Bay Area to operate an office for shipping magnate Cornelius Vanderbilt, Ralston followed. He worked with Garrison again for a while in this city, but then returned to banking. Several partners came and went over the next eight years, but Ralston never lost his wish to create a financial institution that would stand at the center of development in San Francisco and northern California. With that in mind, he gladly made loans to entrepreneurs with great ideas, people who might contribute something substantial and permanent to the area. He also became a major investor in the Comstock Lode, which had been discovered in 1859. The lode took some time to heat up, and it was never to be the bonanza portrayed in some histories. However, when it did boom, Ralston wanted ties between it and San Francisco to be strong enough that the riches belched from the ground there would funnel back to the Bay Area.

In 1864, Ralston created the Bank of California, soliciting 22 of the state's leading businessmen to buy enough shares of stock—at $100 a share—that he'd have $2 million in capital funds. Then he convinced Darius O. Mills, the premier financier of Sacramento, to serve as president of the new money house, although in name only. "I will do all the managing," Ralston explained. For the next 11 years, this town's foremost captain of industry would carry the modest title of "cashier" at his own bank.

SAN FRANCISCO RUNNETH OVER with wealthy men during the second half of the 19th century. Conniving Sacramento shopkeepers-turned-capitalists Collis P. Huntington, Mark Hopkins, Leland Stanford, and Charles Crocker—the "Big Four"— would become obscenely rich after they convinced Congress and President Lincoln to let them construct the western section of the first transcontinental railway. They went on to turn their Central Pacific Railroad (later known as the Southern Pacific) into a California rail and water transportation monopoly that set high rates for its services, punished any- body who refused to pay up, and kept its stranglehold secure (until 1910, anyway) with judicious distribution of bribes around the smoke-filled hallways of Capitol Hill.

The other most significant cabal of Midases featured the four so-called Bonanza Kings—former mine superintendents John W. McKay and James G. Fair, and saloon pro- prietors James C. Flood and William S. O'Brien—who eventually broke Ralston's hold over the Comstock Lode. Like the Big Four, these nouveau riche spent extravagantly, building magnificent palazzi and trying to turn their monetary muscle into political power, whether as national legislators or behind-the-scenes manipulators.

Billy Ralston could be as covetous and cruel as any of those other gentlemen. For instance, after encouraging German entrepreneur Adolph Sutro in 1865 to construct a tunnel beneath the Comstock Lode, which was supposed to bleed off steam and hot water that were plaguing deep-earth miners, he and his business partner, William Sharon, sud- denly turned on the ambitious Sutro and tried to bankrupt him out of Nevada. Six years later, Ralston's greed got the better of his common sense, and he fell for an elaborate dia- mond mine fraud that cost him millions of dollars.

But the sheer acquisition of lucre didn't charge Ralston's batteries. He was thrilled by what he could *do* with the money he made. And he wanted to do *everything*. So he invested in woolen mills and cigar factories; he constructed a multicolumned Bank of

closely held company, Ralston spent $50,000 to $100,000 on surveys and other studies of Alaska. His repre- sentatives interviewed the Russian ambassador in Washington City and made contacts with the Czar. Then just when Ralston seemed ready to ratchet negotiations up further, the U.S. government, which had received copies of Ralston's Alaska research information, announced that it was buying Alaska. The transaction was completed by Secretary of State William H. Seward in 1867. Perhaps as compensation, an official missive from Washington to Ralston acknowledged that "You are responsi- ble for the acquisition of the Territory, for to your correspondence is due the fact that it is now in the possession of the United States."

FAIR IN LOVE AND WAR

Silver King James Fair was strikingly successful in buying his way into Congress. In 1879, running as a Democrat, he defeated his rich rival, William Sharon, in the race for a U.S. Senate seat from Nevada. Business interests in that state were assured that Fair would speak for them—loudly—on Capitol Hill. But he was by no means a spectacular solon. One San Francisco newspaper, recapping the Silver King's six-year term in Washington City, remarked: "About all that can be said for Nevada's junior Senator is that he has had the good sense to sit silent while matters of which he knows nothing are under debate."

☞

California headquarters on the northwest corner of Sansome and California streets, a building meant to reflect the stability and strength of his enterprise; he raised an opulent country mansion for himself and his wife, Lizzie, at Belmont, 22 miles south of the city; he opened the giant California Theater on Bush Street as a lure for high-caliber international performers; and he gave money to widows and grubby street urchins and even Joshua Norton, the colorful former rice merchant who'd allegedly gone mad and proclaimed himself to be the emperor of North America. (As George Lyman observed in *Ralston's Ring,* "No one was ever turned away from Ralston's office who had something to contribute to California welfare or who needed help or a word of encouragement.") To attract visitors and the finest mercantile enterprises to his precious city, Ralston put up an impressive hotel (the Grand) at the corner of New Montgomery and Market streets. Then he turned right around and outdid himself with a second, grander edifice just across the street: the original Palace Hotel.

RALSTON DREAMED SO EXPANSIVELY, so expensively, that his funds were often stretched by the breadth of his interests. In his later years, he seemed always to skirt the edge of calamity. Yet he was unchastened by periodic failures, believing—from experience!—that he was the comeback kid.

But between losses on the Comstock and the Panic of 1873, brought on by bank failures back East, Ralston was forced to start looking for fresh and substantial sources of funds that would float his empire above the westward-flowing tide of red ink. In 1875, he thought he'd discovered a solution. Going further into debt, he and a friend named Charles N. Felton gained control of the private company that brought San Francisco its drinking water. They then offered to sell their stock and watershed to the city for $15 million—half again its physical value. To Ralston, this seemed a win-win deal for both himself and San Francisco. But the local newspapers, especially the *Bulletin* and the *Call*, were irate at the idea of pumping more money into the pockets of rich speculators. Their editorials eventually convinced the board of supervisors to turn thumbs down on Ralston's proposition.

Desperate to cover his assets, the visionary banker borrowed heavily and still found himself short of money. He finally asked William Sharon for help, expecting that the years of trust he'd shown Sharon would bring that financier to his rescue. Instead, Sharon desperately started dumping his Comstock mining shares, depressing the value of Ralston's shares in the process. When word got around on August 26, 1875, that Sharon might be selling out in order to raise money necessary to save the Bank of California, frightened depositors rushed to the bank, anxious to withdraw their funds—funds that, of course, weren't actually there, thanks to its "clerk's" recent profligacy. Ralston was forced to close the doors when his vault went empty.

The next day, a Friday, Ralston was told by his bank directors that he would have to relinquish his control of the institution. He took the news with equanimity and then, as was his usual daily routine, went to work off tension with a swim. He was stroking vigorously from a North Beach bluff in the general direction of Alcatraz Island when watchers saw him thrashing desperately in the cold tide. Cause of death was reportedly stroke, although some skeptics suggested, given what else had happened that day, that suicide might be more likely.

BECAUSE HE HAD BECOME so representative of his times and place, San Franciscans seemed to collectively bow their shoulders just a bit when Ralston died, as if fearing what catastrophe might follow. Billy Ralston had always helped keep doubts about the future at arm's length; now they rose suddenly like Marley's Ghost. Recent concerns

Fair gained more notice as the defendant in an 1883 case of "habitual adultery," brought by his estranged wife, still living in Virginia City. The San Francisco Bulletin filled its broadsheet pages with stories about female witnesses testifying as to Fair's adulterous behavior. Other newspapers across the nation scandalized the divorce in their pages, and it even became a subject for floor debate in the Senate. Fair let the adultery charges go uncontested, perhaps hoping they would receive less extended publicity that way. Eventually, Fair gained custody of his two sons, but he lost his family home in San Francisco plus some $4,750,000 in cash and securities — reportedly the largest divorce settlement ever awarded up to that time.

about Ralston's ability to manage his bank vanished as people praised him as "the father of the city," "the magician of San Francisco." At his funeral, speakers recounted his accomplishments and imagined what he might have done had he lived past age 49. When his casket was transported from the church near Union Square to its burial ground, it was reportedly followed by some 50,000 people, forming a line that covered streets from curb to curb and extended for three miles.

Those folks didn't come only to mourn the passing of William C. Ralston, banker and speculator. They came to shed tears for the end of their innocent dreams.

BIG TROUBLE IN LITTLE CHINA

Mid-19th-century San Franciscans were openly suspicious of, and often hostile toward, foreigners—a funny paradox when you consider that at that time, almost everyone here could have been considered a foreigner. This fact did nothing to stop prejudice, though, especially prejudice exercised against the Chinese.

California's first few Chinese are said to have arrived in the Bay Area in 1848, shortly after gold was discovered at Sutter's Mill. But only four years later, according to *The Annals of San Francisco*, a rough head count of Chinese residing in the Bear State came in at 22,000, with most of those people gathered about the Mother Lode. No trouble arose as long as there was lots of gold to be had in the Sierras; however, as the supply of riches decreased, racial animus increased. To avoid trouble, Chinese miners retreated from the most active gold-seeking areas, instead reworking claims that had supposedly been tapped out or proved unproductive. Even that didn't satisfy some avaricious whites, who prodded Governor John Bigler to increase the 1850 Foreign Miners' Tax in hopes of driving Asians from the goldfields. In the end, many of the Chinese who'd dreamed of finding mineral wealth in "Golden Mountain," as they referred to California, opted instead for more pedestrian ventures with their brethren in San Francisco.

Conditions in China at that time were increasingly miserable. Floods, famine, and skyrocketing taxes (demanded by the Manchu regime to pay off the British after the First Opium War of 1839–42) took their toll on the populace. So, though the opportunities to be had in California weren't as highly publicized in Asia as they were throughout Europe, Chinese men who did hear about this place sailed for the Golden Gate in droves, hoping to fill their family coffers with the fruits of overseas success. "The typical Chinese immigrant of the 1850s wanted to remain in Ka-la-fo-ne-a no longer than necessary," Richard Dillon observed in *The Hatchet Men*, an often painful discourse on San Francisco's early Chinatown. "When he had made his pile—perhaps $500—he would return home to his patient wife and family for a life of relative ease in Kwangtung," a Cantonese province of southeastern China.

The *Annals* estimated that, in 1852, 3,000 Chinese were living in San Francisco— or *Gum San Ta Fow* (Big City in the Land of the Golden Hills). Many of these immigrants went into the local laundry business. The first Chinese laundry in the United States was opened by an entrepreneur named Wah Lee at the corner of Washington Street and Dupont (now Grant Avenue) in 1851. By the 1880s, there were supposedly 1,000 of these laundries scattered around the city. Other Chinese found employment as cooks, cigar makers, domestic servants, and manufacturers of women's underwear.

CLOUDS UPON THE WATER

Clipper ships were created specifically to speed up cargo transport from the industrial East to the rich shores of the Golden Gate. Captain George Gordon's Memnon was the first of this breed to hove into the Bay, in July 1849—only 120 days out from New York Bay. The first great clipper race came a year later. Seven rivals headed west from New York around Cape Horn. The apparent winner, Captain Charles Porter Low's Samuel Russell, arrived here on May 6, 1850, after 109 days at

*sea. But on July 23, Captain George
Fraser's smart* Sea Witch *charged
through the Gate—only 97 days
out from New York.*

*The all-time record, however, went
first to the* Flying Cloud, *which,
under Captain Josiah P. Cressy,
took only 89 days to make the voyage
in 1851. The* Cloud *equaled that
pace three years later, as did the*
Andrew Jackson *in 1860. The end
of the Gold Rush brought an end to
the building of clipper ships. The last
of the grand, or extreme, models
was completed in 1854.*

❦

When, in the late 1860s, the Central Pacific Railroad found itself falling behind schedule in building its section of the transcontinental railway—from Oakland, California, to Promontory, Utah—its director of works, Charles Crocker, arranged to import 15,000 to 20,000 Chinese as cheap labor. The Chinese could lay track much faster and more reliably than Crocker's original Irish laborers, and they were also highly adept at tunnel-blasting. By the time the Central Pacific workers met their westbound counterparts from the Union Pacific at Promontory Point on May 10, 1869, a full 85 percent of their work force was made up of Chinese "coolies." But almost before San Franciscans had stopped dancing in the streets with excitement over the transcontinental's completion, the railroad released all its Chinese workers, most of whom came to San Francisco to live and work—much to the consternation of whites.

The Chinese of the mid-19th century kept very much to themselves. They seemed uninterested in integrating into the San Francisco community; they were even contemptuous of it, preferring to remain among their own people and choosing not to learn English. As Dillon explained, the Chinese immigrant "did not want to be assimilated; on the contrary he preferred to be insulated from the *fan kwai* (foreign devils) all around him." He (or, more rarely, she) tried to stay securely out of trouble by disappearing into the mixed bag that was San Francisco street culture; but traditional dress and coiffures still made the Chinese stand out starkly.

Gathering along Stockton Street—the only roadway where the first Chinese San Franciscans were allowed to rent rooms—and around Portsmouth Square, these quiet immigrants began to form their own village within the larger town, a "Little China" that was every bit as foreign to white San Franciscans as was Shanghai. Even many of the buildings they erected in Chinatown were shipped over in sections from Hong Kong. Merchants banded together to form what were known as the Chinese Six Companies (the foundation of today's Chinese Benevolent Association), designed to maintain order within the community and handle its contacts with the threatening "outside world." Although law-abiding, the Chinese feared police (who reminded them of the violent soldiers they'd left behind), and they tried instead to police themselves. They distrusted courts and lawyers, having been numbed by centuries of proof that fitting in was a saner stratagem for life than fighting injustice. They would accept the authority of the Counsel General of Imperial China before they'd answer to the mayor of San Francisco. They sought to be left to themselves.

White San Franciscans grew suspicious of the Chinese. During the economic depression of the 1870s, out-of-work Caucasians struck out against their complacent, queue-wearing neighbors. City supervisors codified racism by passing laws intended specifically to annoy the Chinese—regulations that prohibited people from carrying basketloads of laundry atop their heads, levied taxes on laundry workers, and fined "any person found sleeping in a room containing less than five hundred cubic feet of space for each person." There was even a law passed in 1876 that prisoners in city jails would be shorn of any pigtails—one of a Chinese man's most prized adornments (a law overturned by the U.S. Circuit Court three years later).

AT THE SAME TIME that many San Franciscans reveled in illicit businesses that had gained a footing in Chinatown, others reviled that quarter for its multiplicity of gambling houses and opium dens. They demonstrated particular contempt for the traffic in slave-girls, who were smuggled from Asia to the Golden Gate disguised as "dirty-faced coolie boys." This trade began in the very early 1850s. Prostitutes accounted for three-fourths of the Chinese arrested in this city at the beginning of the Civil War. By 1869, the *San Francisco Chronicle* reported that "each China steamer now brings consignments of women, destined to be placed in the market." Few of these Chinese girls had come here willingly. Most had been roped in with bogus moneymaking opportunities, often promises of wealthy white husbands. Some were just plain kidnapped. And once they reached this city, their lives usually turned ugly forever. In *The Hatchet Men*, Dillon tells of a *barracoon* (a sort of underworld trading center) situated beneath a Chinese temple off Dupont Street: "Here girls were stripped of their clothing and put up for bid. Those who resisted could be identified easily by the black-and-blue marks on their bodies from bamboo staves wielded by their highbinder masters. The most recalcitrant sometimes bore the sears of hot irons. But they were almost never killed; they were too valuable for that, being worth up to $3,000 each." Nonetheless, these women didn't live long, victims of mistreatment, malnourishment, or disease.

In 1882, the U.S. Congress voted to terminate the flow of Chinese into this country. But rules imposed from without were only one cause of concern for the future of San Francisco's Chinese community. Other troubles were internecine. Some younger Asians felt that their people were losing face (*mien tzu*) in dealing with white Californians; they believed that the Six Companies were no longer able to keep the old interracial relationship balanced. Gangs of hoodlums rose up—not to strike out against whites but, strangely, to punish their own people for their laissez-faire attitudes. "It was a weird class of civil war," Dillon remarked, "a struggle for power among bad men with the good people of Chinatown the pawns and the prey."

These brotherhoods of Chinese miscreants—usually called tongs (literally, "halls")—included both sexes, and "several were captained by maladjusted representatives of the so-called gentler sex," Herbert Asbury commented in his brilliant history, *The Barbary Coast*. Members were often well dressed, clad in frock coats, sombreros, and white ruffled shirts, their hair slicked back. They rarely carried firearms, depending instead on their fists, brass knuckles, and knives. Violence was a way of life in the tongs. In addition, they practiced crooked politics, graft, and blackmail, raking in huge profits for themselves, which were then used to buy heavily into the gambling, prostitution, and drug trades. Mobs of hooligans (the *boo how doy*) would descend upon individuals, or trash laundries and Chinese stores, or burn lumberyards where Chinese men were willing to work for the hated whites. They turned their piece of Golden Mountain into hell on earth.

LIKE THE GANGSTERS of Depression-era Chicago, the blood brotherhood of tongs bowed to no legal restrictions in San Francisco. They ruled Chinatown with an iron fist, from the 1880s until the earthquake of 1906. Most of the credit for finally bringing these gangs down belongs to those Chinese who abhorred the tongs' methods. Accepting their own status as Americans, law-abiding residents of Chinatown sought help from the local police and courts. White San Franciscans, having slowly shed much of the racism that had crippled their relations with Asian immigrants in the past, agreed to help bring law back to "Little China." Their campaign was assisted in an odd way by the tong leaders themselves. The more young thugs who killed each other off in the city's tong wars, the more level-headed elders were able to elbow their way back into leadership positions. By the 1920s, the tong battles were done.

It would take another two decades, though, before the Chinese could again become naturalized American citizens. And not until the 1950s were San Francisco's Chinese allowed to purchase homes outside Chinatown. Today, more than 80,000 people occupy the 18 square blocks of Chinatown—the second-largest Chinese community in the United States (after New York City).

TURTLE WOMAN

One of the most prominent houses of prostitution in mid-19th-century San Francisco was run by Ah Toy (sometimes called Atoy or Achoy), a Cantonese madam "blooming with youth, beauty, and rage." She arrived as sexual chattel in San Francisco about 1850 and may have been the first Chinese prostitute to operate within the city's developing Chinatown. Ah Toy was 22 years old and tall for a Chinese woman. She dressed in the most colorful of garb, and was "alternately the laughing-stock and the plague of the place," according to The Annals of San Francisco. *Ah Toy used her lascivious links with white potentates to purchase her freedom and then set herself up as a prosperous importer of Chinese women for immoral purposes. She survived the negative attentions of the first Vigilance Committee in 1851, and by 1852 was benefiting from (and probably promoting) the start of a great influx of Asian prostitutes into the Bay Area. As she became more confident and more powerful, writes Jacqueline Baker Barnhart in* The Fair But Frail, *Ah Toy used the full weight of the American judicial system on her behalf. She was especially quick to prosecute anybody who "disturbed the order of her disorderly house through attempts to tax the Chinese women," according to Barnhart.*

SHAKE, RATTLE, AND ROLL

"There was a deep rumble, deep and terrible, and then I could see it actually coming up Washington Street. The whole street was undulating. It was as if the waves of the ocean were coming towards me, billowing as they came."

The speaker, a police sergeant named Jesse Cook, who was on duty in the city's produce district during the early morning hours of Wednesday, April 18, 1906, remembered later that he didn't even have to time to react before San Francisco's most violent earthquake smacked him to the ground.

It began just after 5 a.m., shuddering down from the north along the San Andreas Fault with a force equal to 15 million tons of TNT. Forests of redwoods were toppled like so many toothpicks. Ships 150 miles out in the Pacific were jolted, their captains convinced that they had somehow struck a reef or a wreck twisting up from the deep sea floor. Fort Bragg, a blue-collar hamlet on the Mendocino Coast, jiggled and collapsed. The 110-foot-high Point Arena lighthouse, 90 miles north of San Francisco, swayed like a hula dancer before it too disintegrated in a hazardous hail of glass shards and broken masonry. At Point Reyes Station, the quake's epicenter, the morning train south was thrown into the air as its track buckled with the release of subterranean pressure. Boats docked at Bolinas were snapped clear of their moorings, and the town's wharf slipped underwater. South of San Francisco, 14 buildings at Stanford University in Palo Alto were demolished, along with the main quadrangle. Twenty-one men, women, and children perished in San Jose. A telephone operator in San Luis Obispo heard a scream on the other end of the line, and her scratchy connection with Salinas suddenly went dead.

At 5:13 a.m., the shock pummeled San Francisco. The first tremor lasted an excruciating 40 seconds. Then everything quieted for 10 seconds, before the arrival of a second, even stronger wave that endured for 25 seconds. The Richter scale hadn't yet been developed in 1906, but estimates since then have rated this seismic convulsion at 8.3, on a scale of 1 to 10. (By comparison, the October 1989 quake registered only 7.1 magnitude — more than 30 times less powerful than its 1906 counterpart.) Its effects were picked up by seismographs in Birmingham, England, and Tokyo, Japan.

Most of the force was concentrated north and south of San Francisco. The quake was powerful enough, though, to send earth waves, two to three feet high, roaring through the ground, threatening the foundations of even the strongest buildings and bringing lesser edifices down with ear-splitting crashes.

And the quake was only the beginning of a three-day disaster that would bring an end to San Francisco as it was.

ONE OF THE FIRST buildings to go was City Hall, finished only six years before, after three decades of slow work. The shaking caused almost the entire facade of the building to peel away, until all that was left was the metalwork beneath. The once-elegant dome looked like a bird cage.

Streetcar tracks reared up from their bolts and bent around like angry snakes. Long jagged tears opened the concrete middles of streets. Water gushed from broken lines. Gas spit up from rents in the sidewalk. The Ferry Building's tower clock stopped, and the tower itself weaved drunkenly and threatened to give way. Structures erected on landfill that covered old Yerba Buena Cove sagged into the ground, twisted unnaturally, their wood siding springing free with loud whines. At wharves, scaffolding collapsed, chopping boats in half. Hundreds of cemetery headstones tumbled over, all falling toward

~~~~~~

the east. Lights went out everywhere. Horses, spooked by the commotion, by the sparks thrown off from severed power lines, by people screaming all around them, broke their tethers and stampeded through downtown, joining platoons of rats already running for their pitiful lives.

Like some complex nightmare or surreal stage drama, the quake has left us thousands of such bizarre scenes, each one seeming to exist separately, although we know that they are tied together by a natural phenomenon.

In *The Damndest Finest Ruins*, one of the most readable accounts of the April 18 catastrophe, author Monica Sutherland tells of a flophouse lodger who woke in his dirty bed, still partially intoxicated from the night before, to find the furniture around him bouncing up and down on the floor. Looking up at the ceiling in his bleary-eyed confusion, the man saw a crack open up and a child's bare foot come poking through, "like some ghastly hanging lamp." As the building swayed, that crack closed again, "and the tiny foot, snapped off at the ankle, fell down soft and bleeding onto his bed." The terrified transient leapt up and hurled himself from the flophouse window. That act saved his life, for within minutes the building he left behind was rubble.

Above a fire station on Bush Street, Dennis T. Sullivan, the city's activist fire chief, was jolted from his sleep by the belligerent rocking and the crash of chimneys from nearby buildings. Getting up quickly, he rushed toward the back bedroom where his wife had been staying. But before he could reach her, a brick tower from an adjoining hotel punched through the firehouse roof, taking out part of Mrs. Sullivan's bedroom floor. Unable to get a clear view through the resulting dust cloud, the chief stepped forward to see if his wife was all right . . . and fell three stories down through the hole that had been left by the tower. He landed on a fire wagon, his skull, arms, and legs badly fractured.

Sullivan died in a hospital three days later, without enjoying even a moment's role in combating the blaze that might have made him famous.

MEANWHILE, AT THE Palace Hotel, built deliberately to withstand earthquake and fire threats, Italian tenor Enrico Caruso, in town for a week with the Metropolitan Opera Company to perform in *Carmen*, was bawling his head off. Caruso, not inclined to adapt easily to new surroundings, hadn't wanted to visit this city in the first place. When the second temblor of April 18 finally stilled and the cacophony subsided into an equally frightening silence, Caruso was convinced that his life was over. Worse, he was sure that he'd lost his voice. When Caruso's conductor, Alfred Hertz, rushed into the star's bedroom, he found the singer weeping desperately amidst piles of boots, silk shirts, and broken chandeliers. Hertz tried to calm Caruso, but with limited success. Finally, he told the tenor to come to the open window and see for himself that the quake was over.

"The street presented an amazing series of grotesque sights," Hertz later recalled. "Most people had fled from their rooms without stopping to dress, many of them a little less than naked. But excitement was running so high that nobody noticed or cared." Above this melée, Hertz instructed Caruso to sing. And he did just that. At the top of his lungs. At the top of his form. One can imagine the confusion engendered by this tableau. The Queen City of the Pacific Coast was a shambles, women were running down Market Street with babies squeezed against their breasts, men were hobbling along with prized belongings, smoke was rising from the Chinese corners of town . . . and the world's greatest living tenor was bellowing lines from *Carmen* out a fifth-floor window at the Palace. People below stood transfixed by the absurdity and wonder of it all.

THEY DIDN'T REMAIN still for long, for no sooner had the quake ended than the fires began. With all the crossed power lines, upended coal and wood stoves, broken

❧

FLAMMABLE

"San Francisco has violated all underwriting traditions and precedents by not burning up. That it has not already done so is largely due to the vigilance of the Fire Department, which cannot be relied upon indefinitely to stave off the inevitable."

—Citizen's Committee Report, 1905

❧

SINGING FOR HIS PASSAGE

Enrico Caruso had no intention of waiting out San Francisco's earthquake and fire. So, after fleeing the Palace Hotel, he and two members of his company embarked for the Ferry Building, hoping to secure passage across the Bay and then a train heading east. But when they arrived at the terminal, according to Gordon Thomas and Max Morgan Witts, in The San Francisco Earthquake, *the group was told to wait in line along with everyone else. This was too much for the spoiled Italian. "I am Enrico Caruso," he announced. "The singer." When the railroad man appeared unimpressed, Caruso drew out a signed portrait of Theodore Roosevelt that he had carried with him from the Palace and*

☞

vials of ignitable chemicals, and flammable-gas leaks, combined with the dry debris so recently exposed, the city's combustability was at an all-time high. Fifty fires were reported in the first 17 minutes after the quake. Yet not a single fire bell could be heard clanging. Wrecked along with so much else that morning was the fire department's central alarm system, housed in Chinatown.

While the tremors certainly caused havoc in the city, it was fire that sealed its fate. Despite several city-destroying blazes in the 19th century, San Francisco was still built primarily of wood. Chief Sullivan's forces did their best, rushing into the heart of the disaster, braving incinerations so hot that the firemen's hair was singed as they moved in with hoses. But it was all for naught. In most cases, hoses attached to hydrants brought forth little more than a trickle. The 30-inch main lines leading to San Francisco's two primary reservoirs in San Mateo County were broken.

Water pipes within the city were ruptured. Water was leaking everywhere, and little was left to throw onto the flames. Huge cisterns that had been located decades before under major intersections, for use in just such emergencies, ran dry in no time flat. Sewer water was pulled up by the gallon and heaved against the incendiary demons, but it made little difference. Firemen, even the bravest of the lot, were forced into retreat. Half an hour after the earth stopped shimmying, the city was engulfed in great, mephitic clouds of smoke five miles high that convinced onlookers in Oakland and Berkeley (where the earthquake had barely been felt) that San Francisco would be utterly destroyed.

Thousands of refugees fled before the scalding onslaught, carrying their possessions. Mobs rushed to the ferry docks, begging for passage to the East Bay. Some had barely escaped the fires, and their scorched bowlers and flame-fingered dresses showed just how close they'd come to being painful statistics. Through the middle of this panic drove automobiles retrieving the earthquake dead, their bloody, featureless faces staring out at people still hoping to survive the calamity.

Not everybody was unnerved by the disaster building in San Francisco. On the Barbary Coast, the city's center of salaciousness, men and women whooped it up, taking whatever liberties they could in the belief that all was lost and they might as well enjoy their last hours of life. Elsewhere in the city, looting of saloons and liquor stores was commonplace. The threat from mob violence was so acute in North Beach that even the firemen working in that area took to carrying arms. Mayor Eugene E. Schmitz finally proclaimed that law-enforcement personnel "have been authorized to KILL any and all persons found engaged in looting or in the commission of any other crime."

WATCHING THE CITY BURN from high up on Washington Street, Brigadier General Frederick Funston decided it was time for him to do something. Short and slight, Funston was nonetheless known to charge through point-blank gunfire in pursuit of a military goal. After proving his mettle during the Spanish-American War and in the Philippines, the red-headed Funston had arrived at the Presidio in 1901 as second-in-command of California's military department. It was not an easy posting for him. He didn't trust Mayor Schmitz's corrupt administration, for which he was acting as a liaison to the army, and he missed the thrill of battle. But now, with San Francisco staggering on the edge of ruin, Funston saw a chance to exercise his command skills.

Not so surprisingly, the brigadier general didn't consult with Schmitz—a breach of protocol that would be heavily criticized in weeks to come. Nor did he have the approval of his superiors in Washington, D.C., before he took action. Yet he ordered his troops to march right away upon the city and do whatever they could to restore order, end the looting, organize first-aid services, and help extinguish fires. Then "Fearless Freddie,"

shouted, "I am a friend of President Roosevelt. See. He gave me this!" And as the bewildered official studied the photo of the toothsome Chief Executive, Caruso added, "He is expecting me in Washington!" Another railroad man was called over, and the pair consulted for a few minutes. Then the new official said to the beefy tenor, "You Enrico Caruso? Then sing." "Sing! I want to leave here!," exclaimed the tenor. "Sure," the railroader remarked skeptically. "But you sing first." And so the Italian who never wanted to come to San Francisco in the first place was forced to belt out a few lines from Carmen. *Amazingly, it worked. Within a few minutes, Caruso and his party were on a ferry bound for Oakland.*

❧

as he would thereafter be known, telegraphed appeals to the army installations at Alcatraz, in Marin County, and as far away as Portland, Oregon, asking for additional troops to save San Francisco. By mid-morning, he had placed the city under martial control.

In the meantime, the scattered fires coalesced into three major ones—south of Market Street, north of Market near the waterfront, and in Hayes Valley, to the west of City Hall. This last blaze, the so-called Ham and Eggs Fire, was apparently started by a woman cooking breakfast in an earthquake-damaged chimney. Her house caught flame, and the fire spread.

Scattered successes were logged against the conflagration. The waterfront survived because fireboats rushed in to spray down flammable warehouses and sheds, and to fight back the cauldron of fire that was consuming the remainder of downtown. Most of the Jackson Square area survived because a naval force led by a Lieutenant Frederick Newton stretched a mile-long hose from Meiggs' Wharf (at today's Fisherman's Wharf) over the top of Telegraph Hill and used salt water to douse the flames. On the disaster's second day, Italians struggling to save houses around Telegraph Hill broke open casks of red wine—500 gallons of it—and sloshed it all over roofs, floors, walls. Tongues of fire licked at the wine-drenched edifices and backed away in pursuit of drier feed.

But the efforts of firemen and Funston's forces to create firebreaks by dynamiting buildings in the holocaust's path—a practice that had been popular in the 19th century—were a failure more often than not. First, imprecise loading of explosives meant that some shanties, rather than imploding, were blown to smithereens, sending more tinder into the maw of approaching flames or scattering already burning debris onto previously untouched structures. Then, the firebreaks were neither wide enough nor far enough ahead of the calamity to be truly effective. Mayor Schmitz, chary of political fallout from a wholesale demolition of private property, had insisted that buildings be dynamited only if they were in immediate danger of ignition. This caution proved tactically reprehensible.

By the end of that first day, the city was being consumed by one humongous blaze that kept the night sky lighted. Although many people remained upbeat about their chances of survival, others interpreted this as a signal fire marking the very end of the world. Rumors spread of other disasters: Manhattan Island had sunk already, it was said; Chicago was now at the bottom of Lake Michigan; the entire West Coast was aflame. Just before the San Francisco earthquake, news had come that Italy's Mount Vesuvius was, in fact, erupting. All of this convinced the city's more fanatical residents that divine retribution, rather than natural forces, was to blame for their terror. "This is the Lord's work!" they whispered.

THE FIRE CONTINUED for 74 hours, until Saturday morning, April 21, when it finally burned itself out. Rain began to fall not long after that—a little late, but nonetheless welcome. Late, as well, was official authorization from the nation's capital permitting Brigadier General Funston to take command of the situation as he had already done: It arrived by telegram on April 27.

The fire had razed 28,000 buildings—between $500 million and $1 billion in property—over an area of 4.7 square miles, between Larkin Street on the west and 20th Street on the south. Temperatures in the thick of the disaster had reached as high as 2,700 degrees Fahrenheit. "An enumeration of the buildings destroyed would be a directory of San Francisco," novelist Jack London lamented in *Collier's* magazine soon after the terror had passed. "An enumeration of the buildings undestroyed would be a line and several addresses." A few landmarks, such as Telegraph Hill, Jackson Square, and the old U.S. Mint, at Fifth and Mission streets, survived with a minimum of damage. But many of the

BURNING DOWN THE HOUSE

*It's not by mere chance that San Francisco's heraldic emblem features a Phoenix rising from the ashes. This town has been hit repeatedly by fires over the last century and a half. **1849:** The mostly wooden business district burns to the ground on Christmas Day while hundreds of citizens mill unhelpfully around Portsmouth Plaza. Wealthy merchants must pay men to help save their buildings, as well as pay $1 a bucket for the water they use. **1850:** Arsonists are blamed for starting one or more of the several fires that rage through the city during the year.*

☞

Fires on May 4 and 14 burn most of colonial San Francisco. **1851:** *The anniversary blaze of May 3 and 4 returns the town to a ruinous state. Rebuilders have barely gotten underway before another fire, on May 22, sends their work up in smoke, followed by more destruction on June 22. Upset by no less than six town-flattening holocausts in two years and rampant rumors of arson, property owners endorse the actions of the Vigilance Committee.* **1906:** *The April 18 temblor lasts less than a minute, but it sets off a fire that burns for three days. Four and a half square miles (including about 28,000 buildings) are reduced to smoking rubble and up to 3,000 people die.*

places that had defined the character of San Francisco were horribly defaced or destroyed altogether. The elegant Call Building was gutted, as was the Examiner Building, both on Market Street. Despite elaborate fire-fighting preparations (including a private basement reservoir of water), the Palace Hotel was caught in the wash of flame storming up from the south. At the height of the catastrophe, Nob Hill—with all its extravagant alcazars—looked like a lit match head.

About 250,000 San Franciscans, two-thirds of the city's entire population, were left homeless by this disaster. Many of them retreated to Golden Gate Park or the Presidio, where they set up tent cities reminiscent of those that had dotted the town during its Gold Rush frenzy. Some 3,000 other people are believed to have died in the earthquake and fire, more than 10 times as many as perished in the country's second-worst fire, at Chicago in 1871. Mass funerals were held all over town, with many people finding their last resting place in Portsmouth Square. Dead animals were left to decompose, adding the stink of rotting flesh to the pervasive odor of wet, burned wood.

Everywhere, there was a sense that this place would never be the same again. Yet expectation was in the air. "The great calamity . . . left no one with the impression that it amounted to an irrevocable loss . . . ," English writer H. G. Wells explained some years later in *The Future in America: A Search After Realities*. "Nowhere is there any doubt but that San Francisco will rise again, bigger, better and after the very briefest of intervals."

VICTIMS

"In the time of pestilence there are more things to admire in men than to despise."
—Albert Camus, *The Plague*

The disease was sexually transmitted, spread wildly, and had no known cure. Its rumored path of destruction had begun somewhere in Africa. People were advised to abstain from intercourse, or at least to wear condoms. Scourge-bearers often appeared with lesions on their skin and were shunned by the public. Demands were made to isolate these unfortunates, to let them die with their own kind and thus save the majority of the population. Even some physicians, who would treat patients with other noxious ailments, balked at the idea of helping these plague victims. Because the disease's outbreak closely followed an era of sexual promiscuity, clergymen and sanctimonious bigots were quick to charge that it was God's just punishment for sin.

No, this horror is not AIDS. It was syphilis, the pandemic of the 16th century, communicated in large part by prostitutes and disseminated over the face of Europe by amorous military men. Syphilis wrought its damage upon thousands of people, driving some blind, others mad, and killing the rest. In the sexually liberal city of Paris, where syphilis gained an early hold, as much as a third of the population was infected.

Parallels between AIDS and syphilis are obvious. And one could easily make the case that AIDS (acquired immune deficiency syndrome) is to the Bay Area today what syphilis was to Paris of the 1500s. San Francisco, after all, was the first U.S. metropolis to be struck significantly by AIDS and continues to rank above all others in total number of cases. (New York City holds second place.) In 1992, San Francisco became the first U.S.

IF AT FIRST YOU DON'T SUCCEED . . .

Thanks to an aggressive rebuilding program after the city's great earthquake and fire, by 1909 San Francisco claimed more than half of all the steel-and-concrete buildings then standing in the United States.

THE GROUND, SHE'S MOVIN' UNDER ME

1865: San Francisco's first major earthquake traceable to the now-famous San Andreas Fault strikes in October. 1868: The Golden Gate rocks again, causing an eastern reporter to remark that San Francisco is "a doomed city. It needs no gift of prophesy to predict the

☞

city in which AIDS surpassed heart disease as the number one killer of men of all ages. In September 1994, 280 people out of every 100,000 residents here tested positive for the human immunodeficiency virus (HIV) that causes AIDS. Homosexual and bisexual men—still the highest-risk group—accounted for over 8,200 AIDS cases.

JUST AS WITH SYPHILIS, AIDS scares people. Nobody knows precisely the source of the two principal virus strains (HIV-1 and the less virulent HIV-2) that bring on this disease, though some researchers suspect an African simian source. The Los Alamos National Laboratory has suggested that the earliest forms of AIDS may have evolved as long ago as the mid-19th century, but the earliest suspected case may perhaps be dated back to 1959, when a 25-year-old former sailor in England died after suffering skin sores, weight loss, high fevers, and lung infections. Because the disease is linked so closely with sexual activity (still a subject that's not easily discussed in the puritanical United States), and because in its earliest publicized stages it was reportedly a problem only among homosexuals (the Centers for Disease Control originally called it Gay Related Immune Deficiency, or GRID), U.S. response to its spread was slow and half-hearted. Ronald Reagan, who was president when the disease first gained widespread recognition in 1981, refused ever to talk about AIDS with his surgeon general, C. Everett Koop, despite Koop's repeated pleas for action and education. Not until 12 years later, when Bill Clinton moved into the White House, did the U.S. government take its first halting strides toward a consolidated effort at finding a cure for this disease. By then, more than 110,000 Americans had died of AIDS, and it was expected to kill another 500,000 (including as much as 4 percent of San Francisco's total population) over the next decade. With its slow incubation period of 7 to 11 years, many people—including heterosexuals, who account for under 10 percent of the cases, and intravenous drug users, who make up another 25

future, for it is inevitable." 1906: San Francisco is clobbered on the morning of April 18 by the most destructive earthquake in American history (estimated at 8.6 on the Richter scale). 1989: A 7.1-magnitude quake, centered about 10 miles north of Santa Cruz, hits at 5:04 p.m. on October 17. Part of theBay Bridge collapses, and the Embarcadero Freeway sustains such serious damage that it is not only closed but removed. Eleven people are killed, 566 receive injuries of one kind or another, and some 1,800 are left homeless.

❧

percent—may not know they carry the HIV virus until they have already spread it among their sexual partners. Curiously, others may carry the HIV virus and never develop full-blown AIDS.

Fortunately, this city's assault on AIDS was quicker and more aggressive than the national one. Newspapers and other local media have long stressed safe-sex techniques to trim the disease's propagation. They've also played up the risks that drug users run by sharing hypodermic needles. Special hospitals and home treatment care were established to assist people afflicted by AIDS through the late stages of their decline. Word-of-mouth warnings within the city's substantial gay community have had a particularly decisive effect. In 1982, there were reports of 18 new infections for every 100 uninfected gay men in San Francisco. By 1985, that rate had fallen to less than 1 in 100. Doctors pronounced in 1992 that the epidemic had already peaked here and was on the decline.

But it may have been presumptuous to celebrate. There's been more recent concern among public health officials that the city may be hit with new waves of AIDS. In 1993, for instance, the rate of infection climbed to 2 new cases in every 100 previously uninfected gay males. Statistics were twice that high among gay men younger than 25. This may not sound like an appreciable increase, but it could be ominous. Some authorities speculate that the longer the disease remains a tragic fact of life in the Bay Area, the more despairing and less cautious high-risk individuals may become. Surveys seem to bear this out. In 1994, they showed that, despite the constant barrage of safe-sex advertising, one out of every three gay men in the city was not protecting himself against AIDS transmission.

There is no single cause for this dangerous obstinacy. Part of it might be chalked up to fatalism. As one participant at a local AIDS prevention forum blithely put it, "Eventually you're going to get it, so why resist? We're surrounded." There are also

MELLOWING WITH AGE

Grant Avenue, one of Chinatown's busiest and gaudiest thoroughfares, is said to be the oldest street in San Francisco, dating from 1835. Originally called the Calle de la Fundación, it was later renamed Dupont, in misspelled tribute to Samuel F. DuPont, a naval officer and friend of San Francisco's alcalde (mayor). In 1876, after Dupont Street had become synonymous with crime, the four blocks from Bush to Market were renamed again, this time for President Ulysses S. Grant. Following the 1906 earthquake, its entire length—all the way to the North Beach waterfront—was designated in Grant's honor.

illusions among the young that they are somehow invulnerable or that AIDS is a problem for an older generation, not theirs. Other gay men look around at their friends who are dying of AIDS, see how those friends are showered with attention, and decide that having the disease wouldn't be such a bad thing after all. Or they see AIDS as a grim "badge of courage" that confirms their resolve to be openly gay. "I thought if I was HIV-positive, I'd be so much gayer," a thirtysomething airline mechanic told *The New York Times* in 1994.

AIDS HAS DONE more than anything else—more than the annual Lesbian and Gay Freedom Day parades, more even than the 1978 murder of gay city supervisor Harvey Milk—to bring San Francisco's gay and lesbian community together. As they might in a war, the people most at risk from AIDS have had to fight back in concert with each other—against not only the disease but also the homophobes who have tried to stigmatize and further marginalize San Francisco gays. (Wasn't it the French author Camus, again, who wrote that "The first thing that [the epidemic] brought . . . was exile"?)

San Francisco seems always to have had some homosexual activity, even as far back as the Gold Rush, when newspapers talked obliquely about the "Lavender Cowboys," a cadre of gay men who traveled on horseback through northern California's then mostly masculine society. The number of gay men here grew significantly during World War II, when the U.S. military tried its best to muster out homosexual servicemen. A great number of those soldiers were shipped back to the States through San Francisco and many, chary of explaining to their families the precise reason for their discharge, decided to remain in the Bay Area. By the early 1970s, the homosexual community here was spreading out from its base in the Castro District and making inroads into local politics. The city came to be known as America's homosexual capital, and its eccentric sidewalk parade was enriched with transvestites in stiletto heels, women holding hands, and men with colored

THE QUIET KILLER

AIDS became San Francisco's number-one killer of men in 1992. From a total of 8,143 deaths in the city that year, 1,195 were traced to AIDS, outpacing heart-related disease as the leading cause of death for men.

scarves dangling from their pockets to announce their sexual proclivities. (The scarf is apparently a tradition from the Gold Rush era, when there were so few women here that men had to dance with each other and indicated their preference for leading or following by the hue of their bandanna.)

Never before, however, have the foundations of San Francisco's tolerance for "alternative lifestyles" been so sorely tested as they are now in the age of AIDS. If and when a cure is found, will the city be a stronger and more compassionate place . . . or a more divisive and intolerant one?

❦

HOPE IN SHORT SUPPLY

"In traditional medicine, you go to the doctor and get better. With AIDS, you go to the doctor, you go to the doctor, you go to the doctor, you go to the doctor, you go to the doctor, you go to the doctor, you go to the doctor — and die."

— "Richard," San Francisco AIDS counselor and HIV-positive male, quoted in the San Jose Mercury News

❧

ORDER FROM CHAOS

"It is hardly fair to blame America for the state of San Francisco,
for its population is cosmopolitan and its seaport attracts the floating vice of the Pacific;
but be the cause what it may, there is much room for spiritual betterment."
—Sir Arthur Conan Doyle

TRUE LOVE, TRUE LOSS

One of California's most unforget-table love stories concerns a middle-aged Russian count and a young Spanish girl. Count Nicolai Petrovich de Rezánov arrived aboard a Russian vessel in 1806. While attending a celebration at the Presidio that first night, the count had the opportunity to talk and dance with Concepcion Argüello, the enchanting dark-eyed daughter of the garrison's commandant. He was overwhelmed by the delicate beauty and manners of this slender Spanish girl, and though he sailed away with his ship, Rezánov promised Concepcion that he would return after securing permission from the Russian and Catholic Churches

☞

FORTRESS SAN FRANCISCO

By the late 18th century, weaknesses in the Spanish Empire were painfully obvious and were having their effects on California. More energy had gone into spreading Spain's influence than in actually developing the lands over which the country claimed sovereignty. This might have worked if Madrid had encouraged independent growth of its outposts; but it did not, insisting instead on centralized control. Without the right or impetus to be self-sufficient, Spain's many outposts were slow to improve themselves and usually drained more wealth away from the mother country than they ever returned.

All this meant that a place such as San Francisco, at that time as psychologically remote from the Iberian Peninsula as Earth's moon, had trouble realizing the dreams of its founders. The local stronghold—the Presidio—suffered in particular.

Captain Juan Bautista de Anza had planted a cross on the edge of the Golden Gate with great ceremony and optimism in 1776, designating that very strategic site (the location of today's Fort Point) for a new Spanish stronghold. But rather than constructing a post at the point de Anza had proposed, the Spanish, on a tight budget, erected their new fort at a site about a mile inland. A quadrangle of buildings went up, encircled by battlements made of oak and mud. All this was pretty much destroyed during a heavy rainstorm two years later and was replaced by more permanent fortifications, complete with barracks, a commander's residence, and a chapel. And still, the Presidio wasn't up to its job.

WHEN BRITISH CAPTAIN George Vancouver sailed through the Golden Gate in 1792 aboard his sloop-of-war, the *Discovery,* he was surprised to find both the fort and the surrounding settlement in a sorry state. Describing the Presidio, Vancouver wrote that "its wall, which fronted the harbour, was visible from the ships; but instead of the city or town, whose light we had so anxiously looked for on the night of our arrival, we were conducted into a spacious verdant plain, surrounded by hills on every side, excepting that which fronted the port. The only object of human industry which presented itself, was a square area, whose sides were about two hundred yards in length, enclosed by a mud wall, and resembling a pound for cattle. On entering the Presidio, we found one of its sides still uninclosed by the wall, and very indifferently fenced in by a few bushes here and there. . . . Instead of finding a country tolerably well inhabited and far advanced in cultivation, if we except its natural pastures, the flocks of sheep, the herds of cattle, there is not an object to indicate the most remote connection with any European, or other civilized nation."

George Vancouver's call at the Presidio brought some panic to Spanish administrators. They finally sensed that their fort was woefully ill-prepared to guard the Bay against foreign invasion, and ordered the construction of a defensive barricade on the Golden Gate's south bluffs. Finished in 1794, this Castillo de San Joaquin looked more impressive than the Presidio, but it would have done just as little to stop the British or the French or anybody else with cannon-bearing craft from entering the harbor. Its foundations were weak, and its walls jiggled every time one of its big guns went off. "Munitions were in such short supply," wrote popular historian Rand Richards, "that when, in 1806, a Russian ship entered the Bay and fired a friendly salute, the Spanish soldiers had to row out to the vessel to borrow enough powder to fire a return salute."

MEXICO'S HARD-WON INDEPENDENCE from Spain in 1821 brought a decline in the number of troops assigned to the Presidio, as well as still more severe budgetary constraints. By 1825, when the British sloop-of-war *Blossom* hove to off the shore of what would become San Francisco, the 49-year-old installation was decrepit. The *Blossom's*

for a mixed-faith marriage. Nothing more was heard of the count for 36 years, reported Julia Coolley Altrocchi in her book The Spectacular San Franciscans. And then one day, a world traveler named Sir George Simpson brought back news of Rezánov. "Not knowing that Rezánov's faded sweetheart was in the listening group at Santa Barbara," Altrocchi wrote, "Sir George told the story of Rezánov's death on the steppes of Siberia on the very journey that had taken him away from his betrothed. 'Sh . . . sh . . . sh . . . She is here,' stuttered one of Simpson's fellow diners. 'His enamorada is here in the room.' 'No'—Concepcion spoke through the weighted silence—'she died too.'"

❧

captain, Frederick William Beechey, found the Presidio to be "little better than a heap of rubbish and bones, on which jackals, dogs, and vultures were constantly preying." Whether observed from near or far, he commented, "the establishment impresses a spectator with any other sentiment than that of its being a place of authority. . . . But for a tottering flagstaff upon which was occasionally displayed the tricolored flag of Mexico . . . a visitor would be ignorant of the importance of the place."

The passage of Mexico's Secularization Act of 1834, which relieved California's industrious Franciscans of their church land, halted religious practices at San Francisco's Mission Dolores for the next 25 years, and had a generally depressing effect on the area's nascent community. The Presidio and Castillo de San Joaquin were both allowed to molder. The Castillo was abandoned in 1835, and the remains of its munitions were moved across the Bay to what is now Benicia.

The original Presidio saw its last year of military service in 1835 as well. Much of what remained of its structure was subsequently recovered as material for a customs house being erected in the nearby community of Yerba Buena.

THE PRESIDIO WAS almost unrecognizable on July 1, 1846, when, during the Mexican War, U.S. Army Lieutenant John C. Frémont (later a Senator from California and a presidential candidate in 1856) led a boatload of men across from Sausalito to storm the fort as part of the so-called Bear Flag Revolt. Frémont and many of his men were topographical engineers, sent out west on a mapping expedition. They'd entered this brief rebellion against the Mexican government on behalf of American settlers in the Sacramento Valley, and a jolly good fight had been expected. But to Frémont's surprise, the Americans landing at the beach below the fort were met not with gunfire but with absolute silence. Clutching their rifles and pistols, their hearts beating wildly with the expectation of life-or-death combat, the insurgents mounted the hill where the Presidio was supposed to be located . . . and found only one vacated adobe building and the foundations of several others. There were no soldiers. There was no gunpowder. There was no battle to be had. They did, however, happen upon 10 small cannons that dated from the 17th century and probably weren't even in working order. These Frémont "spiked," and the valiant American invaders returned to their ship and Sausalito.

NOT UNTIL THE CIVIL WAR did the Presidio again see a military presence. Union regiments went through their paces on a broad new parade ground. A dozen cottages for officers were raised on the parade ground's east flank, and a hospital was installed on the site. As early as the 1870s, San Francisco's Presidio was opened to the public, and, in the 1880s, the process of reclaiming as parkland 1,383 acres of wind-ravaged dunes surrounding the fort was begun, with the planting of expansive lawns and tens of thousands of cypress, eucalyptus, and acacia trees.

During the 1906 earthquake and fire, the Presidio, like Golden Gate Park, hosted camps for homeless San Franciscans. Fort Winfield Scott was built between 1910 and 1912 as extra protection along the coastline, and more Mission Revival–style officers' homes went up all over the Presidio. During World War II, the Presidio served as headquarters for the Fourth Army and Western Defense Command.

Today, the Presidio looks more like a fort than it ever did in the hands of Spain or Mexico, although its wooded acreage is currently under the management of the National Park Service and has been included as part of the Golden Gate National Recreation Area.

THE LOWLY P.O.W.

The day after Lieutenant Frémont and his "soldiers" made their semi-comic charge into the Presidio, they invaded the village of Yerba Buena, where they arrested one Robert Riley, the captain of the port. They hauled Riley off to John Sutter's colony of New Helvetia as a prisoner of war — the only captive in the only military skirmish that San Francisco has ever known. On July 9, Captain John B. Montgomery and about 70 of his men from the USS Portsmouth came ashore and claimed California for the United States. Frémont's campaign to create an independent republic was over.

MOB RULES

Tuesday, June 10, 1851. Shipping agent George W. Virgin finds that a thief has ransacked his office on Long Wharf, at the end of Commercial Street, and has stolen his small iron safe. He raises an alarm, and only minutes later, a tall, burly former Australian convict named John Jenkins is spotted in the moonlight scurrying down the quarter-mile-long wharf toward a waiting rowboat, with an obviously weighty sack heaved up onto one shoulder. Other men take off after him, but they can't reach Jenkins before he leaps into his getaway skiff and rows vigorously out into Yerba Buena Cove. With pursuing boats rapidly closing in on him, Jenkins stops and tips his booty into the drink. When he's nabbed, he denies knowing anything about a missing strongbox. But boatmen with long-handled tongs fish Jenkins's sack out of the mud and, lo and behold, inside is Virgin's prized property.

Rather than being handed over to the San Francisco police, Jenkins is surprised to find himself taken to an obscure storeroom, where 80 men gather to question him and take testimony from George Virgin. Evidence in the case is examined, but there seems no question of Jenkins's guilt. At midnight, several hours after this kangaroo court began its proceedings, Sam Brannan, real estate mogul and wealthy publisher of *The California Star,* announces to a crowd gathered outside the storeroom that the miscreant will be hanged within two hours at Portsmouth Square.

As Jenkins and a pack of heavily armed men enter the plaza's moonlit western side at the appointed hour, 2 a.m., policemen rush in to grab Jenkins, but Brannan's people repel them. The cops are told that they'll be shot if they try to interfere. With that, a noose is looped about Jenkins's neck. "Every lover of liberty and good order lay hold!"

WHAT'S IN A NAME

The most lasting result of Frémont's brief rebellion came when the lieutenant, taking a close look at the deep, imposing cut that links San Francisco Bay with the Pacific, decided what its name should be. "To this gate," he wrote in his Memoirs, "I gave the name of Chryspolae, or Golden Gate." Sure enough, that moniker appears on the official 1848 map of Frémont's expedition to the West.

Brannan shouts, and a score of men immediately grab the rope to yank Jenkins high off the ground, gagging and swinging. The crowd disperses as Jenkins stills. But Brannan's minions stay until morning, making sure that Jenkins's criminal friends don't claim the corpse before the coroner can, at 7 a.m.

SO BEGAN THE FIRST of San Francisco's two brief periods of vigilante rule. Never before, never since has the city come as close to anarchy as in 1851 and 1856, when apparently well-intentioned citizens sought to take law enforcement into their own hands.

The Gold Rush in California had brought a flood of new settlers and fortune seekers to San Francisco. The city's population exploded, from about 6,000 in 1848 to 25,000 in 1850, taxing inadequate city services and causing tempers to flare. Police were too few in number to keep everybody in line. Conditions worsened during the winters, when miners—who operated most of the year under a fairly loose web of laws—were driven back into town by Sierra snowfalls. A swelling underground of career criminals, including those night-crawling incorrigibles from Down Under, the "Sydney Ducks," and their fellow felons, the American gang members known as "Hounds," preyed on people who could be easily separated from their money or whose homes and businesses presented paltry protection from vandals.

In February 1851, a dry-goods storekeeper named Charles J. Jansen was beaten severely. Businessmen and property owners decided that they must finally band together for their own survival. Their convictions were strengthened in May, when the fifth major fire in less than two years—this one, like so many others, probably ignited by hooligans—leveled the wooden town and brought forth bands of plunderers anxious to lever their advantage amidst all the confusion. Local courts and law-enforcement officers couldn't

FELONS AFLOAT

The city's first prison was the rotting hulk of a Spanish brig, the Euphemia, which had been abandoned in San Pablo Bay. It was converted into a floating prison in 1851, and California's most hardened criminals were relegated to its dismal, rat-infested cells below decks. Ventilation was bad, food on board was worse, and men were allowed topside only when the Bay was clear of fog that could cover an escape (this meant that convicts might have to ☞

stay down in the freezing hold for weeks at a time). In 1852, the Euphemia was towed to San Quentin Point, where prisoners were put to work building the state's first penitentiary. The scow was later returned to Yerba Buena Bay, to become part of the fill that finally created downtown's southeastern corner (the boat's final resting place is near the intersection of Battery and Sacramento Streets).

control these terrorist campaigns, and many scared San Franciscans were tired of seeing acknowledged outlaws freed by wily lawyers.

In June 1851, about 200 prominent citizens gathered secretly at a building owned by Sam Brannan on the corner of Battery and Pine Streets. They railed at the federal and territorial governments' unwillingness to prevent malcontents from settling in the area, and they insisted that stiffer penalties be handed down against convicted crooks.

After hours of discussion and debate, those frightened burghers formed what would come to be known as the First Vigilance Committee. Its constitution left little ambiguity about its mission or its determination: "WHEREAS it has become apparent to the citizens of San Francisco that there is no security for life and property . . . the citizens, whose names are hereunto attached, do unite themselves into an association for the maintenance of the peace and good order of society, and . . . do bind themselves, each unto the other, to do and perform every lawful act for the maintenance of law and order, and to sustain the laws when faithfully and properly administered; but we are determined that no thief, burglar, incendiary, or assassin, shall escape punishment, either by the quibbles of the law, the insecurity of prisons, the carelessness or corruption of the police, or a laxity of those who pretend to administer justice. . . ." The committee went so far as to assume the right to deport unsavory characters and "to enter any person or persons' premises where we have good reason to believe that we shall find evidence to substantiate and carry out the object of this body."

The Jenkins lynching, conducted only hours after the Vigilance Committee had formalized its existence, was a sure sign that Brannan and company meant business. When the vigilantes' opponents tried to prosecute individual members of the committee, a statement was issued declaring that every one of the committee's members took equal responsibility for the Jenkins affair. If any one among them was to be tried for murder, so must they all. It was signed by 180 people.

COMMITTEE MEMBERS HAD another message for malcontents, especially those who frequented "Sydney Town," a treacherous harbor for thieves and Chileno whores at the base of Telegraph Hill (later incorporated into the even-more-colorful Barbary Coast). *Get out,* they insisted, *or we'll kick you out!* A subcommittee of vigilantes even policed incoming ships, and any men who couldn't provide proof of virtual sainthood were turned away from the docks. Some Sydney Towners were hauled off the streets and dumped before regular policemen, along with long lists of their transgressions. Others, mostly small-timers, were spotted fleeing the city on board steamers headed east up the Sacramento River toward the Mother Lode. In all, during the First Committee's reign 14 people were deported and another 14 were ordered to pack their bags and leave California. But the ruffians who remained behind, who defied the vigilantes' intimidation, were the worst of the bunch, intent on revenge.

Nobody doubted that the Ducks and Hounds were responsible for a June 22, 1851, fire that began in a vacant house at Pacific and Powell Streets and swept over most of the local skyline, destroying 18 blocks in the business district. Hundreds of frightened residents at that point decided they'd had enough, and moved out of the city to the East Bay. But the vigilantes saw this arson as a test of their commitment, and they stepped up their activities.

One night in early July, "English Jim" Stuart, an escapee from Australia's prison system and the man responsible for the February assault on Charles Jansen, came out of hiding to rob an English ship docked in the harbor. He had made it as far as the captain's cabin when that old salt and his wife suddenly awakened. English Jim clubbed the captain

GETTING REALLY TOUGH ON CRIME

San Quentin State Prison's reputation as overcrowded and violent is nothing new. It dates back to the 1850s, when severe punishments were meted out as a means of controlling recalcitrant inmates. Flogging was common practice. "At almost any hour of the day or night the screams of a whipped man could be heard," Fred Harrison *wrote in* Hell Holes and Hangings. *"Later, if the convict survived whipping, he was often chained to iron rings imbedded in the stone walls and left to contemplate his sins, sometimes for years at a time," with no toilet facilities or bedding, and little food. Disruptive prisoners might also be tightly straitjacketed and gagged, after which shifts of guards would beat them with fists or clubs. A less labor-intensive penalty was the "shower bath," a high-pressure blast of water from a 1½-inch hose that would be used until the convict bled from his eyes, ears, and nose. The true sadist's discipline of choice, however, was something called "the derrick." Men were hung for hours from a block that allowed only the tips of their toes to brush the floor. What's worse, chloride of lime was spread on the floor, its fumes wafting up to burn and strangle the inmate. Fortunately, most of these brutalities were eliminated by the 1880s.*

❦

with a "slung shot" (blackjack), but the wife grabbed hold of the burglar and screamed until crew members could capture Stuart. After being beaten generously, Jim was delivered to the Vigilance Committee, which now numbered 400 and was itching for trouble. It didn't take long to find him guilty of larceny, especially since the culprit confessed to a long list of misdeeds, perhaps hoping to win mercy. Two hours after the committee decided he should hang, Jim was dangling from a derrick on the Market Street wharf.

The final two executions attributed to the First Vigilance Committee brought a heated standoff with lawmen. Sam Whittaker and Robert McKenzie, known associates of English Jim's, were seized by committeemen and promptly convicted of burglary, arson, and robbery. Everybody knew they would swing, but no immediate date was set. While McKenzie and Whittaker cooled their heels in the vigilante lockup, on August 21, California Governor John MacDougal issued a proclamation addressed to all of San Francisco that condemned "the despotic control of a self-constituted association, unknown and acting in defiance of the laws." The next morning, Sheriff Jack Hays arrived at the vigilantes' headquarters with a gun-toting contingent of cops and a writ of habeas corpus from the governor, demanding the release of the prisoners. The outnumbered guards didn't resist.

But three days later, 36 vigilantes went to the jail under City Hall and, overpowering the sheriff's men, recaptured Whittaker and McKenzie. Within minutes, the pair had their lives choked off by nooses, while hundreds of San Franciscans cheered.

This was the First Vigilance Committee's last official act—the last one that was necessary for some time, causing "a panic in Sydney Town," as Herbert Asbury explained in *The Barbary Coast.* "Its rascally inhabitants left San Francisco in droves, and within two weeks there remained in that vicious quarter only a few dance-halls, saloons, and houses of prostitution, all of which were carefully operated in strict accordance with the law."

HOWEVER, THIS PEACEFUL situation didn't hold. Five years later, violent crime again captured the attention of leading San Franciscans, and the Second Committee of Vigilance came into being. The main impetus for its birth was the street slaying, on May 14, 1856, of James King of William, a member of the First Committee who had become publisher of the *Daily Evening Bulletin.* Many of the men who'd stood behind Sam Brannan in 1851 congregated again to capture and hang King's murderer, James Casey, along with a gambler, Charles Cora, who had recently killed a U.S. Marshal.

Those lynchings stunned the city's criminals. But they had the same effect on California's governor at the time, J. Neely Johnson, who issued a proclamation declaring that San Francisco was in a state of insurrection. The future Civil War general William T. Sherman (at that time a banker in San Francisco) was placed in command of the local militia and told to both fortify strategic locations (such as the State Armory on Grant Avenue) and neutralize the vigilantes. Committee members themselves were ordered to relinquish their weapons and cease practicing outlaw justice.

Unfortunately, Governor Johnson hadn't reckoned on the determination of William Tell Coleman, a broadly mustachioed merchant who was in command of the committee. Not only did Coleman fail to dissolve his group—5,000 members strong—but he had them hunker down more solidly behind the sandbag fortifications that marked their headquarters, a former Sacramento Street warehouse they called "Fort Gunnybags." Sherman's resignation after just a week with the militia (he was discouraged at Johnson's unwillingness to summon more troops to San Francisco), followed by the appointment of a lesser commander, former Texas Congressman Volney E. Howard, only strengthened Coleman's hand.

SPY VS. SPY

The roots of the U.S. Secret Service date back to 1861, when Secretary of State William H. Seward began hiring agents to ferret out Confederate conspirators in the nation's capital and abroad. A year later, Seward split his international and domestic counterespionage efforts and assigned a former San Franciscan, Lafayette C. Baker, to build up a domestic intelligence agency under the Secretary of War's imprimatur. Baker enlisted a coterie of informers and detectives, responsible for not only arresting disloyal citizens and

☞

Members of the Second Committee took it upon themselves to punish not only crooks but also those who opposed the group's extra-legal activities. The committee did not even hesitate to take on Governor Johnson's own representatives, one of whom—Reuben Maloney—tried in June 1856 to guide a flatboat full of ammunition down the Sacramento River, with the intention of resupplying the militia. The cache was captured in San Francisco Bay by Coleman's forces.

Vigilantes subsequently tried to capture Maloney himself. But it was a supremely bollixed escapade. Knowing that Maloney was in the local office of the U.S. Navy Agent H. P. Ashe, Coleman's men lay in wait outside. When Ashe, Maloney, and California Supreme Court Judge David S. Terry exited the building, the vigilantes confronted them. In the ensuing melee, Terry stabbed one of the vigilantes in the throat and was hauled before Coleman's committee for his crimes. He was found guilty of the assault, but since his victim lived, Terry did too.

THE SECOND COMMITTEE finished off its work on July 24, 1856, in classic style, hanging two men who had murdered a doctor. That made four men sent to the gallows that summer, added to 26 lawbreakers who had been deported. Even in the face of threats from Sacramento, the committee had done what it perceived as its work, and couldn't help crowing about it. So on Monday, August 18, more than 8,000 well-armored men turned in their guns and handed the city back over to Mayor Charles Brenham and Governor Johnson. San Francisco's revolution was over—and everybody knew who had won.

"THE CHINESE MUST GO!"

After the economic surges provided by discovery of gold in California and of silver in Nevada, and following the promise of prosperity that accompanied the opening of a transcontinental railroad in 1869, the 1870s proved an economic disappointment to San Francisco. The Panic of 1873, brought on by the collapse of millionaire Jay Cooke's giant New York banking house, led to the closing of financial institutions across the country. Depression conditions were particularly severe in the East, forcing unemployed men and their families farther and farther west in hopes of finding work. During its boom times, California had been desperate for fresh workers. But with 260,000 people arriving in the state between 1873 and 1875, there was suddenly a glut of laborers.

Tensions grew among unemployed San Franciscans, and frustration was directed in particular toward the Chinese, some 20,000 of whom had been brought to the Bay Area under a special agreement to help build the Central Pacific's rail link to Promontory, Utah. After the line's completion, these Chinese toilers were released to find other jobs—or *steal* jobs, as many of their white competitors saw it. In 1870, more than half of the 71,328 Chinese in California were living in San Francisco. By 1875, the state contained about 100,000 Chinese, most of them men willing to work at wages well below those acceptable to the majority of Caucasian laborers. In San Francisco alone, the Chinese accounted for 20 percent of the working population (the same percentage as the Irish), and employers were ready to save a buck by hiring them.

It seemed inevitable that racial conflict would erupt in California. The most shocking incident came in Los Angeles in 1871, when about 20 Chinese people were massacred, most of them by hanging. Violence hit San Francisco hard six years later, in late

LANGFORD'S LAW

Frequented by a rough crowd of shanghaiiers, hoodlums, opium smugglers, and outright murderers, San Francisco's waterfront in the late 19th century was no plum assignment for cops. The lawmen who patrolled the wharves and filthy sea-dog saloons had to be as brave and brutish as their adversaries. It was common, especially among policemen who walked the old Barbary Coast section of the waterfront, to carry not only nightsticks and pistols but also knives that might measure a foot or more in length. They used these sharp instruments at the slightest provocation— and to the bloodiest effect. It was de rigueur for cops of the harbor

☞

precinct, when cornered by thugs, to dispense with their clumsy and sometimes ineffective firearms, and turn to their knives instead, slashing away with all their might. In one story, a sergeant named Thomas Langford is said to have launched right into a group of several hoodlums he found ransacking a Pacific Avenue clothing store. Braving pistol blasts, he wielded his long blade like a pirate, wounding most of the thieves and all but severing the head of one of them. Needless to say, after this near-decapitation, the rest of the gang fled in terror, and Sergeant Langford enjoyed a fearful respect that was unusual even among his husky and violent brethren.

July 1877, when a convocation of thousands of angry workers at a sandlot adjacent to City Hall led to the torchings of several Chinese stores and laundries. This was followed by stonings of Asians in Chinatown.

Local businessmen, wary of full-scale rioting, sought to tame tensions by setting up a Committee of Public Safety under the direction of ex-vigilante chieftain William T. Coleman. Arming 5,000 men with hickory pick handles and sending them out on street patrol, Coleman seemed capable of maintaining the peace. Just two days after he took on his assignment, his "Pickhandle Brigade" quashed an anti-Chinese mob assault on docks that were shared by the Pacific Mail Steamship Company (which hired Chinese workers to crew its ships) and the Central Pacific's Occidental & Oriental Line (a large transporter of Chinese immigrants). Though four men died in the confrontation and a nearby lumberyard (which had hired several Chinese men) went up in flames, Coleman's army was deemed effective. Yet it was disbanded not long afterward, when rioting came to a halt, and replaced with a special police force financed by timorous property owners.

RESENTMENTS DIDN'T GO away easily, however. And strangely, it was a member of Coleman's brigade, Denis Kearney, who rose to become the city's most troublemaking Sinophobe. An Irish immigrant and former sailor, Kearney had owned a small drayage business, but had watched it go under after the Panic of 1873. The loss of his enterprise embittered Kearney, and though he felt an obligation as a small businessman to help Coleman put down labor's revolt, he blamed the Chinese for souring San Francisco's economy. When he discovered that he had a gift for fiery perorations, he determined to foment large-scale anti-Chinese ire among San Francisco's working class.

Kearney had never been particularly fond of the working class. He had been known to call his own blue-collar peers "shiftless and extravagant," too fond of their liquor and tobacco, indolent. However, he was also an opportunist. He could see that anybody capable of controlling this city's large working-class population might enjoy significant political clout. So Kearney decided to volunteer himself as the Voice of the Little Man.

He blustered against the Chinese, against local capitalists, against corrupt politicians—all of whom he claimed were co-conspirators in keeping wages depressed and reducing the number of jobs available to Caucasians. Kearney knew just what his audience wanted to hear, and he delivered it as often as possible and at the top of his lungs. The more outrageous and xenophobic he became, the more hatred and intolerance rolled off his tongue, the more respect Kearney gained among the workers he sought to represent. When Kearney was arrested, as he periodically was, for trying to incite violence, his foes (and surely most of Chinatown) cheered; but he always managed to return to his soapbox, just that much stronger for having survived the establishment's concerted efforts to silence him.

The nativist agitator seemed unafraid that his provocative exhortations might invite assassination. In fact, there was a part of Kearney that longed to be murdered, knowing it would make him a martyr and solidify his followers' narrow viewpoints. So he attacked any conceivable target. He threatened to lynch the "thieving millionaires, the hell-born, hell-bound villains, the bloated bondholders" of Nob Hill. He proposed that when that was done, the next inhabitants of the hangman's noose should be members of the state legislature. Even President Ulysses Grant couldn't escape the spray of Denis Kearney's venom. He charged that the Hero of Appomattox, whose administration had sat on its hands while corrupt business leaders lined their pockets with pelf, should be burned in effigy, if not destroyed in fact.

But Kearney's heaviest vituperative ammunition was aimed at the hated "coolies,"

STORMING THE PALACES

Denis Kearney and his disciples were unsparing in their hateful harangues against local nabobs. "The monopolists who make money by employing cheap labor had better watch out," Kearney proclaimed in one of his sandlot speeches. "They have built themselves fine residences on Nob Hill and erected flagstaffs upon their roofs. Let them take care that they have not erected their own gallows."

One evening in late 1877, several hundred Kearneyites took their fight to the doorstep of their enemies. After marching up Nob Hill, they declared that two of the most prominent mansions there, those owned by railroad

☞

magnates Leland Stanford and Mark Hopkins, should immediately be ceded to "the people" and turned into asylums. While neighboring millionaires cowered in their houses with their loaded rifles and their terrified families, Kearney told the angry crowd of workers that he was prepared to organize a Workingmen's Party club for the Nob Hill area, and that if Stanford would come forward and admit to his multitudinous perfidies, he would be named president of the new club. Stanford, however, was apparently not even at home that night, and he never acknowledged Kearney's invitation.

❧❀❧

the "Yellow Peril," the men who had not had the sense to return to China when their work on the railroads was done. Working himself into a scarlet-faced rage, he told hordes of fellow bigots assembled in San Francisco's sandlots that "the Chinese must go!" That became the battle cry of his new Workingmen's Party of California (WPC), a more-or-less socialist organization that Kearney said would accept "no great capitalist, no political trickster, no swindler or thief" as a member.

"We will fill the [political] offices with honest poor men who will make laws to protect themselves," this sandlot orator proclaimed. "We will send the Chinese home, distribute the land of the grabber, tax the millionaire, make a law to hang thieves of high as well as low degree, elevate the poor, and once more return to the simple virtue of honest republicanism." If achieving all of that meant chaos and anarchy in San Francisco, then so be it. "I'll make a burning Moscow of this city!" Kearney promised. More thoughtful pro-labor activists, even those who agreed with his anti-Chinese sentiments, sought to distance themselves from Denis Kearney. He was too much of a loose cannon.

BY 1879 KEARNEY had reached the zenith of his power. That was the year when California held a second constitutional convention, hoping to satisfy critics who charged that the original constitution of 1849 was not specific enough in its articles to answer the questions and satisfy the needs of an increasingly intricate democracy. Out of 152 delegates elected to that convention, 51 of them owed allegiance to Kearney's WPC and 30 of those hailed from San Francisco. Coalitions were formed desperately between Democrats and Republicans opposed to Kearney's politics, yet the Workingmen's Party managed to convert much of its platform into law, including heavier regulation of railroads and banks, compulsory education, and of course, limits on Chinese employment. (Most of the racist provisions, however, were later declared invalid or unenforceable.)

In the same year, Kearneyites exercised their influence statewide by electing 11 senators and 16 assemblymen to Sacramento, as well as the chief justice, five associate justices of the California Supreme Court, and a railroad commissioner. In San Francisco, the Reverend Isaac S. Kalloch rode the WPC bandwagon straight into the mayor's office.

California was becoming a dangerous place for Asians. It was out of the racist violence of this era that the expression "Not a Chinaman's chance" was coined. With increasingly frequency, Chinese prostitutes were harassed and molested, and their brothels were taxed extortionately. Other taxes were levied on the queues worn by the inhabitants of Chinatown. White gang members made sport of capturing Chinese people and clipping off the ends of their pigtails. There were even local ordinances passed to restrict the number of occupants allowed to inhabit a single dwelling—laws that could be used against the clannish Chinese in general, as well as against Chinese houses of prostitution, when it was convenient.

IRONICALLY, KEARNEY CUT his own political throat by doing so much to popularize the Chinese issue. By 1876, Congress and the White House were both well aware that the balance of electoral votes necessary to win a presidential race lay in the West. Therefore, the values and biases of westerners couldn't be ignored. If California and other states beyond the Rocky Mountains thought it was necessary to limit or reduce Chinese immigration, then Washington, D.C., was going to do just that. So in 1882 Congress, supported by Republican President Chester A. Arthur, passed the Chinese Exclusion Act, which curtailed inflows of people from Shanghai, Peking, and other ports along the East China Sea. The Workingmen's Party got what it wanted, but it lost its binding cause, and disintegrated quickly.

San Francisco spent its xenophobia early, and never again witnessed the levels of anti-Chinese sentiment that became familiar during the mid-1880s in other parts of the West Coast.

. . . AND STAY OUT!

Critics who hoped that the Chinese Exclusion Act would have only short-term effects were disappointed when, in 1888, a new law forbade any Chinese laborer who was temporarily away from the United States to return. About 20,000 traveling Asians were thus cut off from their adopted American homes. In 1892, a 10-year extension of the Exclusion Act was adopted, and a decade after that, Congress voted to extend it indefinitely. Finally, in 1943, the prohibition against Chinese immigration was repealed. That was the same year that San Francisco hosted Madame Chiang Kai-shek at a series of exquisite fêtes.

ASSASSINATED!

If you think that today's politicians sometimes turn prickly over their treatment in the press, it's nothing compared to the reaction that the editor of the *San Francisco Chronicle* got in 1880 when he dared to take some shots—both figurative and literal—at the man in the mayor's chair.

The *Chronicle* was established in 1865 as a free theater guide by a couple of teenaged Jewish brothers from St. Louis, Charles and Michael Harry de Young. By 1868, it was publishing daily as a rival to the *Examiner,* the *Call,* the *Alta California,* and the crusading *Evening Bulletin.* Editor Charles de Young made his name with the biting wit and invective he employed in unsparing measure in his writing. He "never let an opponent off as a 'scoundrel' or a 'thief' if he could be called a 'degenerate, skulking, vile, foul, depraved sewer creature,'" explained Frances Moffat in *Dancing on the Brink of the World.* De Young's purpose in all of this was to encourage order and sanity in his hometown. For his trouble, he was occasionally attacked—verbally, in print, even physically. During the 1870s, de Young and the *Chronicle* lashed out vigorously against Denis Kearney's reform-minded but bigoted Workingmen's Party, a stand that would cost de Young his life.

In 1879, Kearneyites infiltrated the state's second constitutional convention, capturing several significant offices. They also helped Isaac S. Kalloch, a Baptist minister from Kansas (known as the "Sorrel Stallion" for his amorous adventures), win the mayoralty of San Francisco.

De Young railed against Kalloch, who struck back with some insults of his own, including one directed at the editor's elderly mother. Incensed, the editorialist boarded his carriage, sped to Kalloch's church, and promptly shot the candidate in the leg. It wasn't a

CORRUPTED

Denis Kearney ended his public career in scandal, charged with embezzling money from the coffers of the crumbling Workingmen's Party. He tried to recoup his power through involvement in other parties, including the Democrats and the Greenbacks, but by 1884 he had withdrawn from the political ring. According to historian Richard H. Dillon, he'd had the good fortune—literally—to inherit money, which Kearney used to enrich himself further through investments in the wheat crops of the San Joaquin Valley. He died in 1907, as well off as some of the Nob Hill inhabitants whom he had once excoriated.

severe wound, and after being jailed for a day, de Young was fined and released. Kalloch survived to become mayor.

But the politician's son, Isaac M. Kalloch, wasn't about to forgive de Young his impetuousness. Kalloch was further enraged by rumors that the *Chronicle* was preparing to resurrect the story of his father's 1857 trial on charges of adultery in Boston.

ON THE NIGHT OF April 23, 1880, at 8 o'clock, Isaac M. Kalloch, dressed in a double-breasted overcoat and a soft felt hat, walked into the *Chronicle* offices and, spotting de Young at the front desk, drew a Smith & Wesson pistol from his pocket and began firing. Two shots shattered the quiet as de Young dove behind a protective counter. "He was stooping behind the counter," the next day's *Chronicle* reported, "when Kalloch reached over, placed the pistol within a foot of his face as he was looking upward, and fired again, the ball striking Mr. de Young in the mouth." The editor then drew a gun of his own and was staggering back to use it when Kalloch squeezed his trigger again. De Young never even raised his firearm, but fell back instead into the arms of his half-brother Elias. The assassin dashed out the door, according to the *Chronicle*, while his bleeding victim was "placed upon the floor and medical attendance was instantly summoned, but ten minutes afterward, despite medical efforts, HE WAS A CORPSE."

It was young Kalloch's misfortune that, when running from the scene of the crime, he immediately encountered two policemen, who took him into custody. Michael de Young took over as sole publisher of the paper, and though his editorials were not as belligerent as his elder brother's had been, the *Chronicle* continued to seek a directing hand in civic affairs. Even today, it remains under the financial (if not the exclusive editorial) control of the de Young family.

LABOR PAINS

Prior to the 1870s, San Franciscans spent relatively little time or energy protesting their working conditions. Some guilds had been established as early as the 1850s, but they served more of a social than a political function. Those that were more active tended to focus on specific grievances, and they usually disappeared once their demands were met. Beginning with a carpenters' protest in 1849, occasional strikes upset the city's commerce, but scant incentive existed for collective bargaining when work was plentiful and wages in San Francisco were already comparatively high—$5 for a standard 10-hour day (at a time when most American laborers put in 12-hour shifts for $3 or less).

Increasing dissatisfaction with cheap Chinese labor and significant jumps in the number of job seekers venturing here from eastern states finally upset these quiescent dynamics. In search of a coordinated voice, many unemployed whites turned to Denis Kearney and his Workingmen's Party. But Kearney, for all his posturing and rhetorical brutalizing of the establishment, remained firmly a member of the employer class, not a $5-a-day man. His primary interest was in solidifying his own political stature, not in winning real power for the men who complained about lack of employment. In fact, Kearney saw conventional labor unionism as a threat to his leadership.

This obduracy eventually backfired on the Irish firebrand, as many working stiffs who felt underrepresented by Kearney and his people peeled away in the 1880s to start their own labor organizations. Perhaps the most important among these was the Representative Assembly of Trades and Labor Unions (or Trades Assembly, for short), spearheaded by Frank Roney, a Marxist socialist and one of Kearney's more vocal opponents within the labor circle. By the 1890s Roney's followers had enlisted the membership of most San Francisco tradesmen. The concept of collective representation was seeping slowly into the city's various industries.

Not until after the final curtain rang down on the 19th century, though, did San Francisco become a hotbed of labor organizing—and labor violence.

THE BROTHERHOOD OF TEAMSTERS, antagonized by a major drayage firm that hired nonunion workers in open defiance of a closed-shop agreement, called its people to strike on July 20, 1901. In sympathy, dockworkers walked off their jobs to begin the largest strike in the city's history up to that point and one of the longest ever to subdue local commerce. At least half of San Francisco's businesses ground to a halt. It took three months to settle the strike, and by that time four men had died, 300 others had been injured, and one major political figure had seen his career seriously derailed.

That last reference is to banker and lawyer James Duval Phelan, who served three terms (1897–1902) as an activist mayor. The charming bearded son of an Irish-Catholic immigrant who'd made a fortune in California gold mines, real estate, and banking, Phelan was "the very embodiment of elite reform," as historian Michael Kazin wrote in *Barons of Labor.* Following the disappointing one-term mayoralty of capitalist Adolph Sutro, who couldn't make the philosophical transition from private business to public bureaucracy, Democrat Phelan was elected on a "clean up City Hall" platform. He got directly to work on streamlining the city charter, repairing roads and prettifying parks, and initiating the process whereby private transportation lines and utilities could be brought under the municipal aegis. Over the long haul, he did his best to expunge the boss-style politics from San Francisco. If Phelan wasn't a completely virtuous politician (he had been known, for instance, to cast aspersions against Asians when that seemed a politically advantageous act), he was certainly earnest, thoughtful, and apparently

THE BLIND WHITE DEVIL

Christopher Augustine Buckley was to San Francisco what Tammany Hall "Boss" Tweed was to Manhattan—a powerful and corrupt political manipulator. Buckley arrived here in 1862 and won a bartender's post at the Snug Café, an elegant establishment on Montgomery Street. There Buckley accumulated his business and political savvy, and also met William Higgins, the city's premier Republican ward boss. Higgins took Buckley on as his protégé, familiarizing him with the art of machine politics. But in 1873, Buckley bolted from the party and began his rise instead through the ranks of the

☞

Democratic Party, which he felt had a national platform more consistent with his own philosophies. Buckley helped rebuild a Democratic power base that had been weakened by defections to Denis Kearney's Workingmen's Party. By 1882, and thanks in large part to the WPC's decline, the San Francisco Democratic Party was again winning races, and Chris Buckley was its undisputed boss. What made this fact especially remarkable was that sometime in the early 1870s, Buckley had gone completely blind. But the "Blind Boss," as he was known until his dying day, didn't let this stop him. For almost 30 years, he was the chief back-door string-puller in the city's political wards.

꧁꧂

incorruptible—if only because he was rich enough to spurn the lure of graft money. In these respects, he was a welcome change from many of his predecessors.

In general, Phelan, along with other members of America's popular late 19th- and early 20th-century Progressive movement, believed that the corruption of public and private life could be cured, at least in part, by restraining the power of the wealthy minority. They therefore endorsed trust busting, railroad regulation, and a graduated income tax that would take a bigger percentage out of upper incomes than lower ones. At the same time, Progressives didn't entirely trust unionized workers, either, since so many of those workers were foreign-born and might hide anarchistic ambitions beneath their socialistic bombast. The Progressives' natural constituency was the middle class.

The Strike of 1901 put Mayor Phelan in an untenable position. While he agreed that employers were probably mistreating their workers, he didn't want to intervene on the unions' behalf. As a result, he delayed taking action on the walkout. Finally, San Francisco employers demanded that Phelan call in state or federal troops to quash the protest. Horrified by the possibility of martial law, the mayor chose what seemed the least onerous course of action: assigning police protection to strikebreakers.

The spectacle of arrests and clubbings that followed focused the world's attention on San Francisco. Things grew even more worrisome when the police force, augmented by special officers called in for the strike, clashed with union protesters in a bloody battle on September 29, 1901. Governor Henry T. Gage put a stop to the strike three days later, under terms that were never revealed to the public—and that still didn't earn teamsters the closed shop they'd demanded from the start.

Although the walkout was over, Phelan's troubles were just beginning. His actions—or inaction—had managed to antagonize both sides in the waterfront drama. By calling out cops instead of troops to help subvert picket lines, the mayor caused concern among business interests, who worried that Phelan didn't have the guts necessary to hold a town together in tense times. By calling out strikebrakers at all, Phelan convinced union laborers that he was firmly in the pocket of the employers.

In the election of 1901, disaffected workers created their own organization, the Union Labor party, and succeeded in electing as mayor the president of the local musicians' union, Eugene E. Schmitz. The Union Laborites also reintroduced corruption into City Hall, in the form of political-machine boss Abraham Ruef.

WITH THEIR REPRESENTATIVES finally in control of city finances and the police force, local unions set about winning a number of important concessions. After 1908, the *American Mercury* reported, "not a hammer was lifted, or a brick laid, or a pipe fitted, or wall plastered or painted or papered without the sanction of the unions."

But Schmitz and Ruef's prosecutions for graft, followed in 1910 by the bombing of the *Los Angeles Times* building (the work of union militants who despised "General" Harrison Gray Otis's rabidly pro-capitalist newspaper), began to sour Bay Area residents on the labor movement.

A coastwide shipping strike beginning in June 1916 didn't help relations any, either. After weeks of threats from both sides, interspersed with beatings and one striker fatality, San Francisco was shaken seriously on July 22 by a pipe bomb explosion at the corner of Market and Steuart Streets. The blast went off just as Mayor "Sunny Jim" Rolph, bedecked proudly in a 10-gallon hat, was leading a patriotic parade along the Embarcadero. Ten people were killed and another forty were wounded by flying metal fragments and live cartridges. An unscathed Rolph called for immediate action, and two suspects—Tom Mooney, the combative local secretary of the International Workers'

PROPOSAL INTERRUPTUS

Despite his storied appeal to women, Jim Phelan never married. It's said that only once did he come close to walking down the aisle. That was in the early years of his tenure at City Hall, when he was courting a woman described by Evelyn Wells in her splendid social history, Champagne Days of San Francisco, *as "one of the great society beauties." It seems that after a time, this fair society girl determined to leave the West Coast for Paris. Phelan, fearing that he would lose her to some titled European, chose in desperation to ask for her hand. They were riding*

☞

Defense League, and Warren Billings, an associate who had once been imprisoned for carrying dynamite—were convicted separately for the waterfront bombing.

All of that, though, was still small potatoes compared with what happened during the General Strike of 1934.

THIS HUGE WALKOUT couldn't have come at a worse—or more predictable—time. Like the rest of the nation, San Francisco was suffering through the depths of the Great Depression. Between October 1929 and the summer of 1933, stock values plummeted 80 percent, hundreds of undercapitalized banks and thousands of other businesses shut their doors, and the gross national product fell by almost half. By 1934, nearly 20 percent of Californians lived off worker relief.

Waterfront employees didn't see how their conditions would improve without concerted action. During the early 1920s, as anti-union resentments rose again in the Bay Area, employers had managed to all but destroy organized labor's influence on the waterfront, substituting their own weak Longshoremen's Association of San Francisco and the Bay District for the smaller, more potent workers' unions that had previously held sway among local stevedores. This "company union," often called the "Blue Book" union (for the color of its membership books), maintained a semicorrupt atmosphere of favoritism in hiring, opened opportunities for racketeering gang bosses, and encouraged speed rather than safety in the work environment. Dock laborers had never liked the Longshoremen's Association, and they liked it even less when they realized that it had no plans whatsoever to help them survive the Depression. They deserted in droves, joining instead an older and more militant organization, the International Longshoremen's Association (ILA).

The ILA had lost almost all of its followers and power after a failed strike in 1919. But it received an unexpected boost from none other than President Franklin D.

Roosevelt, who in 1933 signed the National Recovery Act (NRA), the first federal legislation giving unions the right to organize and bargain with employers. By the fall of 1934, the ILA had been recognized by the San Francisco Labor Council and had picked up most of the former Longshoremen's Association membership. It was also developing a network of ILA locals in other Pacific Coast ports.

Responsible for much of this networking was a tough-minded, hawk-nosed Australian by the name of Alfred Renton ("Harry") Bridges, who had given up his sailor's career in 1920 to stay in the Bay Area. He'd suffered through the Blue Book system and dreamed of something better for his fellow dockworkers. A big component of this dream was to assemble ILA representatives all over the West Coast, who would draw up and put their unified muscle behind a list of demands on employers. With his encouragement, those representatives finally met in San Francisco on February 24, 1934. They agreed that a walkout would be called in early March unless employers agreed to a bevy of changes, which included a 6-hour day and a 30-hour work week, as well as rules to end the era of company-run hiring halls and give the ILA the right to assign men to work as it saw fit. Roosevelt's NRA people managed to delay the strike, but with employers digging in their heels against the ILA's authority, there was no way to prevent it.

So on May 9, 1934, while newspapers thundered in opposition to strike organizers, local longshoremen refused to show up for work. Some roamed San Francisco's 17-mile waterfront, carrying picket signs and heckling strikebreakers who'd been brought in to unload 100 or more ships congested in the harbor. In the following days, other maritime associations joined the strike, tying up ports and allowing tons of cargo to rot all the way from Seattle to San Diego. Industries in San Francisco closed, and construction of the two trans-Bay bridges was halted. The strike's first month cost the city about

OUT OF SIGHT, OUT OF MIND

Tom Mooney and Warren Billings, the two suspects in the 1916 pipe bomb explosion near the Embarcadero, remained in prison until 1939—despite recurring doubts about testimony that had been used to lock them up. Mooney was sentenced to death, but President Woodrow Wilson commuted his sentence to life imprisonment, wanting to avoid the violence his execution might provoke. By 1939, political passions had cooled, and California Governor Culbert Olson reduced Billings's sentence to time served. Mooney was pardoned.

KEEPING THE FAITH

Union activist Harry Bridges certainly reached the high point of his career during the 1934 strike. But he didn't disappear from the news or the waterfront after that. He spent the next 15 years fighting government efforts to deport him as an undesirable alien. An appeal to the U.S. Supreme Court allowed him to remain in this country. But during World War II, he was forbidden from going near the San Francisco waterfront and the workers he still represented through the organization that came to be known as the International Longshoremen's and Warehousemen's Union (ILWU). Bridges finally died in 1990 at age 80.

✾

$3 million. Violence broke out sporadically along the San Francisco waterfront. And then, on July 5, 1934, the powder keg of anger blew.

"WAR IN SAN FRANCISCO!" the *Chronicle*'s front page screamed the next morning—Friday, July 6—explaining that "blood ran red in the streets of San Francisco yesterday."

Thursday morning had found hundreds, then thousands of men swarming along the Embarcadero, armed with loose bricks, sections of pipe, guns. It seemed as if the city's entire police force was on hand to keep down trouble, but even that wasn't enough. The first movement of trucks threw a spark into the kindling of worker resentments, and after that, San Francisco became "Gettysburg in miniature," as the *Chronicle* described it. Fists flew. Nightsticks were wielded in deadly profusion, filling the air with the sound of cracking skulls. Men in torn clothes ran about, blinded by blood streaming over their faces. Ambulance sirens wailed above the sounds of cursing and fighting, while other workers and curiosity seekers ran for their lives. Tear gas welled up from sidewalks and the middle of crowds, while trucks crawled through the melee. Gunshots snapped their ugly rhythms. When the strikers tried to interfere with the state-owned Belt Line Railroad, Governor Frank Merriam called in the National Guard with its machine guns. Together with the cops, they tried to push the mob back into the city, off the open battle spaces of the waterfront. In the afternoon, haggard strikers took a stand in the warehouse district south of Market Street. There was fought the Battle of Rincon Hill, bloodier than all that had preceded it, leaving two people dead and hundreds injured.

By the end of the day, 64 strikers and spectators had been seriously wounded (half of them by guns). A small American flag surrounded by flowers marked the place where the two workers had been killed, along with the chalked legend "Police Murder."

A funeral was held for the dead dockers on July 9, and a week later, almost all union members walked off their jobs in an extraordinary expression of solidarity. Federal arbitrators were called in to settle the strike, and on July 31, Harry Bridges allowed his men to return to work. He'd won what he wanted: the Federal Arbitration Board ruled that the ILA should be allowed to control all hiring through its own halls.

"A SWAGGERING MORAL IDIOT TO THE LAST"

I ronically, it may have been the reform policies of Mayor James D. Phelan that led to one of this city's sorriest periods of political corruption. Before Phelan's call in the 1890s for a new city charter that would centralize authority in San Francisco, the mayor was little more than a figurehead, with most lawmaking weight vested in the often-corruptible Board of Supervisors. Phelan and his many fellow Progressives were convinced that only a strong mayor, with the warrant to appoint and remove supervisors, could rebalance power in San Francisco's city government. So they were thrilled in 1900 to see their revised charter go into effect, mandating just such a rebalance of power.

No less delighted, though, was an opportunist named Abraham Ruef. A lawyer, real estate mogul, and student of Republican "machine Politics," he recognized the extraordinary power that Phelan's charter gave to the mayor's office. So he set about to control that office and create the most potent political empire San Francisco had ever known. He almost succeeded.

ABE RUEF WAS BORN of French-Jewish parents in San Francisco in 1864.

Rather small, fine-boned, and sad-eyed, in addition to his head of curly hair, he sported a broad, pendulous mustache that he hoped would deemphasize his prominent proboscis. Graduated from the still-new University of California in 1886, Ruef quickly rose through the ranks of the local Republican party, but he was prevented by strong rivals from realizing his dream: to become leader of the San Francisco GOP. Instead, he started looking around for alternative paths to power.

In the summer of 1901 San Francisco witnessed the creation of a significant third political organization—the Union Labor party. While most Democrats and Republicans in town looked upon this turn of events with distaste, the pragmatic Ruef saw an opportunity. He realized that the new party's leadership was made up mostly of parliamentary neophytes, men who desperately needed an expert to tell them how to win elections. And so, in an ostensibly benevolent effort, Abe Ruef took the Union Laborites firmly under his wing.

The Union Labor party opened its premiere convention on September 5, 1901. Its most important order of business was to pick a mayoral candidate. Neither the Democrats nor the Republicans were fielding a strong contender, so there was every chance for a third-party man to win. Surprisingly, Ruef—acting behind the scenes, but in control nonetheless—anointed a political unknown: Eugene E. Schmitz, president of the musicians' union and onetime conductor of the orchestra at San Francisco's principal playhouse, the Columbia Theater. Even Schmitz acknowledged initially that "I have no ability to act as mayor." Yet to Ruef, he was the ideal candidate: 37 years old, Catholic, a native San Franciscan and congenital Republican, a model husband and father, and a gent who could claim both Irish and German blood—thus appealing to the city's two largest ethnic blocs. "He was a man of natural ability, of good intelligence, and keen perceptions," Ruef later said of Schmitz. "He possessed a tenacious memory and an unsurpassable nerve. He

IDEALISTIC YOUTH

Abe Ruef studied classical languages and the fine arts at the University of California, but also demonstrated a healthy regard for civic reform. In what is surely one of the great ironies of all time, the future political manipulator's senior thesis was titled "Purity in Politics."

could 'put up' a better 'front' than most any man I knew." Best of all, though, Schmitz was "a commanding figure of a man," tall, with a thick black beard, and always sharply dressed. Ruef was an early believer in the politics of image. "The psychology of the mass of voters," he once proclaimed, "is like that of a crowd of small boys or primitive men. Other things being equal, of two candidates they will almost invariably follow the strong, finely built man . . ." If he could look like a mayor, Ruef concluded, Schmitz could be mayor.

He was right. With a deliberately moderate labor platform behind him (again, the work of Ruef), and to the utter amazement of seasoned political handicappers, on November 5, 1901, Schmitz pulled in 4,000 more votes than his nearest opponent. Other Union Labor candidates did less well (the party captured only 3 of the 18 city supervisor seats), but that didn't matter. Ruef finally had his big victory.

However, he also had Schmitz. Despite his comforting baritone voice and his respectable "front," the former conductor had zero political intellect or instincts. Ruef's job was to wise him up—fast. Shortly before his swearing-in, the mayor-elect and Ruef checked into a Sonoma hotel under assumed names, and got busy day and night studying practical governance. Ruef had big plans for Schmitz—and for himself. "I saw the Union Labor party as a throne for Schmitz," he recalled, "as Mayor, as Governor—as President of the United States. Behind that throne, I saw myself its power—local, state, national . . . I saw myself United States Senator."

AFTER SCHMITZ MOVED into City Hall, he and his Svengali went from concealing their relationship to flaunting it. Ruef—known by his cronies as "the Little Boss"—composed most of the mayor's official papers. Schmitz directed any sachem seeking help from the city to "see Ruef," either at the lawyer's business offices or at The Pup, a French eatery on Stockton Street near Market, where Ruef stayed late into the night,

GREASING PALMS

During his years in control of City Hall, Boss Ruef grew adept at squeezing graft money from every available source—prostitution, gambling, construction permits, liquor licenses, franchises, street railway companies, and others. Two of his most lucrative bribery connections were Pacific States Telephone and Telegraph Company, which sought to retain its local phone-system monopoly, and the United Railroads Company, whose president—Patrick Calhoun, grandson of renowned statesman John C. Calhoun—eventually ponied up $200,000 to keep the city from requiring that overhead trolley cables be buried at the company's expense.

palavering with office seekers and talking kickbacks (more than half a million dollars worth, by some estimates).

Opposition to Ruef's spreading web of corruption was slow to grow. Labor had been mollified by achieving its goal of a closed-shop town under Mayor Schmitz. Most voters, along with William Randolph Hearst's *Examiner,* dismissed rumors of nefariousness at City Hall, believing it was no longer possible in San Francisco to construct a political machine of such far-ranging criminality. In the elections of 1905, at the very acme of Ruef's infamy, not only was Gene Schmitz returned to the mayor's office, but every seat on the Board of Supervisors was awarded to a Union Labor candidate—some of whom Ruef had picked at random, never guessing that they all might triumph.

This was too much for Fremont Older. The *Bulletin*'s tall, balding, and sometimes brash editor was a confirmed social crusader, a supporter of organized labor, and a friend to such liberalists as attorney Clarence Darrow and muckraking journalist Lincoln Steffens. Older had spent the previous few years investigating and exposing scandal where he could find it. And he was sure he could find it now in City Hall, although his evidence of Ruef's graft was thin, more "hints here and there" than proof, as the editor himself conceded. He needed help to bring Ruef down.

In early December 1905, Older visited President Theodore Roosevelt in Washington, D.C. He explained his suspicions about Ruef and Schmitz, and asked the President to assign two of his finest federal agents to investigate: William J. Burns, a zealous detective with the Treasury Department's Secret Service division; and Francis J. Heney, a special prosecutor with the Department of Justice. Roosevelt agreed to dispatch both men to the Bay Area.

Meanwhile, Older had found two other crucial allies in San Francisco—former mayor Jim Phelan and sugar millionaire Rudolph Spreckels. Both were convinced of Ruef's scoundrelry, and both would be needed to finance the inquiry by Burns and Heney.

THE INVESTIGATION WAS delayed somewhat by the April 1906 earthquake and fire, during which Schmitz proved himself a more inspirational figure than his detractors had expected. But Burns's men were soon again hot on the trail of Schmitz, Ruef, and their Board of Supervisors. They were encouraged along by District Attorney William H. Langdon, an honest prosecutor who had miraculously entered office with the full support of Ruef's forces. By October 20, 1906, Langdon and Heney (appointed temporarily as assistant district attorney) had enough evidence and affidavits to go public with the bones of their coming graft prosecution.

On November 15, a grand jury handed down five indictments against Ruef and Schmitz on the first of several charges: extorting protection money from a series of fancy French restaurants that ran prostitution businesses out of their upper stories. Ruef huffed, "The whole thing is absurd." The mayor, then in New York City, issued statements on his way back to California charging that Langdon and Heney's attacks were politically motivated. Schmitz was arrested when he crossed the state line at Truckee.

TO BOLSTER HIS CASE, Heney trapped a city supervisor into taking a bribe and then, with the promise of immunity from conviction, forced a confession out of him. Soon, similar promises were flying hither and yon, as self-interested supervisors rolled over on their bosses. They even named a few business titans who had bribed Ruef for special favors. The result was more indictments, some of which even found their way into San Francisco's great bastion of prosperity and propriety, the Pacific Union Club.

By March 20, 1907, with 65 indictments hanging over his curly head and Heney offering him at least partial immunity, Abe Ruef, too, agreed to give a full confession. He told enough that Schmitz could be convicted in June of extorting and accepting bribes.

Ruef's turnaround was just one of the graft trial's dramatic episodes. Fremont Older was kidnapped briefly, but released. A house owned by Supervisor James L. Gallagher, who appeared as a prosecution witness, was dynamited. One of the prospective jury members was convicted of taking a $1,000 bribe from Ruef and sentenced to four years in prison. And in mid-November, 1907, Morris Haas, a jury candidate who'd been rejected for being an ex-convict, shot Francis Heney in the courtroom. Miraculously, Heney not only survived but returned to the trial after some weeks. His would-be assassin was found in jail with a bullet through his forehead.

When it finally came time for Ruef to testify in court about bribe-givers, he developed cold feet. Heney tried to make his case against businessmen who had allegedly paid favors to the Ruef-Schmitz machine, but his targets were invariably acquitted.

Ruef wasn't so lucky. He was convicted on one of the 65 counts brought against him and entered San Quentin Prison on March 7, 1911, to begin a 14-year term. The *Call* described Abe Ruef as "the most conspicuous prisoner ever to enter the gray stone walls of a California penitentiary." The *Bulletin,* in its final send-off to the man it had so vigorously helped to bring down, was less generous. It called him "a chipper, impudent, and swaggering moral idiot to the last."

❦

MITIGATING CIRCUMSTANCES

When Abe Ruef entered San Quentin in 1911, he figured that, with good behavior, he might reduce his 14-year sentence to 9 years. However, thanks to the unexpected help of his bête noire, Bulletin *editor Fremont Older, Ruef won parole after serving only four years. He returned to San Francisco — but never to politics. Thank goodness.*

❦

THE MYSTERY OF CHIEF BIGGY

S ome people claimed it was suicide, brought on by hounding accusations from a local newspaper and criticism from citizen activists. Others passed it off as a tragic accident. In fact, nobody knows exactly what happened to Police Chief William J. Biggy, just that in 1908 he set off north across San Francisco Bay to the town of Belvedere—and didn't return alive.

At 49 years of age, the mustachioed Biggy was a distinguished native of this city, the owner of laundry businesses and a onetime state senator. He'd been appointed to the city's police commission by Mayor James Phelan and was famous for spectacular hatchet raids through Chinatown's more treacherous quarters. Biggy was appointed chief of police in 1907. He quickly earned a reputation for conscientiousness and won fame for his aggressive campaign against the so-called Municipal Crib, an Abe Ruef-sanctioned prostitution palace on Jackson Street.

But only a year after he donned the chief's smart billed cap, Biggy was the focus of a vigorous public attack. Much of it centered around the attempted murder of assistant district attorney Francis J. Heney, who was prosecuting political manipulator Ruef for graft, and the subsequent suicide of Heney's would-be assailant, Morris Haas. It seems that even before Haas had the chance to make a confession, which detectives hoped would implicate Ruef in yet another municipal scandal, he apparently shot himself in the head while under guard at the county jail. Since this happened on Chief Biggy's watch, he got slapped squarely with the blame.

The *San Francisco Call* accused Biggy of having "arrayed himself" on Ruef's side and even suggested that the chief had helped smuggle Haas his pocket pistol so that Haas

QUEEN OF
THE TENDERLOIN

Tessie Wall, who became a special target of Chief Biggy's anti-vice campaigns, was not among this city's most reprehensible early 20th-century madams. Yet she was certainly one of the best known. Rumor says that she spent her childhood on the Barbary Coast, but in 1907 Miss Tessie opened her first cathouse in the Upper Tenderloin, a Coast satellite, located between Larkin, Mason, O'Farrell and Market streets. About two years later, she met and married a gambler named Frank Daroux, who was enchanted by Tessie's buxom good looks and her ability to down a dozen or more bottles of champagne without once retreating ☞

could eliminate himself as a witness in the ongoing graft trial. In addition to the *Call*'s concerns, the chief faced accusations of inappropriate behavior. It was said that, while under the influence of spirits, Biggy had smashed a saloon window and attempted to singlehandedly raid a disorderly house on O'Farrell Street managed by Tessie Wall, a well-upholstered blonde whose clientele ran mostly to college boys.

The Citizens League of Justice prepared to file charges against Biggy. Just a day before the chief's peculiar demise, San Franciscans advocating governmental reform petitioned Mayor Edward R. Taylor to investigate the chief's conduct and dismiss him, if necessary.

TROUBLED BY HIS RAPIDLY ebbing credibility, Biggy boarded a police launch on the foggy night of November 30, 1908, and set out for Belvedere to meet with one of his supporters on the police commission, Hugo D. Keil. The chief arrived at Keil's home at approximately 9 p.m., prepared to tender his resignation. But as the commissioner later testified, he talked Biggy into remaining at his post, at least until a formal investigation could be concluded. "I cheered him up and told him not to mind the criticism," Keil told a *Call* reporter the next morning. "While he was disturbed, he did not impress me as having any intention of ending his life."

Biggy returned to his police launch at just after 10 p.m. and instructed Captain William Murphy, the only other man on board, to shove off for San Francisco. The night was cold and the seas were a bit choppy, but nothing seemed amiss until the boat was passing Alcatraz Island. Murphy said it was then that the chief, who had been in the cabin below, came out on deck and started a conversation. Biggy remarked that he was feeling "very badly tonight," but nonetheless offered to take the helm for a while, to give Murphy a rest. "That's all right," Murphy replied, "I'll run her home." And with that, Biggy started back along the slippery deck toward the cabin.

Fifteen or twenty minutes later, at about 11 p.m., with the water growing rougher and the dock at Mission Street not far off the bow, pilot Murphy strode to the cabin to ask Biggy for his help in getting the launch safely to shore. But Biggy was nowhere to be found! "I was terrified as the thought struck me that he might have been lost overboard," Murphy recalled for the press. "I scrambled all over the vessel and to every possible place that he could have gone, but I could find no trace of him." Unable to spot the chief foundering in the water, Murphy sped on to the dock and rushed from there to the harbor hospital, yelling, "I've lost Biggy. He disappeared somewhere between Alcatraz and the city."

Initial searchers had no better luck than the pilot had had in finding Biggy's body. Finally, more than a week later, his corpse was spotted floating in San Francisco Bay.

There were no obvious clues to Chief Biggy's fate. Suicide theorists pointed to his concern over public scrutiny of his department as proof that the top lawman had cause for doing himself in. Yet he hadn't left behind a suicide note, and people who knew Biggy insisted that his religious convictions and his stubborn determination to fight back against charges of corruption weighed mightily against the notion of self-destruction. Gossip that Biggy had been deliberately pushed overboard by Murphy was never taken seriously. Stories about a third man aboard the police launch, someone in the employ of Biggy's enemies, someone with murder on his mind . . . well, they seem to have been nothing more than the product of overactive imaginations.

The official cause of death was finally ruled as accidental drowning, and a new police chief was named. Had it not been for an incident that occurred some two years later, most people in town would probably never have thought about William J. Biggy again. But in 1911 William Murphy, who had piloted the chief's launch on that fatal night,

to the bathroom. Daroux repeatedly tried to persuade Tessie that she should give up her illicit businesses and retire.

When she repeatedly refused, he divorced her. Tessie was furious. She proclaimed that if she couldn't have Daroux, no other woman would either, and in the summer of 1916, she plugged her former hubby three times with a .22-caliber revolver. "I shot him," she claimed later, "because I loved him—damn him!"

Daroux lived, but left shortly after that for New York. In the late 1920s, Tessie sold her resort for a small fortune and enjoyed a respectability in her last few years of life that she'd not known before.

❧❦❧

It took San Francisco some years to get a City Hall that would reflect its pride—or that would even remain standing. The architectural firm of Shea & Shea was commissioned in 1871 to create a grand edifice on the site of Yerba Buena's original cemetery, a triangle of land squeezed between McAllister, Larkin, and Market Streets (across from today's City Hall). Expectations were that the tall-domed building could be completed within two years, at a cost of about $1 million. By the late 1880s, when its skeleton was still exposed to the weather and charges for the work kept going up (final cost of construction was $8 million), bitter locals took to calling the project the "new

☞

was committed to an insane asylum. He was a haunted-looking man by this point, no longer the proud commander of his vessel. Among Murphy's ravings was the frequent cry, in reference to Biggy, "I don't know who did it, but I swear to God I didn't!"

MAYOR OF ALL THE PEOPLE

I t is ironic that the fall of the Barbary Coast, haven of prostitution, licentiousness, drunkenness, and crime, came during the heyday of Mayor James Rolph, Jr., for this man—known familiarly as "Sunny Jim"—was a true believer in a San Francisco that combined high times with discreet lawlessness. Yes, he had originally campaigned for mayor in 1911 on a promise to "clean up" the city's iniquitous enclaves, and he'd won easily against vice-loving incumbent P. H. "Pinhead" McCarthy. But Rolph's idea of cleaning up meant bringing sanitation and sanity, not necessarily sanctimoniousness, to California's most colorful burg.

One of the first changes to come out of his administration, in fact, was the 1911 order establishing the Municipal Clinic, which ran compulsory medical checks on prostitutes every four days and issued bills of good health to all those who passed. Naturally, this brought forth the wrath of San Francisco's pious minority, mostly loudmouthed, sour-faced ministers who denounced the Municipal Clinic as "a blow at marriage" and a shame on the face of a supposedly reputable town. Within two years, Rolph was forced to withdraw police protection from the clinic and cease enforcing the medical examinations of painted ladies. It wasn't long after that that the clinic closed down—and disease was again free to rampage through local cathouses. But that wasn't the mayor's fault.

Sally Stanford, a Bay Area madam who eventually became the mayor of Sausalito, wrote in her memoir, *The Lady of the House*, that "first and foremost," Rolph was for "Live and Let Live, Let Sleeping Dogs Lie, and Don't Stir Up Muddy Water. Also, If You Haven't Tried It, Don't Knock It." This might explain why he evinced no shame in showing up at the annual Policeman's Ball in the company of Tessie Wall, the owner of an Upper Tenderloin pleasure palace. It could also account for his lack of concern about holding cockfights in his own home or tippling a few during the sorry depths of Prohibition. Rolph showed no embarrassment even at his own corniest behavior, whether it was handing out keys to the city with extreme liberality or throwing the first pitch at old Seals Stadium to begin each spring's baseball season.

HE WAS BORN IN San Francisco in 1869 and grew up in the Mission District. After graduating from finishing school, Jim Rolph and a classmate founded a shipping company. That corporation did well enough to allow Rolph to expand his financial involvements, moving into banks and buying up shipbuilding operations. He made millions over the years. But in business as in politics, he was luckier than he was good. Historians T. H. Watkins and R. R. Olmsted wrote in *Mirror of the Dream* that Rolph's "most noteworthy achievement came when he contrived to lose more than $3 million as a shipbuilder after World War I, a disaster from which it took him ten years to recover."

Sunny Jim had been initially reluctant to enter City Hall. After gaining notoriety as the head of a relief committee set up to handle the 1906 disaster, he'd turned down a bid for the mayor's seat in 1909. But he eventually took to the job as a beaver takes to water. He loved the parades and any other excuse for a public appearance, loved pressing the flesh of voters, and loved posing for pictures with fellow politicos or children or, especially,

City Hall ruin." Many people were actually surprised when the masonry exterior was finished in 1898. Two years later, officials were finally able to move in, only to discover that the internal sewage system was debouching its pungent refuse into the basement.

This wasn't the only thing about the new City Hall that stank. When the 1906 quake struck, it found every weakness in this ostensibly sturdy pile. Cheaply built pillars supporting the dome came crumbling down. The structure's masonry facing flaked off in huge, dangerous chunks. Only after the devastation, when the pride of San Francisco was actually in ruins, did inspectors realize that old newspapers and other refuse had been used as building material.

LOVER MAN

It was said that Jim Rolph had been quite the ladies' man before marriage, and that wedded bliss did little to blind him to female charms. Rarely did the mayor pass up the chance to pose for photographs with local beauty queens or visiting Hollywood starlets.

Although no sex scandals beset him in office, Sunny Jim's incessant flirtations did almost cost him the governorship of California. Apparently, during his campaign for the job in Sacramento, his suspicious wife, Annie, hired private detectives to keep track of the mayor, and then made their detailed and scandalous report

☞

members of the fairer sex. Most of all, he loved the city of his birth—and it showed. "You must think of the City as your best girl," Rolph counseled his city engineer, Michael O'Shaughnessy, "and treat her well. Do what you think is best for her interests."

Not everything went well during his time in office—there was the waterfront strike violence of 1916, the First World War, the flu epidemic of 1918, the Great Depression. But it was Sunny Jim's great good fortune to be in charge of San Francisco during an essentially prosperous and optimistic period in its history. People credited Rolph with those high times, even if he wasn't wholly responsible for them. Odder still, San Franciscans came to trust their mayor, something that few of his predecessors could have claimed. It was hard for voters to give up his ebullient leadership, so they kept pushing him back into office. After 20 years (the longest continuous service by any mayor in local history), it was finally Rolph who had to insist on a change.

With an aureate personality to match his nickname, Sunny Jim relished his frequent description as the "Mayor of All the People." He was genuinely glad to connect with his constituents and would talk with anybody, no matter how lowly their station in life, no matter what reflection those contacts might have on his reputation. That's why he had no compunction about being seen with prostitutes or, in one case, inviting Communists who were protesting outside City Hall to come into his office and talk for a while about their grievances.

ROLPH LOOKED EVERY INCH the respectable politician. But he never failed to show at least some distinctive style. Noting the mayor's cherubic face, his neat white hair and mustache, and his easy smile, Sally Stanford was reminded of the entertainer Tennessee Ernie Ford. "In some respects he was a sartorial freak," Stanford wrote of Rolph, "but on him it looked good. He wore a cutaway coat, a black pearl in an impeccably knotted cravat, and he was always seen with a carnation in his lapel. He probably wore one to bed on his pajamas.

"He never wore shoes," Stanford continued, "preferring Western boots with semi-high heels and one trouser cuff draped, Texas style, into the top of the boot. He was probably the last politician in San Francisco to let himself be seen, more than occasionally, in a high silk hat. When he became Governor, he took to wearing huge cattleman's Stetsons. If he'd ever visited India, he'd have worn a turban. He was a hat-minded man."

Sunny Jim had a flair for the dramatic, and he knew just how to pump up a crowd. "Not a large man, he made up for it with a voice that turned the most casual statement into a graceful speech," Stanford recalled. When the First World War ended in 1918 and Market Street was awash in people and the reassuring chords of "The Star-Spangled Banner," Mayor Rolph took center stage to shout, "This is the world's greatest day in the age-long fight between good and evil!" It didn't matter that this was 100 percent, Grade A hyperbole; it was hyperbole that struck a chord of pride and satisfaction in his listeners, and that's all that mattered.

By most accounts, Rolph was less adept at going beyond artifice to tackle the nitty-gritty of political activism. Certainly, many things happened during his years in office. The Municipal Railway was begun. Work commenced on the dam and aqueduct that would turn the once-bucolic Hetch Hetchy Valley (one of John Muir's favorite natural spaces) into the city's main reservoir of water. The phenomenal Panama-Pacific International Exposition was held in 1915 on 600 acres of marshland just north of Cow Hollow. And the present Classical Revival–style City Hall was erected according to designs by architects Arthur Brown, Jr., and John Bakewell, Jr. Rolph was so proud of City Hall, the centerpiece of San Francisco's Civic Center, that he delighted in pointing the four-story building

available to Rolph's political advisors. She warned that unless something was done, "their candidate for Governor in the next election might be a bachelor." One of the advisors, Gavin MacNab, subsequently shared the report with political boss and Rolph supporter Tim Reardon. In The Lady of the House, *Sally Stanford recounts that the two "were thunderstruck by the length, breadth and complexity of their candidate's activities. MacNab had the only reaction worth remembering. He turned to Reardon and said in a broad Scottish accent, 'This mon is a-wastin' his God-given gifts taking any time out at all frrrrrom dooties such as these just to perforrrrm as Mayorrrr.'"*

out to visitors, noting every time that its dome (307.5 feet above the curb) is more than 7 feet taller than the top of the dome on the U.S. Capitol building in Washington, D.C. (The pinnacle of City Hall is actually 30 feet taller than the Capitol's pinnacle.)

But change tended to occur regardless of Rolph's leadership, not because of it. "As a politician," commented authors Watkins and Olmsted, "he displayed all the social and administrative instincts of a doorknob." He wasn't a particularly strong fighter in the corridors of power. During his mayoral years, he buckled easily to critics of the Municipal Clinic, and he buckled again in 1917, when the California Red Light Abatement Act finally stole the life and licentiousness out of the Barbary Coast—a place that had always been near and dear to Sunny Jim's heart.

He has been described as the "drum major of progress," but not necessarily its driving force. When things went right, Rolph was in his element. When they went wrong . . . well, he learned to adapt. Or he failed, as he did to a great extent as governor of California, an office to which he was elected in 1931—at a time when citizens needed innovative and energetic leadership to lift them out of their Depression doldrums, not the laissez-faire style that Rolph took to Sacramento.

It seemed almost calculated that Sunny Jim died of a heart attack in 1934, at a time when he could still be remembered for his early successes, rather than his later failures. As any of his supporters would have readily said about Rolph, he was a political pragmatist. He knew when to cut his losses and move on.

STICKING HIS NECK OUT

The most serious blemish on Sunny Jim's career as governor of California may have been his praising of a lynch mob in San Jose. The mob's violent act—the last lynching in California history—followed the kidnapping and ransom of Brooke Hart, son of a San Jose merchant. Young Brooke disappeared in the fall of 1933. His body was finally recovered from San Francisco Bay in late November of that same year. Only 12 hours after this gruesome find, the boy's confessed kidnappers, John Holmes and Thomas H.

ON THE ROCK

Al "Scarface" Capone. George "Machine Gun" Kelly. Arthur "Doc" Barker. Bugs Moran. Roy Gardner. Alvin "Old Creepy" Karpis. Robert "The Birdman of Alcatraz" Stroud. They were part of a select fraternity, a hard-bitten lot immortalized in American history by the brutality of their actions and their distorted notoriety in the press, but also by the fact that they were all exiled at one time or another to a knotty fist of rock that punches up from San Francisco Bay.

This wasn't just any rock, mind you. It was The Rock. That's what its inmates respectfully called both Alcatraz Island and the "maximum security, minimum privilege" federal penitentiary established there in 1934. As in "no man has ever been granted parole from The Rock," the pained acknowledgment of one Albert Besmanoff (a.k.a. Al Best), a minor purveyor of bad checks who occupied a cell at Alcatraz during its tense early years.

In the long run, The Rock may have been something of a failure—less important as a deterrent to crime than as a cruel public display of the criminal justice system's interest in appearing to act swiftly and significantly against the gangster violence that erupted between the two world wars. But it was always a potent symbol: America's own Devil's Island, a lockup that put many people in mind of the Count of Monte Cristo's rat-infested Chateau d'If. *Time* magazine reflected the prevailing attitude toward Alcatraz when it called the prison "the human zoo of 'the world's most dangerous men.'" It was a dangerous place indeed. And despite the fact that decades have passed since The Rock was turned into a tourist attraction, it continues to exude a fearsome punitive aura.

ALTHOUGH IT'S A MEMORABLE feature of the Bay today, photographed

Thurmond, were taken forcibly from their cells, stripped naked, and brutalized. Holmes, according to one account, was "beaten into an unrecognizable pulp-like thing." Then the pair were hanged in a San Jose park near where they'd been imprisoned. After being advised of these atrocities, Rolph exclaimed, "This is the best lesson that California has ever given the country. We show the country that the state is not going to tolerate kidnapping." For weeks after that, the governor was barraged by commentary in the California and national presses that accused him of insensitivity and backward thinking.

❧

FORT ALCATRAZ TAKEN!

It's only by the best of luck that early photographs of the military post at Alcatraz exist. For security reasons, they were supposed to have been destroyed. They'd been commissioned in 1864 by outpost commander Captain William Winder. A San Francisco firm, Bradley and Rulofson, had done the photographic survey, given the results to Winder's company, and then, realizing that the public might also be interested in seeing details of the fortress, began accepting other private orders for sets of the shots. Meanwhile, Lieutenant George Elliott of the U.S. Army Corps of Engineers, who had supervised the expansion of Fort Alcatraz's defenses, happily sent

☞

incessantly by tourists from Topeka and Tokyo, early Spanish explorers apparently didn't think enough of this 22-acre, guano-covered islet to give it a name. They referred to it only as "rock island." It was the mistake of an English mapmaker in 1826 that led to its immortalization as Alcatraz. The name *La Isla de los Alcatraces,* or Island of the Pelicans, had originally been given to what we know now as Yerba Buena Island.

Not until 1850, when ships carrying gold seekers were passing through the Golden Gate, did Alcatraz gain much attention. To avoid navigational disasters, Congress approved the building of a lighthouse on the craggy outcropping. But that was superseded almost immediately by President Millard Fillmore's order to reserve every strategic point around San Francisco Bay for military use. This included not only Alcatraz but also Angel and Mare Islands, Benicia, Point San Jose (now the site of Fort Mason), the Presidio, and that knuckle of land on which Fort Point sits. Fillmore wanted a citadel on Alcatraz to guard against any warring ships that might penetrate defenses nearer the mouth of the Golden Gate and then bear down upon young San Francisco. Beginning in 1853, the U.S. Army Corps of Engineers set to work building Fort Alcatraz and Alcatraz Light, the West Coast's first American fortress and lighthouse.

Photographs of those original installations are all but nonexistent, but they show a lighthouse standing 160 feet above the Bay's choppy surface, with a lantern that could be seen from about 12 miles out to sea. The island's southern end, once an easy slope, was blasted into a cliff to prevent human assault from the water. Cannons capable of launching 120-pound shot through the harbor channel lined the breastwork, along with closer-range barbette batteries. Neatly ordered pyramids of smooth-bore cannonballs rested nearby. A three-story citadel sat brooding atop the island's humped spine. It was all a very impressive sight from San Francisco's wharves and sandy slopes. But its martial purpose was never realized. The Civil War had no military impact on Northern California, and before the fortress' first year of operation had ended, it was already housing prisoners in a wooden shack below the citadel, mostly Confederate sympathizers shipped over from mainland institutions.

By 1868, Alcatraz had firmly established its usefulness as a bastion, although it was still considered primarily an army fort. The citadel was torn down and replaced by a new bastion with walls 12 feet thick and underground quarters for officers of the garrison. The wooden building that had held prisoners gave way to a brick structure. Some of Fort Alcatraz still exists in bits and pieces around the island—granite from the citadel makes up part of the entrance to the present-day warden's office; supply vaults and cisterns bored into the rock became storage space for the prison; and blue sandstone that once covered a wharf blockhouse was used subsequently in the building of a warehouse (look for the cornerstone inscription "Alcatraces 1857"). But outside of the 1857 sally port (guardhouse), the island's oldest remaining edifice, no aspect of the present architecture would likely be familiar to anybody who did a tour of duty at old Fort Alcatraz.

TROUBLESOME NATIVE AMERICANS from the Arizona and Alaska territories wound up in the Alcatraz stockades in the 1870s. During the Spanish-American War, soldiers returning from the Philippines with tropical diseases were quarantined on the island, along with the many soldiers who came back from the South Pacific under arrest for one reason or another. J. Campbell Bruce wrote in *Escape from Alcatraz*, "The influx of culprits from that conflict so overtaxed Alcatraz that presidential pardons were handed down by the fistful to reduce the congestion." Crowding was again a problem after the 1906 earthquake, because ruined jails in the city shipped their malcontents to the island for temporary incarceration.

a set of the prints back to his superiors in Washington.

The War Department wasn't amused by any of this. In fact, it was desperate to suppress the photographs as soon as possible, fearing exposure of military armaments to Confederate spies. On August 2, 1864, armed soldiers showed up at the Montgomery Street studios of Bradley and Rulofson and seized all the Alcatraz photos and negatives, along with all information relating to the planned public sale of those shots. The Bulletin headlined its report of the seizure "FORT ALCATRAZ TAKEN!"

Until recently, all those early photographs were thought to have been destroyed. However, some have turned up at the Sacramento History Center.

FLYING THE COOP

Although he is known today as the Birdman of Alcatraz, prisoner Robert Stroud would more correctly have been immortalized as the Birdman of Leavenworth, where he was previously incarcerated. It was at that Kansas institution that he'd developed an interest in birds after finding a wounded sparrow in the prison yard and smuggling it into his cell to nurse back its strength. While he retained an interest and expertise in ornithology, Stroud's feathered friends were taken from him when he was transferred abruptly to the maximum security pen at San Francisco in 1942.

Congress declared in 1907 that Alcatraz would become the Pacific Branch of the U.S. Military Prison. Two years later, the cellhouse now so familiar on the Alcatraz skyline was erected atop the island, where the former citadel had stood. Because this new building partially obstructed the lighthouse's beacon, that, too, had to be replaced in 1909. All of this was upsetting for many San Franciscans, who deplored the military prison on that craggy cork in the mouth of the Golden Gate. There was talk in 1914 of transforming Alcatraz into the West Coast's own Ellis Island, an immigration portal capable of processing Europeans who shipped through the new Panama Canal. But nothing came of it.

In 1934, the Department of Justice, which had been nosing around for a secure spot to "bury" the most intractable elements of Depression-era criminal culture, took over at Alcatraz and set about creating an escape-proof penal installation. Gun towers shot up toward the sky. Iron cellhouse bars were replaced with tool-proof steel versions. Tear-gas outlets appeared, along with metal detectors and automatic door-locking gizmos. A sophisticated surveillance system was installed. Guards were not allowed to fraternize with prisoners, and at least originally they numbered one guard for every three inmates, rather than the one-to-ten ratio prevalent elsewhere. A keep-out perimeter 200 yards wide was established around the island and marked with buoys. It was assumed that as long as boats piloted by prisoner accomplices could be kept clear of Alcatraz's shores, escape was impossible. It was said that no one could survive for more than mere minutes in the icy grip of San Francisco Bay.

The feds wanted Alcatraz to be a dead zone, protecting the law-abiding public from what its first warden, a former banker and politician named James A. Johnson, described as "the most perplexing problems—problems for the most part which cannot be solved in other prisons."

THESE "PROBLEMS" WERE generally long-term inmates who'd been shipped in from less secure and less obnoxious federal lockups where they had tried to bribe guards, escape their confinement, provoke prisoner strikes, or otherwise stir up trouble. They might have appeared on FBI Director J. Edgar Hoover's famous Public Enemy List and been sought by Hoover's weapon-toting, publicity-hunting G-men. But there were other jailbirds, too: unlikely criminals who found a home on The Rock, like the army prisoner who earned a federal rap for assault and a $1.50 robbery, or the man who had filched a pig (it was his misfortune to have committed this desperate felony on a protected Indian reservation). Stan Brown, a mail thief from North Dakota who was released from the San Francisco pen in 1941, insisted that "only about fifty of the 300 prisoners rate Alcatraz."

Whether it was for Capone (who arrived on the island with a 10-year sentence for tax evasion), or Bob Stroud, the misnicknamed "Birdman" (he never kept any of his feathered friends at Alcatraz), or just some no-fame shlub with a check-kiting beef over his head, the routine at this prison in its early days was the same. Al Best, who came to Alcatraz in 1934 from a federal pen outside of Washington, D.C., and recorded his experiences on The Rock, wrote that new inmates were taken across the Bay in leg irons, assigned cellblock space and work duties, and sent through the showers. They then received their clothes, beginning with "a blue woolen coat, blue woolen trousers, and two blue woolen shirts. This was the Sunday and holiday uniform. Then two pairs of new shoes (brown, army-style, one for work, one for dress), two suits, medium-heavy underwear, six pairs socks, a blue cap, a belt, a blue handkerchief, and two suits coveralls or union-alls for work. (This is the daily uniform for everyone. It is a blue-gray checkered material, one-piece.)"

Silence was enforced within the walls of Alcatraz. Gifts from the outside were

---

❈

THE INMATE ARTIST

Rumors that Depression-era Chicago gangster George "Baby Face" Nelson was once captured in the ladies' room of a Columbus Avenue tavern seem to have spread with little regard for the truth. However, it is a fact that one of Nelson's chief lieutenants, John Paul Chase, grew up in Sausalito and was a rumrunner during Prohibition before joining up with Baby Face, a hair-triggered associate of bank robber John Dillinger's.

In November 1934, four months after Dillinger was gunned down by FBI

☞

agents, Nelson and Chase were caught in a shoot-out with lawmen in a Chicago suburb. Chase was sentenced to life imprisonment and shipped to Alcatraz, where he gained an early reputation as a trouble-maker. But by 1951, he had mellowed significantly and taken up a rehabilitative hobby: painting. His oils — mostly prison scenes, but also a series of canvases showing the Bay Area from the viewpoint of an Alcatraz inmate — were sold in San Francisco, with proceeds going to the American Cancer Society.

forbidden; however, prisoners who demonstrated good behavior were allowed to write one letter a week to their relatives. Shaving was done in shifts, three times a week. Visitors were permitted once each month, although no physical contact was allowed. (Outsiders sat in a room separated from the prisoner, and the two looked at each other through a hole in the wall.) Everybody going in and out of the prison passed through a metal detector (Best called them "Snitch Boxes"). "Capone's mother visited him once," remembered Best, "and when she went through, the machine buzzed. She was taken by an officer's wife and searched. They found she had an old-fashioned corset with steel in it. What a thing for a woman nearly seventy years old to go through!" It's said that she never again set foot on Alcatraz.

ALCATRAZ WAS NOT a place that condoned resistance to uniformity, whether in appearance or sleeping hours or even dining. Recalcitrant convicts were punished with stints in solitary confinement on D Block, or the "Hole," as it was called. "There are about eight or ten solitary cells in Alcatraz, all painted black so it's dark," according to Al Best. "When a man is placed in solitary, all his clothes are taken and searched thoroughly and then given back to him. He is permitted two blankets and sleeps on the cement floor. Federal law calls for a meal every three days. Outside of that, he gets bread and water daily, nothing else."

Movies were a rare and wonderful treat, shown only on legal holidays, Best explained. "This is looked forward to, but the men are always greatly disappointed—no crime or sex pictures like Mae West, etc. We see all of Grace Moore's pictures, *David Copperfield* and *The House of Rothschild* made a great hit. But the pictures enjoyed most are Shirley Temple's, and many a man cries . . . . Little Shirley Temple is the goddess to every man on the Rock, the Sweetheart of Alcatraz." The image of Scarface, rum-running czar

Bugs Moran, and the Birdman all drippy-eyed after a rendition of "The Good Ship Lollypop" is absolutely priceless.

Since Alcatraz was clearly not the Ritz, escape attempts were inevitable. As warden Johnson conceded, "The first thing a prisoner does is case the joint. They watch everything, every guard. They look and look for a weak point." One of the more incredible attempts to gain freedom occurred in the very early morning hours of Friday, January 13, 1939, when kidnapper and life-termer Arthur "Doc" Barker, youngest son of the Midwest's notorious Ma Barker, somehow managed to flee solitary confinement with four fellow felons. They had made it as far as a cove below the south gun tower and were using their outer garments to rope driftwood together into a raft when their escape was discovered. Jailers rushed the conspirators, their machine guns leveled for action, as a Coast Guard patrol boat flailed its searchlight over the cove and scattered the men.

"Halt!" cried a guard, and then bullets were charging into the deep well of the night. The only one to die in this skirmish was Barker. Historian Bruce recalled that when Doc's bloody corpse was off-loaded at the Fort Mason pier, one guard commented wryly, "Well, he's a lot better off now where he is than where he was."

Other inmates found their escape in suicide. Or they went insane. "No man can stand the routine of Alcatraz for very long," Best warned. "It's impossible for the human brain cells to stay normal under present conditions." Alphonse Capone was one of the first to crack. Concerns about his mental stability were filtering through The Rock as early as January 1938. Soon after that, he was relegated to the prison hospital, where he underwent treatment for "mental disturbances," as the Justice Department reported it. "His condition is in no wise due to his confinement," federal sources added, "but grows out of conditions originating prior to his incarceration." The tale grew that the former Chicago

SCARFACE'S LAST DAYS

Al Capone was released from the federal penitentiary system in 1940 and taken by his wife, Mae, to a walled retreat in Florida. He died in 1947 at the age of 48. The cause of death was reportedly a heart attack, brought on by general paresis and complicated by a stroke and pneumonia. None of his many enemies left behind at Alcatraz shed a tear.

mob boss was suffering from a case of syphilis he'd contracted as a young man. Later stories suggested that he may have been a habitual cocaine user. Whatever the cause of Capone's deterioration, by January 1939 he was moved secretly (with six weights on each leg) from Alcatraz to the Terminal Island correctional institution in Los Angeles Harbor.

IT'S INTERESTING TO NOTE that France cut off its flow of prisoners to the penal colony on Devil's Island, off the coast of French Guiana, in 1938. The United States didn't shut the doors of Alcatraz until 1963, and not because the facility practiced a Dark Ages brand of punishment, but simply because The Rock was too expensive to operate. North Dakota Senator William Lanber testified that it was cheaper to board Alcatraz residents at New York's Waldorf-Astoria Hotel than it was to keep them at the gloomy pen in San Francisco Bay.

ESCAPE TO ALCATRAZ

Outside of a brief headline-grabbing occupation by Native American protesters between 1969 and 1971, Alcatraz has been pretty quiet since the Kennedy years. It was opened to the public as a tourist attraction in 1973, and now caters to visitors (and locals, too) who are curious about the cells where the Birdman, Capone, and others among America's "most wanted" once spent their involuntary confinement. Surely it would have amused those convicts to see people today trying to get onto, rather than off of, Alcatraz Island.

CHAOS FROM ORDER

"Satan is entrenched much more strongly than he should be in this wonderful city of God."
—Billy Sunday, evangelist

ROBBING HOOD

Many times in history truth has become so thoroughly entangled with imagination that it's impossible to separate the two. Occupying one such gray area is Joaquin Murieta, the so-called Robin Hood of El Dorado. Cattle thief, lover, and dashing revenge killer all rolled into one, Murieta had allegedly committed himself to redressing wrongs perpetrated by California's gold-mining generation against Mexicans living north of the border. His legend may have been born of fact, but it was well nurtured in romance, and was further embroidered after his death. A ripe air of mystery hung around the fate of his head, which was severed by lawmen, bottled in alcohol, and taken on a half-century tour around San Francisco and northern California. So oft-repeated and potent is the Murieta legend that it has been propagated by even such redoubtable history experts as Hubert Howe Bancroft and Herbert Asbury.

Here's what little we know—or *think* we know about this infamous 1850s outlaw: A man named Joaquin Murieta did, apparently, exist. He may even have terrorized some Sierra mining camps during the Gold Rush. But while gringos came to blame the majority of the theft and pillaging on a single individual, known simply as "Joaquin," this person may or may not have been Murieta (sometimes spelled Murietta or Muriatta). Indeed, while everyone agreed that Joaquin was bloodthirsty and fearless and approximately 18 years of age, almost nobody could agree on his surname, which was reported variously as Carrillo, Valenzuela, Botellier . . . and Murieta. In all probability, there was more than one Joaquin, given that the crimes attributed to him often occurred simultaneously but hundreds of miles apart.

This was not a good period in which to be of Mexican descent and living on

California soil. The United States had just spent two years in a war against Mexico, and although that war was officially concluded in 1848, the same year gold was discovered in northern California, relations between whites living in the West and their Mexican neighbors were poisoned for many years afterwards. The California legislature went so far as to pass a racially biased Foreign Miners' Tax Law, which levied unreasonably high license fees on anybody except "Americans" who wanted to look for precious metals in the new 31st state. The definition of "Americans" included anyone with white skin. Germans, Englishmen, and other western European immigrants paid the lower fees, while miners from Peru, Chile, China, and particularly Mexico were punished with escalated charges. It wasn't long before the law was repealed, but bad feelings remained. Nobody was terribly surprised to hear of a headstrong Mexican man like "Joaquin" turning to banditry as retaliation against prejudice.

BUT THE MURIETA FABLE offers a far more elaborate and compelling motive for this man's nefarious deeds.

In Asbury's account in *The Barbary Coast*, Murieta arrived in California at age 17 from Sonora, Mexico, to work as a horse trainer for a traveling circus. With him came his young and beautiful dark-eyed wife, Rosita Felix. When the Gold Rush began, Asbury wrote, the Murietas were living in San Francisco, but they quickly packed up their belongings and, in 1849, "staked a rich claim" in Stanislaus County, southeast of the city.

A band of white miners, angered by the Murietas' success, found their camp, beat Joaquin, raped Rosita, and told them both to go back to Mexico. Those same men later accused Murieta of horse theft. When, by way of defense, he led them back to his brother's ranch, from which he said he'd borrowed his steed, the miners promptly hanged the brother, stripped Murieta, tied him to a tree, and flogged him until he lost consciousness.

Joaquin Murieta retaliated—or so the story goes. For the next three years, he engaged in a campaign of vengeance, accompanied by as many as 80 horsemen and the ravished Rosita. "Attired in men's clothing," Asbury explained, "with her black hair clipped short," Murieta's fiery spouse "took an active part in many of his robberies and murders, and remained steadfastly at his side through all the vicissitudes that eventually resulted in his death."

According to the legend, Murieta and his men plundered stagecoaches, stormed mining camps, and eventually shot or knifed every one of those miners who had abused the bandit king and his loving Rosita. He spared no brutality. "The bodies of his victims," wrote Dorothy M. Johnson in *Western Badmen*, "could be identified by his trade-mark method of murder: he roped them around the neck, dragged them around for a while, then tortured them and slashed them with a sharp blade. Sometimes he cut his initial, *M*, for Murieta, on their foreheads."

At the same time, the Murieta myth casts him as California's very own Robin Hood, sharing his stolen riches with his poor countrymen. What loot he didn't give away, he supposedly hid in the Calaveras Forest near the town of Murphy's, southeast of Sacramento. (Some sources suggest there is still $150,000 in the ground out there somewhere.) He was gallant and handsome in a dangerous way, with long black tresses and "a silvery voice full of generous utterance." It was said that he could disguise himself expertly as a priest, an old man, even a fair maiden. Murieta reportedly had spies all over northern California, carried a string of his victims' ears over his saddle horn, and wore a coat of chain mail. Most of these fantastic stories circulated after Joaquin's vicious reign and were propagated by fictionists.

IN MAY 1853, when California legislators considered posting a reward (allegedly

$5,000) for the renegade, all they knew was that his first name might be Joaquin. The law-makers and Governor John Bigler approved the hiring of Captain Harry Love, a former Texan and deputy sheriff from Los Angeles, to assemble a cabal of peacekeepers and hunt down Joaquin. So anxious was Governor Bigler for results (and so worried was he that his legislature would renege on its own offer) that he ponied up his own $1,000 reward.

Love's contingent of 20 men traveled the valleys of the Coast and Cascade mountain ranges. They cut hoofprints into the well-rutted hardpack of El Camino Real. They kicked up dust along trails surrounding the town of San Andreas. They tracked over the sere landscape south of the Central Valley.

As the story goes, in late July 1853, some of Love's rangers finally came upon a band of Mexicans camped just south of Fresno. The band's young leader didn't take kindly to the rangers' intrusion: guns were drawn and triggers pulled. Amidst the shooting, the leader was killed. Several of the Mexicans escaped on horseback; two were captured alive.

Although Love and his men had never seen the murderer called Joaquin, they were certain that the dead leader must be him. So they cut off his head and put it in a bottle of alcohol—proof that they had killed the bandit king.

The head was officially declared to be that of Joaquin Murieta. That was good enough for Governor Bigler, who came through with his reward. Even the legislature paid up.

NOT EVERYONE WAS CONVINCED, though, that Love and his men had killed the mythic desperado who'd earned his reputation under the name Joaquin. On August 23, 1853, after the jarred head was put on display in Stockton, the *Alta California* insisted, "Joaquin Murieta was not the person killed by Captain Harry Love's party at Panouche Pass. The head . . . bears no resemblance to that individual, and this is positively asserted

ARROGANCE IS AS ARROGANCE DOES

According to one oft-told anecdote, Murieta rode into a town somewhere in northern California, only to find a poster that bore this proclamation:

$5,000 — REWARD — $5,000
Offered by the citizens of
Stockton to anyone who
Delivers to the Authorities
JOAQUIN MURIETA
Dead or Alive

Rather than run, the arrogant avenger stopped at the poster long enough to ink an addendum:

I WILL ADD $10,000
TO THIS REWARD.
—JOAQUIN MURIETA

by those who have seen the real Murieta and the spurious head." A woman described as Murieta's wife went to the press, insisting that her husband was still very much at large, probably across the border in Mexico.

Nonetheless, Love's bottle of gore was exhibited in museums and freak shows all over California, and thousands of curiosity seekers paid good money to look at it. Eventually, "Joaquin's Head" was moved to a museum of horrors on Montgomery Street in San Francisco, where the bottle and its hairy contents were lost forever in the San Francisco earthquake of 1906.

Murieta's legend lived on in books, newspaper series, and, decades later, in movies, all of them making it more difficult to separate fact from fabrication. Somewhere along the line, people even forgot about Joaquin's cold-blooded murders and thievery. He became a hero of the West, like Zorro. If anything, Joaquin was even more famous dead than alive.

THE PLUNDERING PO8

This legend begins at a desolate spot just north of San Francisco, between Point Arenas and Duncan's Mills on the Russian River. It was there, in August 1877, that a lone highwayman wearing a long white linen duster and a flour sack over his head stepped out in front of a stagecoach, pointed a double-barreled shotgun at the driver, and forced him to halt. With the horses still sweating and the stage's dust settling in whorls about them, the bandit gave the four-word instruction that would become famous in northern California over the next six years: "Throw down the box."

It was a "deep and hollow" voice, as the coach driver later explained, the sort of voice that brooks no disobedience. But the shotgun was even more commanding. Unhesitatingly, the driver tossed over the wooden strongbox he was carrying for Wells Fargo & Company, and he was relieved when the bandit, with peculiar politeness, told him to ride on.

The box was later found—empty. The mysterious brigand had escaped with $300 in coins and a check for $305.52 drawn on the Granger's Bank of San Francisco. But he'd left something behind—a splenetic rhyme, penned on the back of a waybill, each sentence scribed meticulously in a slightly different manner, as if to confound handwriting analysis:

> I've labored long and hard for bread—
> For honor and for riches—
> But on my corns too long you've tred,
> You fine-haired sons of bitches.

The quatrain was signed "Black Bart, the Po8."

Most people who heard about this crime must have gotten a kick out of Bart's clean getaway and his "Po8try." Wells Fargo, however, was anything but amused. Company offices up and down California were on the lookout for this robber-poet, but the description of him could have fit thousands of men. The Granger's Bank check was never cashed. And Bart let his trail cool for almost a year before he reappeared.

THE NEXT TIME HE STRUCK high in the Sierras, leveling his shotgun at the driver of a stage headed through the Feather River Valley, from Quincy to Oroville. Again

STAGES OF HISTORY

Wells Fargo & Company, a New York banking and express concern founded by Henry Wells and William G. Fargo, opened in San Francisco in 1852. It wasn't the only express transportation service out West, but it's the one people remember—partly because it grew so quickly and partly because its history is entwined with the settling of the West. The Wells Fargo Bank History Room (420 Montgomery Street) provides a quick study in this company's heritage. On view are mementos of the bandit Black Bart, money struck by eccentric Emperor Norton, and a 19th-century Concord stagecoach that made runs along California's frontier trails.

he told the driver to surrender his strongbox, only this time Bart's take was better—$379 in currency, a diamond ring allegedly worth another $200, and a $25 silver watch. He also made off with a U.S. Mail bag.

Bart's doggerel on this occasion was more confident than confrontational:

Here I lay me down to sleep
To wait the comming morrow,
Perhaps success, perhaps defeat,
and everlasting sorrow.
Let come what will I'll try it on,
My condition can't be worse;
And if there's money in that box
'Tis munny in my purse!

California Governor William Irwin posted a $300 reward for Bart's "capture and conviction." Wells Fargo added $300, and postal authorities threw in another $200. The price on his head only led Bart to take more chances. He held up three more stages over the next week, all of them northwest of San Francisco. But never again did he leave a calling card of verse.

Bart's modus operandi rarely changed. He made his stagecoach assaults in wide-open territory, near the crest of steep grades, where horses would be winded and slower than normal. He always had his loose coat and his flour sack with the eyeholes cut out. His rifle was in evidence but never fired. He always cut a "T" into the mail sacks, and he used an old ax to open the strongboxes, then left the ax behind.

Many of his victims described him as a gentleman. A frightened woman once tossed Bart her purse after he had ordered her stage driver to "Throw down the box!" He kindly returned it to her, insisting that all he wanted was the Wells Fargo strongbox and the U.S. Mail bag. Such yarns made Black Bart a darling of the San Francisco press and, later, fine grist for penny-novel writers.

Although his crimes were committed far from civilization, Bart never rode a horse; he walked with a blanket roll and camped out when necessary. Yet he covered a lot of ground, in three separate districts of northern California: north of San Francisco, in Shasta County, and north of Sacramento. Even Wells Fargo was impressed by his stamina, describing the masked adversary as a "thorough mountaineer."

ENDING THE HIGHWAYMAN'S career would be difficult, but James B. Hume, chief investigator for Wells Fargo, was determined to carry out the task. His first big break came when he found some people who thought they had encountered a man who might be Black Bart walking cross-country in the general vicinity of the crimes. The stranger had graying brown hair, with patches of baldness at the temples, two missing front teeth, a mustache, and slender hands that showed no evidence of hard work. They all remarked upon his gentility and added that surely such a well-mannered soul could not be a bandit.

Hume's second break came after what would prove to be Black Bart's last holdup, on November 3, 1883.

In the pre-dawn of that fateful morning, Reason E. McConnell, a driver for the Nevada Stage Company, left the town of Sonora, en route west to Milton. Along the way, he picked up 228 ounces of gold amalgam from the Patterson Mine and locked it into his strongbox, which already contained $550 in gold coin and about 3.25 ounces of gold dust.

Then McConnell made a second stop, for breakfast, at Reynolds Ferry, where he took on a passenger—a 19-year-old named Jimmy Rolleri, who wanted a ride to do a little small-game hunting down the stagecoach road.

McConnell was happy to have the company. But Jimmy wasn't seeing any animals, so when the stage had to go up one particularly steep hill, the teenager grabbed his repeating rifle and said he'd rather walk around it, maybe flush some dinner out of the parched underbrush.

Thus the driver was alone at the top of the hill when Black Bart confronted him from behind a shotgun's double barrels. Bart, hidden beneath his flour sack, sensed immediately that something was wrong. First, he'd watched the stage coming and knew there had been two men, not one, on board. Second, there was no strongbox to be seen.

McConnell lied about Jimmy. He said the boy had gone off in search of stray cattle. Bart wasn't satisfied with the answer but had no time to ponder its implications. He knew gold was on board this stage, and if it wasn't on top, it must be secreted inside. So he ordered McConnell down from his perch and told him to unhitch the horses and lead them over the hill.

While McConnell was doing this, listening all the while to the sounds of Bart ransacking the stage for gold, he spotted Jimmy coming around the hill with his rifle. McConnell couldn't believe his luck! He immediately signaled Jimmy, and together they crept back up the knoll.

Bart was just backing out of the stagecoach with the hidden booty when the sound of three shots exploded over the countryside. Bart darted for the brush, clutching his loot but dropping a bundle of papers. By the time the driver and his sidekick could hustle down the hill, the robber-poet had skedaddled. But there was fresh blood on the papers—Black Bart's blood.

And there was more. Bart had dropped his derby and failed to pick up some belongings that he'd sequestered behind a nearby rock—bags of crackers and sugar, a pair of field glasses, a couple of flour sacks, three dirty linen cuffs, a razor, and a handkerchief full of buckshot. Without too much trouble, the Calaveras County sheriff located the woman who had sold Bart his provisions, along with two other men who'd seen a stranger matching the highwayman's physical description. But the clue that broke the Black Bart case was a laundry mark on that abandoned handkerchief—F.X.O.7.

IT TOOK A WEEK of searching through San Francisco's 91 laundries before detective Hume's special agent on the Black Bart robberies, Harry N. Morse, found an owner to correspond with that mark: C. E. Bolton, a 50-year-old resident of the Webb House, at 37 Second Street, Room 40. And as Morse was talking with the owner of the laundry where Bart had taken his linens, who should walk by but Bolton himself.

He was 5 feet, 8 inches tall, bore his 160 pounds of weight in an arrow-straight posture, and had a light complexion. His deep-sunk eyes were bright blue. He sported a broad white mustache and an "imperial" (a pointed beard growing beneath his lower lip). Photographs show him looking very much like his pursuer, the dogged James B. Hume.

Morse told reporters later that his first impressions of the unmasked Bart were of a man "elegantly dressed, carrying a little cane. He wore a natty little derby hat, a diamond pin, a large diamond ring on his little finger, and a heavy gold watch and chain. . . . One would have taken him for a gentleman who had made a fortune and was enjoying it. . . ."

That was exactly the case, of course, although Bolton—or "Charles E. Boles," the name on a Bible left in his room—denied initially that his gains had been ill-gotten. He

UNFINISHED BUSINESS

How successful was Black Bart as a stagecoach robber? Though he gained fame only after his first "Po8" plundering in 1877, Wells Fargo considers him responsible for 28 stage thefts, beginning in the summer of 1875 and continuing for eight years. Early newspaper reports that he'd netted over $18,000 were surely far off the mark. Unfortunately, Bart never set his own value on what he'd stolen.

claimed to be the proud owner of a mine on the California-Nevada border. Not until he was identified by people he'd encountered during the planning of his final crime did the bandit admit that he'd robbed the Sonora-Milton stage. And even then, it was only because he surmised that with one confession he might escape sentencing for many others. The judge proved him right on that account: Bart-Bolton-Boles got six years for a crime spree that should have kept him imprisoned until his death.

BLACK BART WAS released after serving only four years and two months behind bars. As a prison boat brought him ashore at San Francisco in January, 1888, he was mobbed by reporters. Did he intend to rob stages again? they asked. Bart shook his head. Had he any more verses up his sleeve? Bart seemed to perk up. "Young man," the old highwayman replied archly, "didn't you hear me say I would commit no more crimes?"

At last report, Black Bart was heading south from the Bay Area. He got as far as Visalia . . . and then disappeared forever.

THE WICKEDEST PLACE IN THE WEST

"The Barbary Coast is the haunt of the low and the vile of every kind," B. E. Lloyd wrote in *Lights and Shades in San Francisco* in 1876. "The petty thief, the house burglar, the tramp, the whoremonger, lewd women, cutthroats, murderers, all are found here. Dance-halls and concert-saloons, where bleary-eyed men and faded women drink vile liquor, smoke offensive tobacco, engage in vulgar conduct, sing obscene songs, and say and do everything to heap upon themselves more degradation, are numerous. Low gambling houses, thronged with riot-loving rowdies, in all stages of intoxication, are there. Opium dens, where heathen Chinese and godforsaken men and women are sprawled in miscellaneous confusion, disgustingly drowsy or completely overcome, are there. Licentiousness, debauchery, pollution, loathsome disease, blasphemy, and death, are there. And Hell, yawning to receive the putrid, is there also."

In the 19th century and even into the early 20th, this zone on the edge of San Francisco's financial district may have been rivalled for violence only by Hell's Kitchen in New York City and for prostitution only by the old Storyville section of New Orleans. Yet if you were looking for a combination of those vices, with plenty of gambling halls and vaudeville stages and tragicomic streetpeople thrown in for good measure, the notorious Coast was the place to be.

Growth of the Barbary Coast began right after the Gold Rush, when gambling dens sprang up in close orbit around Portsmouth Square. At the same time, near the base of Telegraph Hill massed a community known as "Sydney Town," which included not only prostitutes, swindlers, and fearless thieves, but members of two significant street gangs, the "Sydney Ducks" and the "Hounds." Slowly but surely, these twin centers of vice expanded until they finally merged into a single whole, with once-reputable Pacific Street serving as the main conduit of sin between the shoreline and the business district. The name "Barbary Coast" came into popular usage during the 1860s, probably the idea of some long-forgotten salt who saw similarities between this parcel of San Francisco real estate and the still more villainous Barbary Coast of North Africa.

At its height, before the 1906 earthquake, the district encompassed everything from the downtown waterfront all the way west to Grant Avenue, with Broadway and

OUTRAGED OBSERVERS?
Newspaper reporters of the 19th century usually denounced the Barbary Coast. But their prose frequently showed an intimate knowledge of the neighborhood. "The Barbary Coast! . . . " announced a Call writer who returned in 1869 from an exploration of its raucous shores. "That stink of moral pollution, whose reefs are strewn with human wrecks, and into whose vortex is constantly drifting barks of moral life, while swiftly down the whirlpool of death go the sinking hulks of the murdered and the suicide! The Barbary Coast! . . . on which no gentle breezes blow, but where rages one wild sirocco of sin!"

AND TO THINK, JOHN D. ROCKEFELLER ONLY GAVE AWAY DIMES

Among the sharpers who came to make their fortunes in San Francisco during and just after the Gold Rush was Bill Briggs. Every street urchin knew exactly where his Montgomery Street gambling parlor was located, for Briggs had a peculiar superstition: he believed that coins of denominations less than one dollar were unlucky. Therefore, at about four o'clock every morning, after his business had closed down for the night, Briggs would gather up all the spare change left behind on tables and toss it into the street. Fights were not uncommon among the gamins who considered Briggs's superstition good luck for them.

Clay streets marking its general northern and southern limits. Chinatown served as an essential lascivious adjunct, and fetid pockets of prostitution could be found as far away as Union Square.

A survey made in 1870 discovered that the underworld population of the Barbary Coast numbered 20,000, 3,000 of whom made a living by selling their bodies. The rest spent their days shanghaiing drugged seamen, running ribald theaters, burgling homes and offices, operating protection rackets that extorted money from small businessmen, and managing the extensive array of drinking places to be found in this zone. Liquor was never in short supply. One block of Pacific Street alone might boast as many as 10 saloons, shouldered up against each other. With such competition, watering holes had to be creative if they wanted to attract customers. One chained a grizzly bear beside its entrance. Many others, explained *Scribner's Monthly* magazine in 1875, "have organs that invite patrons to dally. . . . [They] play overtures, marches and tasteful variations. Other bars have bands, still others pianos. And some, in addition to a band, keep a female staff capable of waking thirst in a stone."

IT'S NOT HARD TO UNDERSTAND why many citizens were shocked and repulsed by the life of this quarter. They heard reports of men who'd just won money at poker tables being bludgeoned in shadowy doorways. They heard about Chinatown's dank opium dens (26 of which were operating in 1885), where smokers reclined on wooden bunks and puffed long pipes. They were told of bars from which besotted ne'er-do-wells vanished through trapdoors, only to wind up crewing on ships bound for Panama or the South Pacific. And they learned about alleyways called Bull Run and Moketown and Dead Man, where "the houses are all saloons and are filled with the very dregs of society," to quote the *San Francisco Call.* "Oaths and curses that exhaust the most degrading expressions of sin strike harshly on the ear. Ribald song and bawdy jest float through the polluted atmosphere with the squeal of fiddles and tumming of banjoes. Sometimes in the midst of the noise there is a shot, a curse, a shriek, a groan, and another hulk whirls down the dark whirlpool of death."

Found here were such venues as the Boar's Head, where the height of entertainment was a sexual engagement between a woman and a giant pig. At another dive, a rank grotesque known as Dirty Tom McAlear would consume any noxious liquid or foul food given him in exchange for a few pennies. (He was finally arrested in 1852 for "making a beast of himself.") Anybody unfortunate enough to wander into that small subsection called the Devil's Acre, bounded by Broadway, Montgomery, and Kearny Streets, was almost asking for a beating, especially if he dared to belly up to the bar at an underground saloon called the Slaughterhouse.

The Barbary Coast was also home to a daily parade of the desperately poor, the haunted and crazed, the roaming lepers from Chinatown, the depressed men and desperate women who might greet the evening with a cocked revolver in their mouths or a deadly dash of laudanum in their whiskey. Is it any wonder that the first Pacific Coast branch of the Salvation Army was founded here in 1883? Or that the Barbary Coast could support not one but two street-corner preachers—"Old Orthodox" and "Old Crisis"—who came every Sabbath to warn of the evils that had trapped so many of their listeners in this fearsome corner of the globe?

PROSTITUTION WAS ALWAYS the main order of business in the Barbary Coast, transacted on three basic levels. At the bottom were the "cribs" and "cowyards," where white and black women rented narrow stalls marked off by curtains and charged 25 to 50 cents for their services. A customer wasn't allowed to remove any of his clothes in a crib, except for his hat, which always had to be doffed out of sheer politeness.

One rung up from the cribs were the dance halls, which offered very unpracticed entertainment along with "pretty waiter girls"—some as young as 12—who served men whatever their hearts and libidos craved. Women received a commission for every drink they sold, on top of their wages of $15 to $25 a week. If a gent proved at all stingy, then "the well taught fingers of his female entertainer opens the pockets that a fool's generosity cannot and he is quickly relieved," the *Call* explained. If the man succeeded in staying sober enough to hold onto his wallet, the woman's next alternative was to hustle him upstairs into one of the private bedrooms.

A variation on the dance hall was the melodeon, where dancing was strictly forbidden, and, though "bawdy songs" and "obscene witticisms" were the order of many days, the pretense of presenting legitimate theater was maintained. Indeed, the child star Lotta Crabtree appeared at the Bella Union, a famous hall at Kearny and Washington Streets. Criminal connivances were discouraged in these places, and streetwalkers were prohibited. However, as in the dance halls, melodeon performers were expected to peddle liquor between the acts, and special curtained boxes were available to any roué who wished to get better acquainted with the charms of a particular would-be actress.

Finally, at local prostitution's ostensible upper end could be found the parlor houses. More refined than their competition, these businesses were run by madams, and were commonly operated out of former private residences that sported antique furnishings and maids. Here a man might be allowed to spend the night with a cocotte of his choice— for the right price, of course (usually $5 to $30).

EFFORTS TO RID the Barbary Coast of debauchery were infrequent and mostly ineffective. They commonly resulted in one or more well-publicized but innocuous prosecutions, such as the case in 1879 of a woman dancer who was hauled into court for showing too much leg when she performed the cancan. But little was done to permanently exorcise the Barbary Coast—much to the relief of corrupt local politicians. Even the vigilantes of 1851 and 1856, who'd used intimidation to clean up the city, caused only a minor decrease in this district's sordid prosperity.

The area simply thumbed its nose at laws intended to rein in its behavior. But what legislation and even lynchings couldn't do, fire ultimately accomplished. Hardly anything remained of the town's criminal carnival after the 1906 disaster. Sodom and Gomorrah on the Bay had finally succumbed.

Saloons and cathouses all had to be rebuilt—and they were, and the patrons came back to celebrate the Barbary Coast's rebirth in raucous style. But on the whole, wrote popular historian Herbert Asbury, "the district underwent a radical change after the earthquake and fire. The decade that followed . . . was an era of glamour and spectacularity, of hullabaloo and ballyhoo, of bright lights and feverish gayety, of synthetic sin and imitation iniquity." There remained a foundation of vice, but atop that was created a sort of diabolical Disneyland, through which moneyed folk could go slumming and think themselves awfully naughty. Many residents even took some peculiar pride in the fact that, in addition to all of its many virtues, San Francisco also hosted the self-proclaimed "wickedest place in the West."

The Barbary Coast's days were numbered, though. In 1913, the police force decided to crack down on drinking and dancing. A year later, the California legislature passed the Red Light Abatement Act, which allowed the city to seek legal means in closing down bordellos. In 1917, police began to forcibly eliminate houses of prostitution. Despite a brief attempted resurrection during Prohibition, the flames of San Francisco's private Hell flickered into darkness.

PROFIT AND LOSS

Most of the cyprians who wound up in parlor houses were poorly educated girls who'd traveled to San Francisco hoping to score their fortune or marry an heir, but instead had been forced by poverty into these circumstances. Once in a while, though, some female of good breeding actually volunteered for this life.

In either case, their chances of long-term success were minimal. Even the best-kept women burned out after five or six years. Those who had a head for business might then open parlor houses of their own. The rest wed the first available lout, or grew sick and died.

"YOU HAVE PUT THE NOOSE ABOUT THE NECKS OF BOTH OF US"

THE BRYANT STAKES

*Among the incidents that won brash
Charles Cora fame in gambling
circles was his 1835 conquest of
"Colonel" J. J. Bryant, a 20-year
veteran of high-stakes play who
owned some of the profitable entertainments at Vicksburg, Mississippi.
After Cora had bested him at several
games, the colonel was determined to
teach the younger man a lesson.
First he won Cora's favor, buying
him gifts and presenting him to local
Southern belles. Then he asked*

Charles Cora had seen his share of American gambling towns, but it didn't take long after he stepped off the crowded side-wheeler *California* in late December 1849 for him to realize that San Francisco was in a class by itself. This would be the place, Cora decided, where he'd finally make his mark.

He just didn't figure on dying in the process.

Born in Genoa, Italy, in 1816 and brought as a child to Natchez, Mississippi, Cora had been playing cards, especially faro, since he was 16 years old. Many of his opponents, remembering how he'd taken them for a month's or a year's wages, were convinced that the dark-eyed Cora possessed some sixth sense about the value of each card dealt him. Only that, they believed, could explain his amazing run of luck throughout the South.

The single most providential event in Cora's life, though, may have been his introduction to Arabella (or Clara Belle) Ryan, a beautiful young courtesan who accompanied him to San Francisco and later became the city's most powerful parlor house madam.

THERE ARE TWO VERSIONS of Belle's background. In one version, she grew up as the sheltered daughter of a Baltimore cleric, only to be seduced at age 17 by a suitor who then fled town after learning he had impregnated her. Her father, shamed by his daughter's behavior, obdurately threw her out into the cold. She somehow made her way to New Orleans and there gave birth to a child who died soon afterwards. Depressed and with no money or hope of returning to her family's succor, she wandered one day down around Tchoupitoulas Street, an early avenue of vice in New Orleans. There she encountered a finely dressed older madam who offered her help. Convinced that she was already beyond Christian redemption, the minister's daughter proceeded to re-create herself as a stylish courtesan.

By all accounts, Belle was a rare beauty, slender and flawlessly complected, with dark hair and lustrous hazel eyes. She was working in a high-class bordello when Charles Cora first laid eyes on her. He was so awed that he determined to win her heart. When a friend and fellow gambler mentioned a similar fantasy, Cora offered to flip a coin for wooing rights. As usual, the Italian's luck put him on top.

The alternate version of Belle's life claims that her Irish Catholic father was no minister at all and that she'd entered into the bawdy trade, along with her sister, Anna, after they'd both sewn dresses for women who worked at the Lutz, a Baltimore bagnio that was much in favor among English sea captains. Belle eventually left her sister behind and moved to Charleston, South Carolina, where she took up with a man who was later killed. After that, she drifted to Louisiana, where she encountered Cora.

WHICHEVER ONE OF THESE tales is true—if indeed either of them is—the fact remains that Charles Cora and Belle Ryan met in New Orleans in 1848, and left the South for California at the height of the Gold Rush, ready to earn a handsome profit with their special talents. They lived first in Sacramento, traveled north to Marysville in 1850, then moved on to wild, Mexican-flavored Sonora.

By November 1852, Cora and the woman who now called herself Belle Cora looped back to San Francisco. Here Belle bought a two-story wooden building at the corner of Washington and Dupont (now Grant) Streets. Hoping to avoid negative attention,

to borrow $10,000. After Cora obligingly came up with the money, the colonel challenged him to a no-holds-barred game of faro. Bryant figured that Cora's good fortune couldn't last forever, and it would be rude justice for the colonel to beat Cora with his own loot. But not only did Cora win back the grubstake Bryant had borrowed, he thereafter loaned the colonel another $25,000—and won that too! Bryant was so furious at himself and Charles Cora both, that he refused to pay off his IOUs.

she left the exterior as plain as possible, concentrating instead on interior appointments, which were said to rival those in the city's priciest mansions. Further smart decoration was provided by Belle's employees, allegedly the loveliest prostitutes to be found in the city, who charged the highest price the market would bear.

Three years later, Belle moved her business to a two-story brick affair on Pike Street (now Waverly Place, the "Street of Painted Balconies"), located between Dupont and Stockton Streets—right in the middle of an area that already boasted at least 100 similar enterprises. Even more plush than her previous digs, this second house reflected the prosperity of both Belle, who had turned 28 in 1855, and her 39-year-old lover. Cora, a regular at San Francisco's finer gambling parlors, was reckoned to be worth about $400,000 in 1855.

The couple exploited their familiarity with and acceptance by the local gentry. In a city still not overly constipated by moralizing social stratification, they were counted as fully vested members of the nouveau riche. Belle's business enjoyed a clientele heavy with jurists, politicians, and the randy, big-spending scions of San Francisco grandees.

SO IT WASN'T UNUSUAL for this pair to show up at the grand American Theater on November 15, 1855, to see a new play, *Nicodemus,* or, *The Unfortunate Fisherman.* Nor was it strange that, during an intermission, some of the men on the main floor, turning to recognize their favorite madam seated beside Charles Cora in the expensive first-balcony seats, should have waved and laughed and smiled at her in greeting.

But all this was too much for the wife of U.S. Marshal William H. Richardson. Seated immediately in front of Cora and Belle, Mrs. Richardson thought all the ruckus was directed at her. She was infuriated! Being a lady, she ordered the marshal down in her stead to break up the hooting. When he learned what the true source of the excitement was, Richardson returned to the balcony and demanded that the gambler and his mistress vacate the premises. Cora, of course, refused. The theater manager was unwilling to oust two such powerful members of the community, no matter what their professions. Finally and haughtily, the Richardsons left instead. But the marshal took with him his anger at being bested by a mere gambler and his whore.

The following evening, Charles Cora and Marshal Richardson both happened to be at the Cosmopolitan Saloon. A doctor who knew both men separately decided that what they needed to soothe their tension was to be formally reintroduced over whiskey. That did help, at least for a while. But later, outside the groggery, the men exchanged insults and Richardson threatened to slap Cora's face. A fight was averted only because Cora retreated into the bar, grumbling that he wouldn't draw on a drunken man.

One more night passed. Then on November 18, 1855, Charles Cora was busily tipping back a few at the Blue Wing Saloon on Montgomery Street when someone told him that he had a friend waiting outside. This "friend" turned out to be Richardson, who had been heard earlier in the day vowing vengeance against Cora. The two men talked sotto voce for a spell, and then strolled off together down Montgomery, turning east on Clay toward Leidersdorff Street. Suddenly they stopped. Depending on the witness, Cora either shoved Richardson back against a building and went for a derringer with his right hand, causing the marshal to scream out "Don't shoot, I am unarmed!"; or the gambler grabbed Richardson by the collar, and when Richardson reached for his weapon, Cora was ready on his own trigger.

In either case, Marshal Richardson dropped dead with a bullet fired point-blank through his heart.

CHARLES CORA SURVIVED mob calls to "Hang him! Hang him!" and was

Five years later, The Annals of San Francisco, *reporting on this city's fondness for poker, faro, roulette, and other games of chance, remarked,* "Gambling was the amusement—the grand occupation of many classes—apparently the life and soul of the place." *Gaming houses that might contain a dozen or more tables would be* "continually crowded, and around the tables themselves the players often stood in lines three or four deep, everyone vying with his neighbors for the privilege of reaching the board, and staking his money as fast as the wheel and ball could be rolled or the card turned."

*San Francisco cardsharps frequented
the Parker House, just off
Portsmouth Square, where it was
said that on any night game operators might have half a million
dollars in gold stacked on their
tables. Other wagerers showed up
next door at the El Dorado, where
musical groups and paintings of
voluptuous nudes along the walls
kept everybody entertained between
hands. There was always a game to
be found somewhere, even during the
three years — 1854 to 1857 — when
California state law made gambling
or running a gambling house a
felony. (Open gambling wouldn't
finally be outlawed in San
Francisco until 1873.)*

taken into custody by police. A coroner's inquest the next morning reviewed all the available evidence and determined that the crime had been "premeditated," but left the definitive judgment to a grand jury. Asked by the court whether he would like to appear in that next hearing with counsel at his side, Cora answered with inadvertent humor, "I don't wish to appear at all."

It fell to Belle to hire lawyers for her beloved. She turned to Colonel E. D. Baker, a nationally known courtroom strategist and star orator. But after taking Cora's case (for a reported fee of $30,000), Baker began to waffle in the face of criticism by the local press, which had pronounced Cora's guilt even before the beginning of his trial. "We have come to the conclusion," opined the *San Francisco Herald*, "that the killing of General Richardson was a most atrocious murder. He was assassinated in cold blood, without a single effort at resistance. . . . The deceased gentleman was of a most kind, generous and noble nature. That such a man should fall by such a hand is to be everlastingly deplored." It took all of Belle's persuasive wiles to keep the barrister from ditching his latest client.

These were wild times, for sure. And they were made all the wilder by James King of William and his *Bulletin*. (King, a previous resident of the Washington, D.C., area, got his unusual name by appending his father's first name onto the end of his own in order not to be confused with 13 other James Kings living near the nation's capital.) King wielded his paper's editorial might like a blunt instrument, striking at anybody who threatened to upset civic equanimity. The tactic drove circulation up, but it wasn't the best way to win friends in a town often cleaved by corruption. King had so many enemies that he carried a gun just to ensure that he'd make it to work each morning.

One of his enemies was James P. Casey, a friend of Cora's who had once served 18 months in Sing Sing Prison (for stealing furniture from his prostitute-mistress) and who was now both the editor of a weekly political broadsheet and a San Francisco city supervisor. In retrospect, it's clear that James King of William signed his own death certificate when he antagonized Casey.

CORA'S FIRST TRIAL BEGAN in January 1856. Witnesses said alternately that the gambler had shot an unarmed man and that he was acting in self-defense. The jury deadlocked, forcing another trial.

Cora might have won easily the second time around—if editor King hadn't continued to strike vindictively at him, if James Casey hadn't responded in his Sunday *Times* editorials with increasingly personal attacks against King, and if the *Bulletin* hadn't finally pronounced on Wednesday, May 14, 1856, that based on his political skullduggery and defense of criminals Supervisor Casey deserved "to have his neck stretched."

All those "ifs" added up to disaster on the afternoon of May 14 when, leaving his office on Merchant Street, King turned to see James Casey, 15 paces away, raise his Navy Colt revolver and point it straight at him. "Draw and defend yourself!" Casey is supposed to have shouted—an instant before he closed his finger on the trigger. King fell, his gun still undrawn. Casey gave himself up to police and was taken to a cell adjacent to Charles Cora's. The gambler, hearing what had happened, took a few minutes to appraise the balding, heavily sideburned 27-year-old editor, and then said, "You have put the noose about the necks of both of us."

THOSE WORDS WERE PROPHETIC. As King was being attended by as many as 20 physicians, William T. Coleman was recruited by irate businessmen to head a Second Vigilance Committee. The committee's first goal was to force justice's hand in the cases of Cora and Casey.

Public sympathies were with the vigilantes. On Sunday, May 18, about 2,600

YOU BET!

Emphasizing San Francisco's devotion to the dice, the dealer, and the draw card is the fact that it was here, according to frontier gambling historian Robert K. DeArment, that the expression "You bet!" originated. "It derived from the gambling table as a shortened form of the commonly heard dealer's question, 'How do you bet?' or 'Do you bet?'" DeArment wrote in Knights of the Green Cloth. *"By the 1860s a New York correspondent would report that 'You bet!' was the most popular and most used expression heard in San Francisco."*

vigilantes descended on Sheriff David S. Scannell's jail, armed with knives, guns, and a 6-pound cannon. They demanded Casey's release. The sheriff, backed up by only 30 officers, complied. But when they wanted Cora too, Scannell refused. He reconsidered only after the cannon was aimed at his office door and primed for firing.

Alerted to these lethal shenanigans, Belle came running, but she arrived only in time to see her lover chained and carted off to a makeshift cell at the vigilantes' "Fort Gunnybags," a commandeered warehouse on Sacramento Street. "Good-bye, Charley," she's said to have called out as Cora was led away, "I've done all I can to get you clear." Cora's luck had finally run out.

The vigilantes held a show trial on May 20, during which Casey and Cora were represented, prosecuted, and judged by members of the Vigilance Committee. The "trial" went quickly, interrupted only with the news that James King of William had died just before 1:30 p.m. By evening, both men had been convicted and sentenced to hang on the same day as King's funeral.

On his last morning of life, sometime before noon, Charles Cora and Arabella Ryan were finally married in his cell by a Catholic priest. Just after 1 p.m., Cora and Casey were led to a pair of elevated wooden platforms. Casey insisted on making a stem-winding last-minute speech and then, with the nooses properly snugged and an anxious crowd milling below, the prisoners' platforms dropped and the two men literally reached the ends of their ropes.

IT'S BEEN SAID THAT Belle Cora buried her husband at Mission Dolores Cemetery and then spent the rest of her life in semiseclusion, selling her house of prostitution and becoming the benefactress of respectable charities.

But don't believe everything you hear.

SWEET JUSTICE

Fifty-four years after Belle Cora's demise, an enterprising San Francisco journalist named Pauline Jacobson became fascinated with her saga. She learned that Belle had tried to arrange for a burial plot beside Charles Cora at Mission Dolores, but had been told there was no extra space. As a result, Belle had her husband's remains reinterred at Calvary Cemetery and, upon her

☞

According to Curt Gentry's *The Madams of San Francisco*, Belle not only remained in the harlotry business after Cora's demise, but she spent her remaining years winning revenge against the men who had arranged or endorsed his execution. She allegedly bankrolled or had a stake in two scandalous newspapers, both of which spread lascivious innuendos about members of the Second Vigilance Committee and their supporters. Before she died of pneumonia on February 18, 1862, at the age of 35, Belle had toppled more than a few pillars of her community. Gleefully.

READY! AIM! . . .

San Francisco's foremost contribution to American dueling lore was the 1859 face-off between U.S. Senator David C. Broderick and David S. Terry, chief justice of the California Supreme Court—a blood contest so controversial that it finally put an end to all dueling in California.

Broderick was born to Irish immigrants in 1820 and grew up defending himself around the rougher quarters of New York City. In early adulthood, he made a living mostly as a saloonkeeper and fireman, but profited handsomely on top of that as a ward heeler for Tammany Hall, New York's growing Democratic political machine. He left Manhattan for San Francisco in 1849.

Well connected to New York Democrats and possessing formidable political skills, within two years of his arrival Broderick was president of the California senate and "dictator of the municipality," as Jeremiah Lynch put it in *A Senator of the Fifties: David C. Broderick of California.* Taking a page from the Tammany manual, "Boss" Broderick created

death, was buried next to him. Jacobson, searching for the graves, found them overgrown and forgotten. She mounted a successful campaign to move them to a common plot at Mission Dolores. Then she wrote a highly sympathetic series about Belle Cora for her newspaper. Hardly any living soul noticed how ironic it was that its publisher should be the San Francisco Bulletin. *James King of William was probably spinning in his grave.*

❧

a strong partisan political structure in the city. Nobody was nominated or elected to office in San Francisco during the 1850s unless he had received Broderick's blessing. The Democratic boss handed out political endorsements as gifts, always expecting something in return—usually money. An 1851 survey of the San Francisco elite listed Broderick's worth as only $30,000, much below that of real estate pioneer James Lick (with a reported $750,000), merchant W. D. M. Howard ($375,000), and the fulminating newspaperman Sam Brannan ($275,000). But Broderick's bank deposits grew quickly after that. By historian Herbert Asbury's calculus, the former saloonkeeper probably pulled down several hundred thousand dollars every year in "favors" from officeholders. It wouldn't be too much to say that the rise of the Second Vigilance Committee in 1856 was brought about in part by public disgust over the Broderick machine's extensive graft—including its looting of the city treasury.

Annalist George R. Stewart once described Broderick as "a responsible leader." But historian John P. Young, in *San Francisco: A History of the Pacific Coast Metropolis*, describes Broderick's political methods as "utterly vicious . . . he shrank from no infamy which would promote his objects." The boss wasn't above surgical applications of violence when it seemed necessary to maintain his order in town or his wishes at the polls, and he had a small troop of "enforcers" on his payroll who were well practiced in the art of intimidation.

"If we can only escape David C. Broderick's hired bullies a little longer," wrote *Evening Bulletin* editor James King of William, acknowledging Broderick's threat, "we will turn this city inside out, but we will expose the corruption and malfeasance of her officiary." King was one of the few men in town brave enough or stupid enough to publicly oppose the boss's rule. He regularly published lists of men who sought political office through the power of their pocketbooks and alluded to covert real estate deals through which Broderick could profit at public expense.

BY 1859, BRODERICK had expanded his influence well beyond the state's borders, winning a seat in the U.S. Senate and thus fulfilling one of his longtime wishes. Biographer Jeremiah Lynch quoted Broderick as saying, "To sit in the Senate of the United States as a Senator for one day, I would consent to be roasted in a slow fire on the plaza."

But his participation in national affairs came at a tumultuous time. Tensions between Northern abolitionists and Southern proslavery members were building. Broderick was identified with forces that opposed the extension of slavery in the West. On this issue, as on others, his influence as a politician was not memorable, but his stated views created trouble for him among some passionately proslavery Southerners in the Democratic Party—men such as David Terry, chief justice of the California Supreme Court.

Terry was a truculent former Kentuckian who was more adept at creating enemies than at making friends. But until the slavery question burned the bridges between them, the judge and Broderick had gotten along quite well. Broderick had come to Terry's aid after the judge stabbed an agent of the Vigilance Committee in 1856. The politician is even credited with paying $200 a week to John Nugent, editor of the widely read and antivigilante *San Francisco Herald*, in exchange for editorials that defended Terry against mob "justice." (Charges against the jurist were eventually dropped after his ostensible murder victim suddenly recovered.) What ultimately soured their relationship were two caustic remarks. The first was made by Terry, who told a Democratic gathering that "Broderick's professed following of Douglas meant not Stephen Douglas the statesman, but Frederick Douglass the mulatto." The second came during breakfast the next day, when Broderick read the chief justice's feeble attempt at insult and told an acquaintance with him at the

loan to a gambler; no rightful claim was more easy of collection. Nor were these men, though most dangerous on certain points of professional prerogative, by any means habitually quarrelsome. On the contrary, they were often the peacemakers of a fierce crowd whose explosive passions were stirred, constituting themselves an extemporaneous vigilance committee, in the name of the law and order they had themselves set up for the occasion; and then woe to the refractory!"

table that he no longer believed Terry to be an honest man. It just so happened that one of Terry's friends was seated nearby, heard this broad slander, and demanded that Broderick withdraw it or be challenged to a duel.

NOW, THE POLITICAL BOSS was from New York, where questions of personal probity were weighted with far less significance than they were in Terry's native South. Broderick could, in good conscience, have refused to apologize for his comment about the judge and also ignored the opportunity to engage in an *affaire d'honneur*. But Broderick agreed instead to take Terry on.

The choice of weapons fell to the judge, as the aggrieved party, and he selected a pair of 8-inch, single-shot Belgian-made dueling pistols that belonged to his neighbor, Dr. Daniel Aylette. Reports are that Terry practiced with these guns for two months prior to his face-off against Broderick—he apparently wanted every advantage he could find—and in that time Terry realized that one of the pistols had a particularly sensitive trigger. This weapon he calculatedly left to the use of his opponent.

The Broderick-Terry duel was originally scheduled for Monday, September 12, 1859, in a ravine near Lake Merced, in what is now the city's southwest corner. But the combatants failed to keep their arrangement sufficiently under wraps, and San Francisco's chief of police showed up to stop the duel before it had even begun. Broderick and Terry were both arrested—after all, dueling was officially prohibited by California state law—and weren't released by a judge until later that day. Before retiring to their respective homes, the men quietly agreed to meet on the following morning at the same place.

When the judge and the politician, both trailing their retinue of "seconds" (assistants), appeared again beside Lake Merced, they found 60 spectators, including some of the city's most highfalutin power brokers. Rules were discussed, and then the opponents

MURDEROUS MEMENTOS

The so-called Aylette Pistols, used in the 1859 duel between David Broderick and David Terry, have been preserved and are now part of the collection at the Museum of Money of the American West, in the basement of the Bank of California's main branch at 400 California Street (between Montgomery and Sansome).

stepped back until they were 10 paces apart. "Gentlemen, are you ready?" asked a second, and he began counting to three. But at the count of one, Broderick's hair-triggered Belgian weapon discharged accidentally, its ball firing into the dirt at his feet. The count continued: *two*. Terry raised his gun and took aim at his now defenseless enemy. *Three!* There was a sharp crack, and a bullet went through Broderick's right lung. The crowd gasped.

Taking stock of the senator's body, Terry is supposed to have remarked disappointedly, "The shot is not mortal. I have struck two inches to the right."

BUT IN THIS, HE was mistaken. Bleeding and huffing for air, Broderick was taken 12 miles north in a wagon to Fort Mason, where he was nursed for the last three days of his life. During his final agonies, the 39-year-old solon is supposed to have said, "They have killed me because I was opposed to the extension of slavery and a corrupt administration," but that sounds like tripe concocted for partisan appreciation.

Judge Terry left San Francisco not long after the duel and joined the Confederate Army. After the Civil War, he returned to California and again was associated with scandal when he acted as legal counsel in one of the Gilded Age's most bizarre sex intrigues.

David Broderick, on the other hand, was laid in state at the Union Hotel on Kearny Street. On September 18, 1859, 30,000 people showed up to pay him a final, moving tribute. A lengthy procession of San Franciscans (by some accounts, the line was at least a mile long) followed the casket to its burial site at Laurel Hill Cemetery, west of downtown. Though he'd accumulated more than his share of enemies in life, in death Broderick was championed as a martyr for the Union cause.

YOU CAN'T KEEP A DEAD MAN DOWN

Laurel Hill Cemetery, the final resting place of Senator David Broderick, no longer exists — the land within the city limits became too valuable to be occupied by dead people. In 1902, city fathers forbade any more burials in San Francisco proper. The process of moving graves outside of town began about a dozen years later. (Only those souls at Mission Dolores and the Presidio's National Cemetery remained behind.) Forty-seven thousand graves were moved from Laurel Hill Cemetery, some two-thirds of which went to Cypress Lawn, south of the city. Many of the old tombstones were employed as fill material along the Ocean Beach seawall.

THE BODY SNATCHERS

O f all the "businessmen" who sought to scratch out a living in the Barbary Coast, none was so notorious or ingenious as Shanghai Kelly. Built like a fireplug, with unruly red hair and a huge beard, Irishman Kelly made his living as one of mid-19th century San Francisco's most successful "crimps," or "shanghaiers." In other words, he did whatever was necessary to procure crews for outgoing ships—not always an easy task when you consider the barbarous reputations of many of the captains who sailed into the Bay. (Local boy Jack London was hardly exaggerating the breed when he created his scurrilous captain, Wolf Larsen, in *The Sea Wolf.*) Is it any wonder, then, that Kelly and his fellow crimps were forced to employ some rather unorthodox methods of persuasion—everything from drugging, to intoxication, to clubbing men over the head with a black-jack—in order to fill their recruitment quotas?

During the 1870s, Kelly ran a three-story saloon and boardinghouse for seamen at 33 Pacific Street. Even though many sailors understood the risks they faced by visiting Kelly's joint, its attractions were often hard for a lonely, overworked, and love-starved salt to resist. Free liquor was in abundance. So were free women, and Kelly sanctioned any sort of debauchery as long as it softened up his patrons for their next nautical assignments.

Like other crimps, Kelly employed "runners" who would trudge out into the muddy streets surrounding the saloon, armed with whiskey and pictures of the nubile lovelies awaiting at Kelly's place, and do whatever they could to convince seamen, miners, farm boys, or any other naïfs that they owed themselves a night of carousing on Kelly's tab. Once through the saloon doors, however, suckers were plied with the house liba-tion—an evil brew of schnapps and beer, liberally laced with laudanum or opium. They were then given cigars—known as "Shanghai smokes"—that were also doped up with opium. And as the poor "pigeons" fluttered with sybaritic overload against women entertainers, Kelly or his henchmen lured them over one of three trapdoors situated just in front of the bar and then yanked a lever to release the latch. Beneath the doors, tidewater lapped up from the waterfront. Kelly kept a boat down there, tethered to a pillar of the house. The catch of the day would eventually be hauled up, robbed, stripped of any good clothing, and kept in a heavily drugged stupor until he could be sold into slavery at sea.

ON ONE FAMOUS OCCASION during the mid-1870s, Shanghai Kelly found himself without a ready supply of impressible sailors, while three ships stood off the Golden Gate, waiting anxiously for fresh crews. Kelly thought long and hard about what to do, and finally decided that his only recourse was to throw a party.

It probably wasn't really Kelly's birthday, but nonetheless he announced that he would be celebrating with a boisterous bash aboard the rented paddle-wheel steamer *Goliath*. He invited as many Barbary Coast habitués as were interested in sharing a splendiferous spread—kegs of beer and barrels of whiskey, and food enough to stuff an army. But after 90 male guests had stumbled up the gangplank, Kelly announced that the ship was full, and the *Goliath* steamed out of the Golden Gate. Revelers quickly shed their initial concern about the Irish crimp's motives and drank to his health . . . and kept drinking, until after about 2 hours, the drugs that Kelly had slipped into the liquor took hold.

The guests collapsed en masse, and whilst they were out, Kelly chugged alongside those three vessels in need of crews, hoisted equal helpings of his comatose complement onto each, and sailed back to San Francisco. It would take hours before his fellow partiers woke to find themselves on an unexpected and extended sea voyage.

How did Kelly explain the disappearance of all those men, you may ask. Well, he

A SLOW BOAT TO CHINA

The term "shanghaiing" probably originated in San Francisco, and it had only a passing association with Shanghai, China, which, in the 19th century, was still a hardscrabble fishing port. During the early years of this city's development as a shipping center, nobody sailed between the Bay Area and China—it wasn't considered a profitable route. To get there, you'd have to sail all the way around the world. Pretty soon any lengthy and treacherous sea excursion, especially one that was taken involuntarily, came to be known as a "Shanghai voyage."

In The Barbary Coast, *Herbert Asbury related an anecdote about a Chilean crimp named Calico Jim, who "shanghaied six policemen who were sent, one after another, to arrest him. Soon afterwards, [Calico Jim] left San Francisco. When his victims returned from their enforced cruise, they pooled their resources, chose one of their number by lot, and sent him to South America to search for the crimp. After several months the policeman came upon Calico Jim in the streets of Calleo, Chile, and shot him six times, once for each shanghaied officer."*

never had to, for good fortune offered itself in his path. On the way back to the city, Kelly just happened upon the ship *Yankee Blade*, which had foundered on a rock west of Santa Barbara. The gallant Kelly loaded the *Yankee*'s crew and passengers onto the *Goliath*, and then returned to a hero's welcome at the Market Street pier. So happy were the survivors, and so intrigued by the story were San Francisco's many newspapermen, that apparently nobody thought (or cared) to ask Kelly what had become of the pestiferous lot he'd taken out onto the Pacific in the first place.

CRIMPS WERE FAMILIAR to sailors everywhere, from Sydney, Australia, to New York City. On the West Coast, San Francisco's reputation for the practice was rivaled by Port Townsend, Washington, and Portland, Oregon. But shanghaiing in San Francisco was raised to a high and heinous art by men such as Shanghai Kelly, Jimmy Laflin, George Reuben, Billy Maitland, and Horseshoe Brown. Each of them practiced a different type of treachery and deceit and had a particular claim to fame. The religious crimp, Mike Connor, for instance, swore on a Bible that every gob he hired out had passed 'round the Horn, and was therefore worth a few dollars more for his valuable experience. What Connor failed to explain, of course, was that rather than Cape Horn, he was referring to the cow's horn at the entrance to his establishment, which every sailor through his doors was obliged to circumnavigate.

Women were rare in this trade, but they did exist. Miss Piggott ran a most dangerous boardinghouse on Davis Street during the 1860s and 1870s. Mother Bronson, famous for attacking rabble-rousers with her sharp teeth and ham-sized fists, had a place on Steuart Street. And a sometime prostitute known as the Galloping Cow was unsparing in her application of the bludgeon as a means by which to collect her human stock.

Shanghaiing began in San Francisco shortly after the Gold Rush, when ships sailing into the Bay were almost immediately abandoned as their crews headed for the goldfields. By 1852, when the Australian gold rush was at full steam and demands for seamen at a record high, two dozen teams of crimps operated along the shore of Yerba Buena Cove; a decade later, this form of abduction had become a staple, if not stable, local business. Sailors were chattel in San Francisco, and it wasn't unusual to hear stories of some being shanghaied two, three, or even more times. For the right sum of money, anyone was a crimp's target. It's said that many early local murders went unsolved because the protagonist or his victim or both were plucked from the streets, filled with "Mickey Finns" (disorienting concoctions of liquor spiked variously with snuff, morphine, or laudanum), and then hustled off to sea, either to disappear elsewhere in the world or to have their dead bodies dumped overboard.

Vessels were lucky to drop anchor before being assaulted by large "Whitehall boats," the standard craft among shanghaiing runners. Like pirates, these come-on artists—typically of imposing stature and well armed with revolvers, knives, and brass knuckles—would scale the sides of ships and do whatever they could to convince seamen to desert their captain for the high life of the Barbary Coast. Runners passed around drugged bottles of whiskey or rum, followed by obscene pictures and promises to find them a spot on board some decent ship bound for the sunny South Seas.

After that, the *San Francisco Times* reported in 1861, "The crews are shoved into the runners' boats, and the vessel is often left in a perilous situation, with none to manage her, the sails unfurled, and she liable to drift afoul of the shipping at anchor. In some cases not a man has been left aboard in half an hour after the anchor has been dropped."

Sometimes this kidnapping was even done with the complicity of the captain, who had every right to pocket the final installment of a deckhand's wages if he ditched his ship

WHAT A DOPE

The term "Mickey Finn" has come to represent a wide spectrum of noxious alcoholic potions, all of which are designed to disorient a person long enough for someone else to steal from and subjugate him or her in some manner. Luc Sante explained in Low Life, *his vivid account of New York City's criminal past, that the classic Mickey Finn was "named after the proprietor of Chicago's Lone* without permission. A commander who planned to lay over in town for a few weeks or months would pay less to replace an entire crew than he would to keep them on his payroll and idle for all that time. And then he'd pass the cost of procuring a shanghaied crew onto the new recruits, under one pretense or another.

Runners could be no less ingenious at supplying ships with crews than they were at kidnapping them off. Nikko, for instance, a Laplander associate of Miss Piggott's, specialized in padding out his shanghaied crews with stuffed dummies. As a special touch, he'd trap a rat in each of the sleeves, just to make them look more realistic. The dummy's twitching was taken for a sign of life, and the rats' muffled squeals were interpreted as the moanings of a seriously intoxicated man. Other runners mixed loads of live sailors with corpses . . . and even the occasional cigar store wooden Indian.

BY THE EARLY 1900S, however, crimping gave its last gasp in San Francisco, the victim of seamen's unions, the decline of tramp-shipping, and a 1906 Congressional act that set the punishment for shanghaiers as one year in prison or a $1,000 fine or both.

THE UNCOMMON COMMERCE OF MAIDEN LANE

Time and natural disaster combined to transform what was once salacious Morton Street into the thoroughfare that now appears on maps as Maiden Lane. Today this chic and discreet passage, located just off Union Square between Stockton

Star and Palms Saloon, who supposedly bought the recipe from New Orleans voodoo operators. . . ." What the precise original recipe was, however, is not clear. Some sources suggest that cigar ashes in beer might have been enough to daze drinkers; others list snuff and laudanum as ingredients. Sante could say only that the Mickey Finn "was often described as being more volatile and more potentially lethal, if more effective, than chloral hydrate."

Street and Grant Avenue, is lined with fashionable boutiques and hosts the Circle Gallery Building, an understated yet significant Frank Lloyd Wright creation. But just a century ago, you'd have found this same shadowy, two-block lane bordered with some of the city's busiest houses of prostitution, where a particularly popular trull might entertain as many as 80 to 100 men in a single lucrative evening.

Although Morton Street was somewhat southwest of San Francisco's official red-light district, it profited from prostitution for more than 40 years, thanks to the variety and storied sexual abandon of its female tenants. Mexican women commanded the lowest rates (25 cents), followed by black, Chinese, or Japanese women (50 cents); French women (75 cents); and American women, who received a whole dollar for their services. "Even higher prices than any of these, however, were sometimes obtained by prostitutes of unusual youth and attractiveness, and particularly by red-headed girls," according to historian Herbert Asbury. "It was a popular superstition in San Francisco for many years that a woman with auburn tresses was exceedingly amorous, and that a red-haired Jewess was the most passionate of all. A pimp who owned two or three such girls was on the highroad to fortune." Curiously, it was a madam and former prostitute known as Iodoform Kate who, in the 1890s, set the success standard on Morton Street. She invested money she'd saved over the years in at least a dozen iniquitous dens and then set each one of them up with a red-headed Jewish woman. When Kate retired, it was with a fortune in the bank.

THE BUSIEST TIME along Morton Street was Saturday night, when men lined up for their few minutes of ersatz tenderness. At slower times—usually during daylight hours—women reclined in casement windows, wearing nothing from the waist up. There wasn't anything subtle about the business that was transacted here. There didn't have to be. Cops happily turned a blind eye to the goings-on, except on those occasions when boisterous shooting got out of hand or someone was killed with a knife.

Various outraged ladies' groups and religious crusaders tried over the years to shut down Morton Street (later known as Union Square Avenue and Manila Avenue), but only for a brief reform period in 1892 did its red lights dim. It took the fire of 1906 to finally sweep this area clean of its unholy commerce.

Maiden Lane supposedly got its name from a jewelry center in Manhattan. But anybody who knows the history of this street has to wonder whether the jeweler who suggested its designation had something quite different in mind.

"THIS IS WHERE THE FIREWORKS START"

His real name was Carl Thomas Patten. But at the height of his influence, in the years when the Oakland evangelist and his wife were skimming the greatest profits from their gullible flock with hollow promises and thunderous threats of damnation, he called himself C. Thomas Patten. The "C," he insisted, stood for "Cash."

Prosecutors agreed, during his long and well-covered trial for theft in 1950, that "Cash" was indeed an apt nickname for this flashily dressed, Western-drawling, Stetson-topped Bible thumper. Money was the very bedrock of his religion. Patten didn't plan to wait for his rewards in Heaven. He wanted a hefty share of them on Earth, too. And he wasn't afraid to admit it. Even his ties had dollar signs on them. Today's most recognizable salvation peddlers couldn't hope to compete with Patten's holy hucksterism. Here was a man almost genetically predisposed to preach in people's ears and pick their pockets at the same time. If there was a nonlarcenous bone in his body, it could only have been found through major surgery. Call him God's own grifter.

SIX FEET TALL, weighing 218 pounds, and always seen in cowboy boots, Patten was appealing in a good ol' boy sort of way, with a mouth full of corny anecdotes. His background was plump with colorful sins. He was expelled from high school for running a liquor still in the school's basement and later was arrested for transporting stolen cars across state lines. His spouse, Bebe Harrison, had learned how to flimflam the faithful at the knee of Aimee Semple McPherson, that shouting sermonizer who'd run the prosperous International Institute of Four-Square Evangelism in Los Angeles (before court actions and an illicit tryst in 1926 put the kibosh on her career).

Patten's real strength was in knowing when to coax his followers and when to threaten them instead. In a report after his trial, *The Nation* recounted "Cash's" efforts one year to raise $3,514.60 for a special project. With only $1,250 in pledges and time for collections running out, Patten suddenly turned on his parsimonious congregation and bellowed, "God is going to slap you cockeyed in about two minutes!" When even that didn't open the floodgates of financing, he proclaimed, "This is where the fireworks start. God has been talking to one man here for five minutes. I don't know whether he is going to knock him off his seat or not. God is going to . . ." With that, reported *The Nation*, Patten "broke off with 'Bless you, Jesus,' and the people said 'Amen.' Evidently, the sinner had reached for his wallet."

The Pattens had spent a decade on the Pentecostal revival circuit before settling in Oakland. They set up residence first in a small, rundown tabernacle where Bebe, dressed

AND SO CATS SHALL INHERIT THE EARTH

A visiting undertaker from Oklahoma tried to make small talk with a clerk at the Palace Hotel. "Of course we've all heard about your salubrious climate," he remarked, "but I suppose people die pretty often, even in California, don't they?" "No," the clerk retorted. "Only once."

like Sister Aimee, in cascading white robes, doused her East Bay proselytes with exhausting rounds of fire and brimstone, while "Cash" collected the money. "If God told me that money is here, it is *here*. That's a fact," he'd shout. "How many say Amen? Hallelujah to His glorious name . . ." Squeezed into a tuxedo, Patten would then bound around the stage, encouraging folks to give till it hurt, all in the name of the Lord, while collection platters were passed about by teenaged Bible-school girls wearing sweaters embroidered with a "P"—for Patten.

IT'S SAID THAT BETWEEN 1944 and 1948, the preaching Pattens deposited $1,354,706.75 in their personal bank accounts. Bebe had her gowns made by Adrian of Hollywood. Her hubby filled his closets with 200 pairs of cowboy boots and racks of tailor-made suits. Servants were at their beck and call.

The pair raised at least $250,000 to purchase the Oakland Women's City Club as a new home for their growing flock. Monthly church collections rang in at $40,000. And after opening a religious school that claimed to have earned accreditation from the University of California (it hadn't), the Pattens enrolled about 300 students, which brought in another $50,000 over five years.

"Cash" Patten's spiritual salesmanship could raise funds for just about any purpose. When he fancied an English bulldog named Bozo, he hit up Bebe's followers for $269.70. When Mrs. Patten bore twin daughters, everybody was asked again to reach deep into their pocketbooks. On an apparent whim one day, Patten announced the pending construction of a 10-story tabernacle on a hill high above sinful San Francisco; within half an hour, donation platters filled with $10,000 in cash and pledges. (The temple was never built, of course, but the money was never returned.) Prosperous defense-industry workers and others who herded into the Pattens' church weren't suckers; they were "social outcasts and urban misfits," according to *The Nation*. Often hailing from the South, they clung to organizations that reminded them of home and made them feel that they belonged to a community. "Cash" played on their insecurity, and he rarely faced any dissent.

HIS BIG MISTAKE came in 1947, when he unexpectedly sold the Oakland church, school, and grounds to the Loyal Order of the Moose for $450,000, then hid the money. Tabernacle members were flabbergasted. After all, they'd heard "Cash" himself promise that their church was "going to be God's house until the hinges rust off the door."

The sale not only broke the spell that Patten and Bebe had held over some Oaklanders, but it sent dissatisfied followers to the local district attorney's office. Though "Cash" protested vigorously that he had stolen nothing, he was indicted for grand theft, fraud, embezzlement, and amassing money under false pretenses.

Patten's trial lasted 84 wild days. The courthouse corridors were packed daily with supporters of all ages, toting Bibles, chanting hymns, wearing those "P" sweaters, and cheering every time "Cash" appeared. Placard bearers demanded that the United States allow for religious freedom. Testimony was often punctuated with "Amens" from the audience. Patten acted unperturbed and tried to put a good spin on every shred of evidence against him.

But it was hard to justify his heavy losses at Las Vegas casinos or the fact that the Pattens owned *nine* expensive automobiles and a cabin cruiser, all purchased with congregation funds. When detectives for the prosecution ventured out among the Pattens's misled flock, calling out their own version of "Can I get a witness?" there was no shortage of affirmative responses. In his encyclopedic *Hustlers & Con Men*, criminal historian Jay Robert Nash wrote that the Pattens' own cleaning lady testified that she'd given up her life savings to "Cash" after he singled her out during one Sunday's services as "the meanest woman in Oakland."

"People give it to me . . . " was Patten's simple excuse when asked why he'd fleeced his flock. "I'm the man who keeps the wheel lubricated to keep the spiritual machinery working."

In the trial's 19th week, Patten supposedly suffered a heart attack. The legal proceedings were removed to a hospital auditorium, where the defendant showed up every day in "pale champagne-colored pajamas" and listened from a cot or a wheelchair as witnesses cast him as less a saint than a sharper.

In June 1950, Cash was finally convicted on five counts of grand theft, worth 5 to 50 years in prison. He told reporters, "There'll be a battle royal before they get me behind bars." But the heavens were silent . . . and so were the folks who'd stuck with Patten through the trial. He was led off quietly to begin what would be only a three-year sentence. He got out in 1953, to discover that Bebe had managed to hold onto part of their flock but none of their previous power. And in the remaining six years of his life, there wasn't a damn thing that C. Thomas Patten could do to change that situation. You see, one of the provisions for his early parole was that he never again try to raise money.

Thank heaven for that.

WHAT A LONG, STRANGE TRIP

"San Francisco is not a city . . . it is a midway plaisance."
—Frank Norris, *The Octopus*

"ONE OF US WILL HAVE TO DIE"

I n the twilight of Thursday, November 3, 1870, the ferry *El Capitan* departed from the Oakland Wharf on the last leg of its last round-trip ride of the day. The boat was the pride of the Central Pacific's transbay fleet, a large side-wheeler with wheelhouses at both ends. After the crossing from San Francisco, which had carried many commuters who spent their work days in the big city but lived in quiet towns across East Bay, the return trip seemed almost empty.

On the upper deck were William H. Kentzel, captain of the Harbor Police, and a prominent Comstock Lode lawyer named Alexander Parker Crittenden. Crittenden was seated on a bench along the aft cabin deck. His wife had her left arm hooked through his right one, and three of their seven children were gathered nearby. Mrs. Crittenden, who had just returned from a train trip to the East, was talking with her husband when a tall, well-proportioned woman in a brown waterproof cloak, her face covered with a heavy veil, suddenly stepped purposefully toward the attorney.

By one account, the tall woman charged, "You son-of-a-bitch, you are the very man I have been looking for." But other witnesses said there was no statement at all, that the first noise they heard was the sharp report of a bullet being discharged from a four-barreled revolver straight into Crittenden's heart.

Dropping her pistol on the deck, the woman strode toward the cabin, passing several passengers. After a few minutes, Captain Kentzel and one of Crittenden's sons found the murderer inside the cabin, unveiled, appearing rather calm. When questioned she said, "Yes, I did it. I don't deny it, and I meant to kill him. He ruined both myself and my child." Kentzel made his arrest, and when the ferry docked at San Francisco, he escorted Laura Fair to jail.

"Oh, my God! Oh, my God!" she was heard to repeat later in her cell, as if she had only just realized the significance of her act: she had finally killed her longtime lover, a man she had once dreamed of marrying.

CRITTENDEN'S MURDER and Laura Fair's trial captivated San Francisco. Local reporters, with a nose for scandal, took their coverage of the affair to ridiculous and sometimes libelous extremes. The extensive publicity caused the murder to become what one district attorney later described as the "most important case . . . ever tried upon the Pacific Coast." Laura Fair's courtroom trials resulted in verdicts on both her actions and, to a lesser extent, the male-oriented Victorian society that had helped drive her to her crime of passion.

The defendant was portrayed as a woman unlucky in love. An *Alta California* reporter remarked in 1871 upon Laura's charms: her magnetic personality, sensuous lips, high bust, and eyes that were "blue and vivacious in expression." She seemed to have no difficulty in attracting men, only in attracting the *right kind* of man.

Born Laura Ann Hunt in Mississippi in 1837, she had first been married, at age 16, to a New Orleans liquor dealer who died soon afterwards from sampling too much of his own hootch. Her second husband was a violent drunk who once forced Laura onto their marriage bed and then emptied a pistol into the headboard behind her. Soon after, Laura escaped to California with her mother, Mary Lane.

In 1859, Laura married her third husband, a struggling attorney named William D. Fair, and gave birth to a daughter, Lillias Lorraine. This marriage ended tragically when her husband committed suicide the following year. After a brief stint running a rooming house in Sacramento, Laura, her mother, and infant Lillie boarded a stage bound for Virginia City, Nevada, where they set to running a 37-room boardinghouse for men drawn by the Comstock Lode.

It was there that Laura was introduced to A. P. Crittenden.

HE WOULDN'T HAVE BEEN every woman's fantasy lover. Balding and thin-lipped, with eyes that records call "cold," Crittenden was 47 years old (or 21 years older than the widow Fair) when he first rented a suite at Laura's Tahoe House. However, he had squeaked his way through a West Point education, had served in the California legislature, and was a successful lawyer for Comstock silver-mining companies. Laura was intrigued, and by late 1863, as she contended later in court, she had become happily engaged to this self-confident man. What she allegedly did not know, as they shared a bed in the Tahoe House, was that Crittenden was already married.

In early 1864 Crittenden's formidable wife, Clara, arrived in Virginia City with some of their brood, forcing Crittenden to move out of Laura's boardinghouse and in with his wife. But Crittenden managed to convince his wife that Laura, who he said was only his landlady, should be allowed to socialize with them. If Clara Crittenden wasn't wise to her husband's philanderings, she may have been the only one in Virginia City. And if she did know, she was doing her best neither to acknowledge the liaison nor to provoke a divorce from her wealthy husband.

Not that Crittenden didn't promise Laura over and over again that he was going to leave his wife and lead Laura to the altar instead. And she believed him, penning notes full of affection and anticipation. "How long, oh, darling," she asked in one early missive, "must I wait—'my love-watch keeping'—tell me." Even when he didn't leave his wife, Laura refused to believe that Crittenden would betray her. She did everything she could think of, even marrying a fourth time, in the hope that this would drive Crittenden into her arms for good. It was a foolish plan, although it got his attention. The jealous Crittenden demanded that Laura divorce immediately (Crittenden even helped engineer the court case), and then, once the pair had reconciled, announced that he was sending his wife away. He swore that she would not be returning.

Laura believed that she had won at last. But a man who was busily furnishing a new house in San Francisco for Laura and her beloved mentioned to her that he would have to complete his work quickly—because Mrs. Crittenden was due back at any time!

"If Mrs. Crittenden returns," Laura shouted at the astonished workman, "one of us will have to die!" A month later, she was on board the ferry *El Capitan* with a gun aimed at her lover.

THE CASE OF the People of California against Laura D. Fair began on March 27, 1871, and lasted 26 days. The prosecution's attack was based on its conviction that the lubricious widow Fair had done something far worse than murder a man: she had threatened society with moral decay. This crime, proclaimed District Attorney Harry Byrne, "is one of the practical results flowing from this modern system of free love, by which religion and law, virtue and purity, and all the moral qualities which made the true man on earth are sought to be sacrificed at the polluted shrine of those who would convert society into one mass of corruption. . . ."

Laura's lawyers, meanwhile, used the insanity defense. While the defendant sat pale and subdued in her black dress and hat, doctors and lawyers both argued that the dead man had led Laura on with self-serving lies, until the roiling frustration inside her took violent command of her actions.

The all-male jury took only 40 minutes to return a guilty verdict. Laura, sentenced to hang, acquired the dubious distinction of being the first women ever condemned to death by the State of California. But she never made it to the gallows.

Among the curious effects of Laura's trial was that it incited suffragist fury in San

HEREDITARY HARDSHIPS

Whatever happened to Laura Fair's daughter, Lillias? It seems she grew up to be a beauty like her mother. In 1892, the 32-year-old won a newspaper contest for the prettiest woman on the Pacific Coast. Twenty-one years later, after a mediocre stage career in which she used her married name, Lillias Lorraine Hollis, she was found dead of starvation in a New York apartment.

Francisco. Both Susan B. Anthony and Elizabeth Cady Stanton showed up to testify on her behalf. The weekly *Golden City* described Laura as "a poor, wretched, friendless woman . . . [who] in a fit of ungovernable anger, inspired by jealousy, kills the learned 'universally respected man' whose acts were identical with hers, whose excuse for these acts were, to hers, as a grain of sand to a mountain of granite. . . . Hang this woman, and the very name of San Francisco will be odious for ages to come." Even the *Alta California*, which had done as much as any other paper to stir up opinion against Laura Fair, questioned "whether the purposes of justice would be imperiled were her sentence commuted to life imprisonment."

Before even the foundations of a gallows had been built, a stay of execution was ordered. A second trial in September 1872 reversed Laura Fair's conviction, a decision viewed with outrage in some quarters of town. Crittenden's son, Jimmy, even tried to shoot his father's mistress, but Laura escaped unharmed.

Laura went on to lecture about her courtroom travails and wrote an account of the trial called *Wolves in the Fold*. She moved to the East Bay for a few years, and San Franciscans pretty much forgot about her. In fact, when she died in 1919, at the age of 82, it took the city two whole days to make the connection between the deceased and the femme fatale who, almost five decades earlier, had supposedly threatened to reduce society to "one mass of corruption."

BILKING THE BARONS

After four tedious days on horseback, riding blindfolded across the western Rocky Mountains, "General" David Douty Colton was nearly blinded by the bright sunlight that assaulted his retinas when the mask was suddenly removed. The politician and mining promoter could barely open his lids, much less see what he'd been told might be the world's fourth-richest diamond field and the first to be discovered in America.

As his pupils slowly adjusted, he could make out the two secretive prospectors with whom he'd been riding, Philip Arnold and John Slack. And he was ultimately able to focus on the features of a sandy western plateau, including boulders and some vaguely shimmering anthills nearby.

Dismounting, Colton walked deliberately toward one of these hills. It seemed to be covered with diamond dust! He probed at the mound with his boot, and as Arnold stepped forward with a knife to help him, they knocked loose one raw diamond. Then another. Colton was beside himself with excitement. Prospectors had been clawing through the dirt of the Arizona and New Mexico territories for years. So far, there had been only scattered garnet strikes—no diamonds. And now this!

Colton bounded around the plateau like a greedy Easter-egg hunter, picking up diamonds as well as rubies, sapphires, and emeralds. Colton had pocketsful of riches by the time Arnold halted his search, saying that he'd spotted Indians nearby and it wasn't safe to stay any longer.

The mining promoter was reblindfolded and led away, back to the train that would return them all to San Francisco. But this time he was smiling. He knew his employer would be happy with the results of his expedition. William C. Ralston was always happy when he had the chance to make money—lots of money.

IT WAS THE YEAR 1871. Had it been three decades earlier or later, chances are that news of a vast treasure-trove in the West would have been met with more skepticism. But the unlikely California Gold Rush and the Nevada silver boom that had followed it were still fresh in everyone's mind. "No man of authority would have been brash enough to say dogmatically that there were no diamond fields in the United States," wrote Herbert Asbury years later, recalling Colton's big adventure in *The American Mercury*.

And of those who were the first to learn of the diamond strike, none knew much about geology. David Colton had never even seen a diamond field, much less judged one's authenticity or value. A trained geologist would've recognized immediately that the jewels waiting to be harvested from that high, scrubby land couldn't all exist naturally within the same matrix. But trained geologists were about as rare in the Old West as, well, diamonds.

Arnold and Slack were counting on that very naïvete. It allowed them to engineer one of the most audacious frauds in American history, a scheme that eventually suckered not only Ralston but a skein of other mid-19th-century notables, including New York editor Horace Greeley, General George B. McClellan, the shrewd English financier Baron Rothschild, and master jeweler Charles Lewis Tiffany.

The drama began in the summer of 1871 when a teller at the Bank of California in San Francisco was approached by a pair of seedy-looking miners who wanted temporary safekeeping for some valuables. The teller assumed that the buckskin bags plopped down on his counter contained gold dust or maybe nuggets, but instead he found diamonds and other raw gems. Writing out his receipt, the teller couldn't help but inquire about the source of this uncommon wealth. But all Arnold would say was that they'd been prospecting in one of the West's many desert regions.

As the con artists expected, the teller reported this news to his immediate superiors, who passed it along to Ralston, the bank's owner and guiding spirit. Ralston was intrigued, both because he was a potential investor in any diamond mines and because he imagined what benefits might accrue to his beloved San Francisco if it became the trading center for yet another valuable mineral. After some consideration (and, according to one published source, after Ralston's jeweler clandestinely authenticated the miners' poke), the financier sent for Arnold and Slack, who were found playing faro and emptying a bottle of whiskey between them.

Phil Arnold feigned surprise at Ralston's summons although, in fact, he'd spent most of the previous two years laying the groundwork for just such a meeting.

NO ORDINARY FLIMFLAMMER, Arnold had engaged in several gold-seeking schemes in California. With his cousin, John Burchem Slack, he developed a successful claim near Marysville in the early 1860s, which the pair eventually sold for $50,000. By the late 1860s, however, gold mining was no longer as easy as it had been, and Arnold decided he could do better. So while Slack drifted off to Arizona, where he ran a mine near Prescott, Arnold moved to San Francisco and did some bookkeeping for the Diamond Drill Company. The pay wasn't high, but then it wasn't really the salary that he wanted — it was the education.

"By the spring of 1871," A. J. Liebling explained in a 1940 *New Yorker* account of the scam, Arnold "knew as much about diamonds as anybody on the coast." Equally important, he knew who *didn't know* about rough diamonds — and that included all the jewelers in San Francisco.

Ralston was not aware of all this, of course. Nor could he have known that, just before meeting up again with Slack in St. Louis, Arnold had gone to Europe, where he bought uncut and imperfect precious stones, spending what was left of his profits from the Marysville mine sale. About $12,000 in precious stones were in the bag that he and Slack deposited at the Bank of California. The balance had been "planted" at their bogus claim site.

The financier assumed Arnold and Slack were what they appeared to be: prickly, small-time miners with a rather bumpkinish suspicion of businessmen. Arnold's bona fides could even be confirmed by a friend of Ralston's, George D. Roberts, a mining promoter for whom Arnold had once worked as an operations manager. Ever optimistic, Ralston hoped that over time he could win Arnold and Slack's confidence *and* their diamond trove. It was the costliest misjudgment of his career.

Arnold and Slack cleverly told the banker that they wouldn't consider selling the controlling interest in their strike. *But,* they acknowledged coyly, they did need a grubstake to start mining. Ralston refused to negotiate further until he had confirmation of their discovery. It took a couple of meetings to reach a compromise, but finally Arnold and Slack agreed to escort the self-styled "general," David Colton, to their claim—provided he was blindfolded as soon as they reached Rawlins, Wyoming, the railroad station closest to the alleged diamond mine.

ARNOLD AND SLACK EXECUTED so many twists and turns and double-backs on the ride to the site that Colton had nary a clue as to his exact whereabouts. All he could report later to Ralston was that on the acreage Arnold and Slack showed him, gems were as easily picked as cherries.

The banker was hooked, especially after a jeweler told him that, though Colton's stones weren't worth a great deal by themselves (maybe a few hundred dollars), they could be merely the tip of a king's ransom hidden deeper in the soil. Before another week was out, Ralston had given the prospectors about $50,000, placed $300,000 more in escrow for them, and promised an additional $350,000, payable after inspection of their field by a trained mining engineer and the establishment of a company that could fully exploit their strike.

Thinking he might need several million dollars to fund a full-scale gem-mining operation, and unable to bear that cost on his own, Ralston set about enlisting the financial assistance of select investors. He convinced General George Dodge, a local real estate and mining operator, and William M. Lent, who had thrown in with Ralston on several previous ventures, to take an interest in the Arnold-Slack claim. Promoter George Roberts was also welcomed into the fold. And he cabled an invitation to London, where his friend Asbury Harpending, a mining magnate, was then touting American mining securities. Ralston's cable to Harpending was so full of hyperbole that it cost him $1,100 just to send. It also briefly convinced its recipient that Ralston must be either duped or totally insane to believe that the West could expect a diamond rush. "Don't be so sure about that," Baron Rothschild counseled Harpending. "America is a very large country. It has furnished the world with many surprises already. Perhaps it may have others in store."

By the time this cabal of capitalists could all gather together, in May 1872, San Francisco was buzzing with rumors about Ralston's latest gamble. Diamonds, rubies, even pearls were said to have been dug up at what was being called the American Golconda. The excitement recalled the gold and silver fevers of years before. Even local jewelers seem to have been seduced by all the publicity. Only that and perhaps narrowness of experience could explain why, when Ralston showed them the bijouterie accumulated from the Arnold-Slack claim, those ostensible gem experts estimated its value at $1,125,000—

⁂

CONFEDERATE CALIFORNIA?

Asbury Harpending, one of the secondary players in the great diamond hoax, was also one of the principal financiers behind a plan to create a Republic of the Pacific, a nation sympathetic with the South's Confederate cause. As a captain in the Confederate Navy during the Civil War, Harpending helped concoct a bizarre plot to take California and Oregon for the Confederacy. Step one was to capture the steamship Oregon *at sea, and then intercept two ships that were loaded with gold.*

☞

far more than the $20,000 or so that Arnold had actually paid for the stones.

Phil Arnold certainly hadn't underestimated the gullibility of San Franciscans. His bravado was sorely tested, though, by Harpending's announcement that he was taking the jewels to New York City, where they could be shown to financiers and also be properly evaluated by none other than the estimable Charles Tiffany. And both Arnold and Slack were expected to go along.

Lesser swindlers might have headed for the hills after this news, but Arnold was a man with "the intuition of a great poker player," as Liebling wrote. If he harbored any concern that Tiffany could blow the lid off his confidence game, it was masked by his charges that the San Francisco "slickers" were again trying to pull a fast one on him and his partner. To smooth the miners' feathers, Lent was forced to pay them another $100,000 in earnest money.

WHILE ARNOLD AND SLACK roamed the streets of Manhattan, a most august body of money men greeted Harpending at the Madison Avenue mansion of Samuel L. M. Barlow, a New York corporation lawyer whom Ralston had hired as a legal advisor. Among the legends facing Harpending were bankers August Belmont and Henry Seligman; General George McClellan, former Union Army commander and onetime presidential candidate; Horace Greeley, *New York Tribune* editor; and General Benjamin Franklin Butler, who had gained not-altogether-favorable renown through his wartime occupation of New Orleans and was now a corrupt U.S. representative from Massachusetts. All of these worthies were prospective investors in the West's latest bonanza, with Butler serving an additional purpose as someone able to help pass legislation that would ensure Ralston's hold on new diamond lands.

"Gentlemen," Tiffany began, holding up one of the stones, "gentlemen, these are beyond question precious stones of enormous value. . . ." The rest of his statement might as well have been delivered in Zulu, because by that time everyone was preoccupied with thoughts of the new El Dorado.

Two days later, Tiffany delivered a final statement from his lapidary saying that the stones were worth $150,000. Ralston and Harpending fairly burst with excitement. Arnold must have smiled, too, for he knew that the nation's foremost jeweler had just assessed his gems at more than 20 times their actual value.

All that was left before Ralston would hand the prospectors the last payments for half of their strike was an inspection of the site by a mining engineer. While this was being arranged, and while the tycoons on both coasts wrestled for control of the corporation to handle diamond mining in the West, Arnold and Slack announced that they were heading home. What they actually did, though, was book passage to Europe and there spent somewhere around $50,000 on the worst raw diamonds they could find in London, Amsterdam, and Antwerp. These they used to re-salt their trumped-up claim. The pair had finished their work by the time Ralston's people hired as their mining engineer, one Henry Janin, said to be the greatest mine expert then living in America—even if he, like Colton, had never actually *seen* a diamond mine.

ARNOLD AND SLACK'S second commissioned expedition to the gem fields was almost identical with the first, except that more people went this time, including Janin, Lent, Harpending, and General Dodge. Again, after exploring the immediate claim (where there were plenty of barely hidden jewels) as well as the surrounding 3,000 acres (where the engineer found no gems, but assumed only that the wealth must lie farther beneath the surface), Janin pronounced the site authentic. Based on the precious stones he found, he further estimated that the land might yield $5 million an acre. "With a hundred men and

CITY SUCKER

It's astounding that Horace Greeley should have taken a flyer on William Ralston's diamond mine project, for only a year before, he'd been stung by yet another embarrassing confidence game. That one was engineered by a well-tricked-out Englishman calling himself Lord Gordon-Gordon. Playing to Greeley's doubts about the business practices of robber baron Jay Gould, Gordon-Gordon sought the editor's help in forcing Gould to resign as director of the troubled Erie Railroad. The lying lord said he'd already bought a sizable chunk of shares in that railway, and was willing to take on co-investors like Greeley who wished to see the Erie line "cleaned up." Naturally, word of ☞

this imminent takeover leaked out. Gould, who had used the Erie operation as a front for a variety of unethical schemes in years past, didn't believe the threat at first. But after being convinced by Greeley of Gordon-Gordon's veracity, Gould gave the Englishman cash, 20,000 more shares in the Erie, and a written resignation as insurance that he would thereafter act honestly on the railroad's behalf. By the time Gould discovered that Gordon-Gordon was a phony, most of the lord's railroad shares had been sold, and he'd boarded a train for Canada. Living in Manitoba, Gordon-Gordon managed to fight off extradition for a while, but after finally agreeing to stand trial for his larcenous ways, he shot himself through the temple.

❧

proper machinery," Janin told Lent, "I would guarantee to send out a million dollars in diamonds every thirty days." Such wealth was unparalleled in mining history.

Ralston quickly closed the deal, paying the prospectors the remainder of the $700,000 he owed them—a suspiciously small sum, it should have seemed, in comparison with the alleged worth of their claim (but then, Ralston always did consider them rubes). Arnold went back to his family in Kentucky; Slack is said to have become a coffin maker in St. Louis before moving to New Mexico and dying at age 76.

In July 1872, a company was incorporated to develop the Arnold-Slack claim: the San Francisco and New York Mining & Commercial Company. Capitalized at $10 million, this enterprise issued 100,000 shares of stock, all sold to 25 of the Pacific Coast's highest-ranking financiers as well as Baron Rothschild in England. Lavish offices were established in San Francisco, and mining operations were set to begin in the spring of 1873.

But in early November 1872, three government geologists were motivated by curiosity and professional pride to investigate the so-called American Golconda. Clarence King (who founded the U.S. Geological Survey), Allen D. Wilson, and S. F. Emmons had already explored the region where the Ralston riches were said to be sprinkled, and none of them had seen so much as a pinch of diamond dust. Could they possibly have overlooked such a find? And if not, what other explanation was there?

It didn't take them long, after finding the property that Henry Janin had marked off for Ralston, to confirm their suspicions. Unlike the poseur geologists who had preceded them, these men knew that diamonds, sapphires, rubies, and emeralds could not exist together in the ground, much less in the tree stumps and clearly man-made "anthills" where Arnold and Slack had secreted them. There was also an unnatural consistency about the grouping of these sparklers: every time the geologists located a diamond, they found about a dozen rubies nearby. But it was King's German cook who provided the clearest proof of the deception when he unearthed a gem bearing the marks of a lapidary's tool!

King quickly telegrammed Ralston with the bad news. "The alleged diamond mines are fraudulent," he wrote. "Plainly they are salted. The discovery is a gigantic fraud. The company has been pitifully duped."

Once explained, the hoax seemed obvious. And when the *Evening Bulletin* gave a general outline of the ploy to its readers on November 27, 1872, all of San Francisco laughed at how easily the West's kings of commerce had been fooled by a couple of dumb-looking miners. An embarrassed Ralston reimbursed all 25 of the shareholders in his diamond mine company, paying out about $400,000 from his own pocket. Asbury Harpending won and lost a fortune on Wall Street, but was always dogged by guilt for the part he'd played in Philip Arnold's scheme.

AND ARNOLD HIMSELF? An angry William Lent tracked him down in Elizabethtown, Kentucky, where the old prospector had spent some of his ill-gotten gains on a large house and livestock. Arnold pleaded innocent when Lent brought a $350,000 civil suit against him, and he even produced copies of Janin's positive geologist's report and Tiffany's high-ball valuation of the gems Harpending had showed him as proof that Arnold and Slack really had found a diamond field. Bets were that Arnold could win his case in a trial, but he chose to settle with Lent, giving the San Francisco capitalist $150,000 in exchange for immunity from future litigation.

Some of his neighbors said that Philip Arnold had enough money left over to set him up for the remainder of his life. But Arnold decided that what he really wanted to do was follow Ralston's example and open a bank in his hometown. Unfortunately, Arnold's bank took business away from a rival institution. Relations between the competitors grew heated, leading to physical blows and finally a shoot-out in front of a local saloon. Arnold tried to defend himself, but he had lousy aim and took a load of buckshot in his shoulder. The wound healed, but left him weakened. He died of pneumonia a year later, never having fully enjoyed the fruits of one of America's most successful claim-salting ploys.

ALL BARK, NO BITE

Like other cities that had declared their sympathies with the Union, San Francisco was in a partying mood after the Civil War ended. Residents turned out enthusiastically to celebrate visits by General Philip Sheridan, General William Tecumseh Sherman (a former San Francisan who had run a bank in the city after the Gold Rush), and General George Brenton McClellan (despite his having been relieved of his command of the Army of the Potomac by President Lincoln in 1862). Until the mid-1890s, just about any high official from the Union command could expect to be received in San Francisco with open arms and keys to the city. Some cranks thought these honorary affairs merely gave the city another excuse to party . . . and they were probably right. But the fêtes did help heal political divisions caused by the war.

The most regal reception was reserved for Army general and former President Ulysses Simpson Grant. Some 20,000 people elbowed onto Telegraph Hill in 1879 just to watch the general's ship, the *City of Tokio,* sail through the Golden Gate on the final leg of a tour that had taken Grant around the world. Many more turned up on flower-arched

Market Street to greet his entourage and to listen to multiple rounds of "When Johnny Comes Marching Home." Grant was then forced to sit through the city's longest parade to date, a processional of firemen and drill teams, interspersed with calliopes and marching bands, all of which played "When Johnny Comes Marching Home," as if the Hero of Appomattox wasn't already sick to death of that ditty.

The whole shebang must have cost the city handsomely, impressing the former chief executive, whose corrupt administration had taken money seriously—and often. However, it was only the beginning of Grant's reception in San Francisco, a place he still remembered (though not fondly) from his days as a junior officer at the Benicia arsenal. Later, the ex-President was welcomed to a lavish dinner at Senator William Sharon's estate at Belmont, where 1,500 guests were served some 15,000 oysters and 100 cases of champagne. On another night, he was heralded with a fireworks display over the old City Hall and Hall of Records.

BUT IT WAS GRANT'S first day in the city that San Franciscans would remember best—not only the marching bands and waves of cheering veterans but also the general's performance later at the Palace Hotel.

After the parades, with his ears still ringing from cymbal crashes, the aging war hero and politician was finally loaded aboard a carriage pulled by matching snow-white steeds and escorted to the Palace Hotel, where crowds lining all six balcony levels of the Grand Court cheered wildly at Grant's entrance. As columnist Herb Caen recounted 70 years later, the uproar was so substantial that "a Chinese waiter on the upper balcony leaned over to see what all the shouting was about. Only one thing was wrong with this understandable gesture: the waiter forgot he had a tray full of dishes on top of his head. They landed squarely in the President's lap."

Grant tipped his hat to his admirers, but he smiled only faintly, which seemed odd, and then he disappeared into his suite. Calls for an encore appearance began immediately, but it was a long time before Grant came back out into the Grand Court, looking very uncomfortable. He took only a quick bow from his balcony, mumbled a few words, and then silently endured eight stanzas of "The Battle Hymn of the Republic" before finally retiring for the night.

Few knew that Grant's restraint was brought on not by modesty or fatigue, but by the fact that a careless steward on the *City of Tokio* had pitched his false teeth overboard sometime during the voyage from Honolulu.

THE CASE OF THE BOGUS BRIDE

America's Gilded Age (roughly 1868 to 1900) was a prime breeding ground for sex scandals. One of the most baroque of these involved former Nevada Senator William Sharon and young Sarah Althea Hill. Sharon, the Comstock Silver King who had finished building the luxurious Palace Hotel after his business partner William Ralston's death, was elected to the U.S. Senate in 1875. Though his homes consisted of an apartment at the Palace and Ralston's former country estate in Belmont, 20 miles down the peninsula from San Francisco, Sharon wielded his $15 million fortune to convince the Nevada territorial legislature that he, better than anyone else, could represent Nevadans in the nation's capital. (U.S. senators were elected by members of their state or territorial legislatures until the 17th Amendment to the Constitution was ratified in 1913.) He remained in Washington, D.C., until his term ended in 1881, then returned to San Francisco.

According to *Bonanza Inn*, a spirited Palace history by Oscar Lewis and Carroll D. Hall, Sharon "was a pale little man with a large head, ladylike hands and feet, and cold blue eyes. . . . He was not popular, but he was constitutionally unobtrusive. The town accepted him for what he seemed to be: an aging, dapper, sedate little figure, important only because of his millions."

So it came as quite a shock when Sharon was arrested for adultery in September 1883. And it was surprising not least because he was assumed to be a widower. His wife, Mary Ann, had died in 1875.

THE ALLEGATION WAS BASED on a secret marriage contract that Sharon had supposedly signed in 1880. The plaintiff, Miss Sarah Althea Hill, an attractive and educated woman from Missouri, claimed to have met Sharon in 1880, when she was 27 and recovering from a broken love affair and recent suicide attempt. The 60-year-old Silver King had been charming. "He made himself agreeable for an old gentleman," Hill said of Sharon, "recited some poetry [including Byron's *Maid of Athens*] and sang 'Auld Lang Syne.' . . . He began telling me how he liked the girls and how the girls liked him, and couldn't I learn to like an old man like him?" Sharon's interest in her attentions came with more than a little incentive—he offered her $500 a month to sleep with him, she said, later upping that to $1,000.

But the aggrieved woman claimed that she'd held out for something more: a marriage contract, which she subsequently produced in court. According to that somewhat soiled document, on August 25, 1880, Sharon had promised "in the presence of Almighty God, [to] take Sarah Althea Hill, of the City of San Francisco, Cal., to be my lawful and wedded wife. . . ." He had insisted, however, that their nuptials go unpublicized. Shortly thereafter, Sharon had set her up in a suite at the Grand Hotel, located across the street from the Palace but connected by a bridge.

The senator enjoyed the company of dear "Allie" for more than a year. But that casual arrangement ended suddenly. Recovering from what he believed to be a life-threatening illness, and realizing that his death might have left Hill with all of his money, Sharon asked for the return of the marriage contract. He further requested that Hill sign another document, this one proclaiming that she *was not* his wife and had no legal right to his fortune. Even before she'd responded, Sharon sent her $7,500 cash and asked the Grand Hotel manager to see to her ouster. A distraught Hill rushed to Sharon's suite at the Palace, but he wouldn't see her. "That afternoon," she explained in court, "I went out to my grandmother, and when I returned to my home I found every door of my rooms taken off, the bells out and the carpets ripped up. I had only my furniture and the bare floor. My maid had fled in fright and I was left alone. . . ."

Such acts only incited her wrath. But they were nothing compared with her discovery that Sharon had another lover, and perhaps also a child by that same lady. Hill— still in possession of her contract with Sharon—sued him for infidelity, asking for a divorce and an equal division of the property he had accumulated since their private nuptials, something in excess of $5 million.

He confessed to philanderings involving a number of women, then countersued Hill for fraud, saying her "marriage contract" was a forgery.

THE LAWSUITS WOULD carry on for six years, making their way through several courts. Hill's attorney was Judge David S. Terry, the former chief justice of the California Supreme Court, who'd faced off against another U.S. senator, David C. Broderick, in 1859, and killed him in a duel just southwest of town. Terry's prosecution of the case against Sharon was no less headline-worthy. In court, Hill claimed Sharon had tried to coax her to give up his marriage agreement with her, and that when she claimed to have mislaid the paper, he choked her until she fainted and then, fearing her dead, stuffed her inside his bedroom closet at the Palace Hotel. "When she revived," wrote Lewis and Hall, "Sharon, delighted to find he had not committed murder, agreed to a reconciliation." Sharon's attorney countered with allegations concerning Hill's own promiscuity. The defense also made much of her interest in love potions, fortune-tellers, and the supernatural. Both sides in the case charged that the opposition was buying off witnesses.

In December 1884, Judge J. F. Sullivan ruled in Allie Hill's favor, granting her a divorce and $2,500 a month in alimony from Sharon. The Silver King appealed the decision to federal court, but Sharon didn't live to see the outcome. In a last message to the newspapers on November 5, 1885, he announced, "I am exceedingly weak in body and suffer great physical pain, but my mind is perfectly clear. In this condition I declare that I never proposed or offered marriage to Sarah Althea Hill at any time or in any form. . . ." He died eight days later, at age 64—six weeks before a judge from the United States Circuit Court decided that Allie Hill's marriage contract with Sharon was, indeed, bogus.

Hill's need for succor at this point seems to have been well answered by her lawyer, David Terry. The pair were married in 1886. He was 62; she was 30 years his junior. Many people said that, outside of his duel with David Broderick, wedding tempestuous Allie Hill was the most daring act Terry had ever committed.

Terry now appealed his wife's case to the Federal Supreme Court, this time fighting Sharon's heirs. The presiding judge was Stephen J. Field, a U.S. Supreme Court justice making the rounds from Washington, D.C. Field was also an old adversary of David Terry's. Hill had waited more than two years for this decision, and her calm

SOMEONE TO WATCH OVER ME

Adding to the otherworldliness of the battle between William Sharon and Allie Hill was the regular presence in the courtroom of Mary Ellen "Mammy" Pleasant, a well-known black boardinghouse keeper and alleged Voodoo Queen, who was said to have sunk $100,000 into Hill's case, hoping to be repaid that much and more from a judgment against Sharon. One observer, obviously affected by Mammy's sinister reputation, couldn't keep his eyes off her smile—"a smile that causes the observer to make an involuntary comparison with the tombstones in a graveyard on a very dark night, with a bit of red fire thrown in."

demeanor had begun to crack under the pressure. While Judge Field read his decision against her, she bolted from her seat and accused His Honor of taking bribes. She was ordered from the courtroom. But when a federal marshal tried to remove her, Terry struck the marshal a "terrific blow" on the mouth. Several guards had to restrain the husky, 6-foot-3 attorney, while Hill was dragged kicking and screaming from the courtroom. Terry later tried to pull a knife on the armed marshals, and a loaded revolver was found in his wife's satchel. Incensed by the outbursts, Field tossed both of them into Alameda County prison for contempt of court. Terry served six months, his wife three, during which she suffered a miscarriage.

ONCE FREED, TERRY appealed the contempt and forgery cases to the U.S. Supreme Court, and took the divorce suit to the California Supreme Court—but lost in all three cases.

At the crux of their defeats, Terry and Hill decided, was Judge Field. They plotted revenge, but Field had long ago returned to Washington.

And then on the night of August 13, 1889, Mr. and Mrs. David Terry boarded a Southern Pacific train at Fresno, bound for the Bay Area, where Terry was to appear in court the next day. As fate would have it, this same train was ·carrying Judge Stephen Field, accompanied by a bodyguard, deputy U.S. Marshal David Neagle. Allie Hill was the first to spy Field in the dining car, and she quickly fled to her room to grab a gun. Meanwhile, Terry stepped directly up to the judge and slapped him across the face. When Neagle jumped between the two men, Terry reached for his breast pocket. But before he could reach it, Neagle explained later, "I raised my six-shooter . . . and held it to him and shot twice in quick succession." Terry died. Hill was restrained in the doorway a moment later, and a loaded pistol was removed from her purse.

When it turned out that Terry had been unarmed, Field and Neagle were arrested for murder. The governor of California had to intervene personally to free Field, and Neagle was released only after it was argued that by protecting the judge against attack, the bodyguard had acted "in pursuance of a law of the United States" and under obligation from none other than President Benjamin Harrison.

Allie Hill—a widow at least twice over—continued pushing for a share of Sharon's millions, but the courts wouldn't listen. Even her contested marriage contract was destroyed when her house burned down. Her interest in spiritualists increased, and she tried to contact her late husband. Her storied beauty deteriorated quickly, and her gray-streaked hair went uncombed. She became a familiar apparition around town, standing dumbly in the rain or strolling (significantly) through the Palace Hotel's lobby, a woman gone mad. In 1892, she was finally committed to the State Hospital in Stockton, where she stayed until her death in 1937. She was 84.

THE GREAT RAT ROUNDUP

We commonly associate bubonic plague with Europe. During the 1,200 years between 540 and 1666, three pandemics of this pestilence—including the so-called Black Death (1346–1361)—reduced Europe's population by about 137 million and caused significant disruption of society. But San Francisco has also experienced outbreaks of this contagion.

The first episode occurred at the close of the 19th century, following reports that the Black Death had risen Lazarus-like in Bombay, India, and was wending its way to northern California via Hong Kong, the Philippines, Japan, and Hawaii. As the city's defense, a quarantine station was set up on Angel Island. Ships arriving from trans-Pacific ports had to be certified plague-free before being permitted to land. Several deaths in Chinatown in 1900 confirmed the presence of the disease and increased plague anxieties. But City Hall, fearful that a wholesale quarantine of San Francisco would disrupt business and commerce, tried to sweep the whole panic under a rug. In *Eradicating the Plague in San Francisco*, Frank Morton Todd recounts that Mayor Eugene E. Schmitz even "refused to approve the printing of health reports and vital statistics, and attempted to remove from office four members of the Board of Health who persisted in the statement that the plague existed in the city." But doctors and sanitation workers knew that something had to be done, so they mounted their own information campaign, which kept the death toll to 113 people, almost all from Chinatown.

In 1907, the Black Death surfaced again in Chinatown. And again, City Hall hesitated to act. Many people refused to believe that San Francisco could be revisited by this disease. They assumed that Chinatown's utter destruction during the recent fire had completely wiped out any harmful bacteria. The effect of doubt and hesitation was that within months a dozen more people died.

In the summer of 1907, the number of plague cases stood at 55. City officials finally had to take action against the disease, and decided that the most effective means of eliminating it would be to find and exterminate the principal carriers of bubonic plague: San Francisco's many rats.

San Francisco mounted what historian Todd called "the most intensive rat hunt in history." A bounty of 10 cents a head was offered for every rat that could be trapped and brought to one of the local health centers. More than 11,200 buildings were disinfected and 1,713 were demolished. Concrete replaced wood in any floors or sidewalks where rats might hide. It was a mammoth task, and a comical one too, as hundreds of men in ties and bowlers pursued tiny tails down fetid alleyways and through saloon basements.

But it worked. Health officials were pleased to see that the more gnawing mammals they rounded up, the fewer new cases of bubonic plague were reported. The last human victim was counted in February 1908, a month in which 84 diseased rodents were destroyed. The hunt continued until November of that year. By that time, 160 San Franciscans had caught the disease, and 77 of them had perished from it. More than 150,000 rats were captured, every one of which underwent bacteriological scrutiny at a central laboratory.

History is silent on what lasting damage this campaign may have done to the local reputation of rats.

"I'M DYING, I'M DYING, HE KILLED ME"

It was a tragedy offering the perfect mix of elements to capture the attention of a nation just then becoming infatuated with the successes and excesses of Hollywood: sex, alcohol, an allegedly brutal film star, and a tragic young starlet. We will never know exactly what happened on the night of September 5, 1921, in a suite combining rooms 1219,

*American humorist and journalist
Irvin S. Cobb, who'd spent years
negotiating the tides of taxis that
flowed up and down streets in New
York City, should have been used to
the sometimes kamikaze-like nature
of such vehicles. Yet, while visiting
San Francisco for the 1920
Democratic National Convention, he
contended that venturing into local
cabs was a particularly white-
knuckled endeavor. "Something
seems to tell me that if I am not
killed in one of San Francisco's
taxicabs, I shall be killed under
one," Cobb wrote. "The youth who
has been driving me about is a
lineal descendent of Ben Hur."*

1220, and 1221 of the St. Francis Hotel. Yet it left an attractive, dark-haired model dead, and put an end to the soaring career of the silent-film comedian known as "Fatty" Arbuckle.

His real name was Roscoe. Born in 1887, a full 16 pounds, he grew into a 270-pound, baby-faced actor who employed his rotundity to the best slapstick advantage. American filmgoers embraced him simply as Fatty. In his day, he was the King of Fun-Makers, star of such films as *The Dollar a Year Man, Brewster's Millions, Fatty on the Job*, and a film that would take on painful significance in later years, *Fatty's Flirtation*. He was once as well known as Charlie Chaplin, Mary Pickford, and the celluloid cowboy Tom Mix, and was especially famous for his pie-throwing buffoonery. Film critic James Agee once wrote that Arbuckle "had satanic marksmanship with pies. He could simultaneously blind two people in opposite directions." Such a hot commodity was he that, just before his downfall, he had inked a contract with Paramount Pictures for $3 million—a truly astonishing figure for the times.

Arbuckle had stayed at the St. Francis so often that the hotel used him in its promotions (along with car maker Henry Ford and politician William Jennings Bryan). San Francisco loved him. On the same Labor Day weekend that he checked in at the St. Francis, Bay Area residents were streaming into the Haight Theater for his latest feature-length series of misadventures, *The Travelling Salesman*.

IN THE EARLY AFTERNOON of September 5, two days after his arrival in the city, Arbuckle was relaxing in his hotel-room parlor, his feet snugged into slippers, a bathrobe tied about his prodigious middle, when a knock at his door announced nine friends from Hollywood, along with bottles of bootleg gin secreted inside plain brown bags. Fatty rang for room service delivery of food and a Gramophone with a stack of records.

Included in these impromptu festivities were two women who had wheeled up from Los Angeles the day before with Arbuckle's agent. First came Maud Delmont, a dour-faced showgirl who had formerly made a sideline of procuring willing women for showbiz fêtes, then blackmailing the men who showed her charges the most intimate attention. With her came comely Virginia Rappe, a 25-year-old actress whose star had dimmed some since her appearance on the cover of the sheet music for "Let Me Call You Sweetheart."

From here, the facts become fogged amidst conflicting court testimony and self-serving salaciousness in the press accounts. But it seems that sometime during that evening, after downing at least three gins with orange juice, Miss Rappe became noticeably uncomfortable and left the parlor. Not long afterward, Arbuckle pardoned himself and padded into his bedroom.

Suddenly he came back, saying that Rappe was very sick and in need of assistance. Several guests followed him into the bedroom, where they found the slender ingenue moaning on the bed, her clothes in some disarray. Efforts to communicate with her were useless. Seeing no other way to revive her from what they assumed was drunkenness, they filled the bathtub with cold water and dunked her in. Arbuckle called downstairs for help, and when a doctor, the hotel manager, and the house detective showed up, the actor helped them carry Rappe to an extra room down the hall, where she was expected to sleep off her intoxication. Other than offering to pay for Rappe's extra room, Fatty took little further interest in her plight. He left the hotel that night for dinner and a personal appearance at a theater, and returned the next morning to his home in Hollywood.

Four days later, he found himself on the phone with a *San Francisco Chronicle* reporter. Did Mr. Arbuckle have a statement to make? Make about what, Fatty asked. Why,

Virginia Rappe's death that very morning, of course, along with Maud Delmont's subsequent accusation that Arbuckle had raped the starlet during his party.

"Arbuckle took hold of her and said, 'I've been trying to get you for five years,'" Delmont had told the media. Then, she said, he dragged Rappe off to his bedroom, slammed the door, and remained inside with her for an hour until screams were heard and Delmont herself had to kick the door to make him open up. She said that the slapstick king was wearing Rappe's Panama hat; that he slurred, "Get her dressed and take her back to the Palace [Hotel]. She makes too much noise"; and that before her cold bath, Rappe had moaned, "I'm dying, I'm dying, he killed me."

The official cause of death was peritonitis, a fact that was buried in the small print. Had it not been for Arbuckle's fame, the case might have slid from the headlines and never gone to trial.

Instead, Fatty returned to San Francisco to face the charge "murder of a motion picture actress" in the first degree (it was later reduced to manslaughter). District Attorney Matthew Brady was quoted as saying, "I will spare no effort to punish the perpetrator of this atrocious crime, although I know that I will be opposed by the cleverest lawyers which money and fame can purchase."

Even before his trial began, Arbuckle was tried and convicted by San Francisco's scandal-loving press. The *Chronicle* published stories with headlines such as "ARBUCKLE NEVER AIDED HIS FAMILY, STEPMOTHER SAYS." The *San Francisco Examiner* sought ever more vivid descriptions of Arbuckle's "orgy," finally describing it as a "bestial, sordid, revolting tragedy." Pictures of Virginia Rappe appeared in papers next to cartoons showing Arbuckle as the spider within a malefic web. Locals suddenly shunned Fatty's movies and preachers wove Sunday sermons around his alleged moral transgressions.

HISTORY'S LOSS

Amazingly, the transcripts of Fatty Arbuckle's trials were destroyed in 1972 after gathering dust for a half-century in the basement of San Francisco's Hall of Justice.

Once in court, however, Arbuckle's self-defense was persuasive. On that fatal night, he said, he'd gone into his bedroom to change for dinner, found Rappe sick in the bathroom, and carried her to his bed before alerting his guests to her condition. District Attorney Brady tried to impugn Arbuckle's testimony, but the cards were stacked against him. Maud Delmont's lurid tale was contradicted by other witnesses dug up by Pinkerton detectives, and she didn't show up in court. It was suggested that Rappe's demise may have resulted from a botched abortion or complications from a virulent case of the clap. The prosecution's own witnesses confessed that they'd been coerced into supporting Delmont's chronology of events. Arbuckle's first two trials ended in hung juries.

Trial number three began in March 1922, and lasted less than a month. The jury this time deliberated for only 2½ hours before finally declaring Roscoe "Fatty" Arbuckle innocent.

BUT IT WAS A PYRRHIC VICTORY. Five days after Fatty's exoneration, the censorship office of the Motion Picture Producer's Association declared that Arbuckle's films would no longer be shown in theaters. By December 1922, the ban was lifted, but the damage was already done. People could no longer bring themselves to laugh at the pudgy comedian without imagining him violating the much frailer and more physically appealing Rappe.

Arbuckle retired from acting in 1923. He later took his pie-throwing talents to the vaudeville circuit and even tried directing some Warner Brothers films under the pseudonym Will B. Good. When he died of a heart attack in 1933, at age 46, he was buried at Woodlawn Cemetery in the Bronx borough of New York City—about as far away from the source of his troubles as he could be taken without leaving the United States.

POSTHUMOUS PROTECTORS

Fatty Arbuckle's wife, Minta Durfee Arbuckle, proclaimed the actor's innocence until she passed away in 1975, at age 86, but by then, nobody cared anymore. Virginia Rappe enjoyed her own posthumous defender. After her demise, Rappe's sweetheart, film director Henry Lehrman, shaped the rest of his days around her memory, visiting her grave weekly until he perished in 1946.

A SOLDIER IN
THE PEOPLE'S ARMY

I t's a parent's worst nightmare: one of your grown children is kidnapped. Later that child finally surfaces to say that she would rather die than return to you. She accuses you of capitalistic "crimes." She condemns you, calling you a "pig."

No wonder so many people were shocked when Patricia Campbell Hearst —heiress to the media empire started by her grandfather, William Randolph Hearst —was abducted from her Berkeley apartment in 1974. Her twisted trail from debutante to desperado worried other fathers and mothers, none of whom could guarantee that their own children wouldn't also one day abandon them, only to turn up later in the cyclopic eye of a hidden camera, brandishing a semiautomatic rifle during a bank robbery.

"It's terrible!" said Randolph A. Hearst, Patty's father, after the famous heist. "Sixty days ago, she was a lovely child. Now there's a picture of her in a bank with a gun in her hand."

PRIVATE-SCHOOL CHEERLEADER. Debutante. A conscientious student at Menlo Park College and the University of California, Berkeley. A young woman engaged to be married. This was Patty Hearst before her bizarre saga began. Just prior to becoming a missing person, she'd been selecting a china pattern with her fiancé, Steven Weed. She was no enemy of The System. Her family *was* The System. Nobody could imagine that she would become famous in San Francisco as a revolutionary.

Then, on the night of February 4, 1974, three members of the Symbionese

Liberation Army (SLA) broke in to Patty's flat, beat Weed with a bottle, and stuffed the screaming bride-to-be into a car trunk.

At first, it seemed like a conventional kidnapping. Patty's father, editor and publisher of the *San Francisco Examiner*, was a wealthy man. Law-enforcement agencies and other observers expected the SLA to extort money from the Hearst family, and they weren't disappointed. In a scheme that was apparently supposed to emphasize the SLA's populist commitment, its leaders forced Randolph Hearst to donate $2 million worth of food, to be distributed around poor neighborhoods in San Francisco and Oakland.

Nine weeks passed without further word from the SLA; then Berkeley radio station KFPA received a set of seven tapes on which Patty Hearst could be heard denouncing her old life and committing herself to the SLA's anti-establishment cause. "I have chosen to stay and fight," she said. She condemned her father as a liar, insisting that his concern for her well-being and that of "oppressed people" was no more than a sham. And Patty maintained in forceful tones that she had not been "brainwashed, drugged, tortured, hypnotized, or in any way confused." She just wasn't the person she once had been. That much was obvious from the snapshot that came with the tapes: it showed Patty Hearst cradling a rifle in front of an SLA poster emblazoned with a cobra.

TWO MORE WEEKS came and went. Suddenly Patty was back, again on tape. This time, it was a videotape from a branch of Hibernia Bank, located in the Sunset District, southwest of downtown San Francisco. Recorded on April 15, 1974, the tape showed five people—four white women and a black man—walking boldly through the doors of the bank with semiautomatic carbines readied in their arms. "We're from the SLA!" one of them announced. And while cashiers gathered stacks of money in hopes of saving their own skins, a member of the holdup gang introduced a pretty dark-haired

A POISONOUS PAST

Before the SLA's kidnapping of Patty Hearst, the group had already been implicated in several criminal incidents, most notably the 1973 slaying (with cyanide bullets) of Oakland's school superintendent, Marcus Foster.

woman who looked just like the third of Randolph and Catherine Hearst's five daughters. Only now she was calling herself *Tania*.

The bandits made off with $10,960, and discharged a few rifle rounds gratuitously as they fled. Shortly thereafter, two SLA members—Emily and William Harris—were spotted in a clumsy Los Angeles shoplifting attempt. From a parked car outside of the store, Patty/Tania opened fire, spraying bullets to cover their escape.

Agents from the Federal Bureau of Investigation (FBI) were frustrated. At times, as many as 300 agents worked the case, and yet Patty/Tania and the handful of other SLA followers remained at large. During the first year of Patty's abduction, the FBI tracked the group to one or more hideouts, but agents always arrived after the SLA had cleared out. Rumors of Patty Hearst's whereabouts were so numerous that a special FBI unit in San Francisco was assigned just to follow them up. There were Patty sightings in Mexico City, Hong Kong, Los Angeles, Cuba, Algeria. As the hunt for the Hearst heiress dragged on, law enforcement personnel got jumpy: American women were detained at the Mexican border while guards checked out their identification; a young woman in Virginia sued the FBI after agents barged into her apartment, convinced that she was the elusive Patty.

On May 17, 1974, a lead brought more than 400 FBI agents, along with a small battalion of armed policemen, to a tiny house in the south-central area of Los Angeles. Millions of Americans watched the shoot-out live on television as the SLA defended their latest safe house, refusing to give up. As many as 5,000 rounds were fired from government guns. No one knew if Patty was inside. The house erupted in fire and was quickly reduced to a rank pile of char. Investigators later found half a dozen bodies, including that of the SLA's principal muscle man, an escaped black convict by the name of Donald DeFreeze, but there was no sign of William Randolph Hearst's granddaughter.

It would've been easier for the *federales* had the SLA been larger and easier to infiltrate, or if Patty Hearst had made attempts to contact somebody from her previous life. But they struck out on both counts. Not even the FBI had heard of the SLA before the group kidnapped her. Her messages to the outside world were few and far between. On a tape recording received by KFPA on June 7, 1974, Patty/Tania offered a tribute to William Wolfe, one of the SLA members who had perished during the FBI's pitched battle in Los Angeles. "His love for the people was so deep," she said, "that he was willing to give his life for them." And she added, "We loved each other so much."

PATTY AND SLA MEMBERS Emily and William Harris kept running. They were in New York for a time, trying to go underground with the Weatherman, one of the most violent of this country's revolutionary sects during the Johnson and Nixon years. But with so much attention and legal heat focused on Patty, she was a liability to her captors. Other underground revolutionaries shunned her and the SLA in the interests of their own survival. At one point, FBI agents tracking her movements accidentally came upon one of the Weatherman's hideouts on West 92nd Street. After that, an investigator told *Time* magazine, "The word went out to keep away from her."

So Patty and the Harrises went to Pennsylvania's Pocono Mountains, where they hid out at a farmhouse near the town of South Canaan for a time, again fleeing just before the FBI closed in. This time, however, they left a crucial clue in their wake: a red Volkswagen camper had been seen near the farmhouse. Authorities didn't find the van, but they did find its previous owner. He told them that he'd sold it to a woman named Kathleen Soliah, who gave him a post office box in San Francisco as her address. Soliah was known to have been connected with SLA members in the past.

A check on the post office box revealed that letters and messages were being picked up for the occupants of two separate addresses: one in the Mission District and another just north of the Daly City line. Agents mounted a stakeout at a Mission District apartment, dressed in the most transparent of disguises—sandals, beards, and beads. Nobody who saw them was fooled by the lawmen, but the couple who lived there didn't see them, and, on the afternoon of September 25, 1975, the FBI nabbed Emily and William Harris after they took a jog around nearby Bernal Park. In their apartment were found 40 pounds of black explosive powder, shotguns and pistols, and plenty of ammunition.

Less than two hours later, the noose tightened around another apartment that had been rented on Morse Street about two weeks before by a man who called himself Charlie Adams (he turned out to be Stephen F. Soliah, Kathleen's 27-year-old brother). Two women—one tall, another short—were known to occupy the flat with him. None of the flatmates had attracted suspicion. Yet, when an FBI agent and a San Francisco police inspector went to check it out, the door was opened by none other than Wendy Yoshimura, a familiar Berkeley artist and radical who had escaped after being implicated in an abortive 1972 bombing plot. Behind her stood a thin, slightly pale figure—Patricia Campbell Hearst.

"Don't shoot," said the 21-year-old heiress. "I'll go with you." And she did—first to an arraignment and then to the San Mateo jail, where she listed her occupation as "urban guerilla."

WITH STATE AND FEDERAL beefs hanging over her head, Patty could have been locked up for life. But in March 1976, she was finally convicted only for bank robbery and felonious use of firearms, drawing a seven-year sentence. She spent just portions of the next three years in prison, with time out during appeals, and was released in February 1979—five years after her odyssey had begun.

Was she a willing revolutionary or a coerced hostage? The FBI believed that she had committed her crimes knowingly and with loyalty to the SLA. As to why she would have detoured into the revolutionary life, psychiatrists speculated after her capture that Patty Hearst's motives were far more complex than loyalty to the SLA's cause. They claimed that she represented a much larger population of disaffected rich kids who, in their search for approval and meaning, allowed themselves to be used by powerful forces—whether the Weatherman, the SLA, or Charles Manson's murderous "family."

Patty Hearst later married and moved to New England; she described herself to a reporter as politically conservative. In a 1988 interview with *The New York Times*, she doubted that she "was ever as liberal as I thought of myself in college." She said the SLA "raped me mentally, physically, and emotionally, and they stole my reputation." She talked about being a kidnap victim: how she was locked in a dark closet for 57 days, how she "cried and cried, the horrible feeling inside all the time of having to be with [the SLA]." Yet, when pressed to tell whether she knew and agreed with what she was doing when she helped rob the Hibernia Bank or shot up that Los Angeles storefront, Patricia Hearst Shaw turned enigmatic.

"The human mind can't be wrapped up and delivered," she told the *Times*. "Troubles can't be summed up in easy packages. There should be questions. Life isn't simple."

IMPROBABLE DREAMS

*"Make no little plans. They have no magic to stir men's blood
and probably will not be realized. Make big plans. . . ."*
—Daniel H. Burnham, architect

OUR OWN PRIVATE XANADU

ECONOMY CLASS

Better than your run-of-the-mill hostelry, but no rival of the Palace Hotel, Robert Woodward's What Cheer House "provided such homey comforts as open fireplaces in public rooms, a thoughtfully selected library for its guests, and the first à la carte restaurant service in San Francisco," according to Lucius Beebe and Charles Clegg, in San Francisco's Golden Era. *Visitors who craved solid service but didn't want to empty their wallets to get it often stayed at the What Cheer.*

On almost any given weekend day during the Victorian age, swarms of bearded men in top hats, women in tents of white chiffon, and overdressed children streamed through the gates of Woodward's Gardens. The city's premier family entertainment grounds, Woodward's offered wild, weird, and wonderful attractions that almost unfailingly charmed its visitors. As popular historian Samuel Dickson once wrote, Woodward's Gardens was "the most glamorous, the most exciting place in all the exciting city of San Francisco."

Owner Robert B. Woodward hadn't intended to become the Walt Disney of his time. Dignified and rather sullen, with a Lincolnesque arc of beard covering his square chin, he had come to California with the forty-niners. By the 1850s and early '60s he was known principally as the proprietor of a five-story hotel called the What Cheer House, at Sacramento and Leidesdorff Streets. This enterprise proved so successful that before long Woodward was able to invest in other businesses. But he sank much of his money into improvements to his estate on 14th Street, between Mission and Valencia, property that had once belonged to explorer-politician John C. Frémont. Woodward slowly developed a substantial Victorian residence orbited by gardens, fountains, and a hothouse for the nurturing of grapes. To satisfy his taste for the finer things of life, the hotelier also created his own private art gallery, curated by Virgil Williams, a landscape painter who later helped found the School of Design, a fine-arts institution. (Williams's school still survives, only now it's known as the San Francisco Art Institute, housed on Russian Hill.)

AT THE TIME, San Francisco was sprouting theaters and opera houses but was still a long way from being considered a cultural capital. However, the nouveau riche created by the Gold Rush were learning how to distinguish high art from artistic high jinks. To help along their education, but more importantly to benefit the U.S. Sanitary Commission (precursor to the Red Cross), in November 1864 Robert Woodward agreed to open up his art gallery for the enjoyment of a select list of elegant guests.

How impressed those gilded mortals must have been, stepping through the Pompeian-frescoed antechamber of Woodward's gallery on their way to an oval display area where paintings and busts were displayed together in splendid superfluity. Julia Cooley Altrocchi recalled the gallery opening in her book, *The Spectacular San Franciscans*: "In the Gallery the contributors to the Sanitary Commission found 66 fine pictures, most of them copies of the old masters and California scenes by San Francisco's own Virgil Williams, who had spent several years painting and collecting abroad (at Woodward's behest), a few works by the local [Albert] Bierstadt and others, [Chauncey Bradley] Ives' statue of *Rebecca at the Well*, and Hiram Powers' famous sculptural piece, *California*."

Following up that first benefit with similar ones, Woodward's efforts to bring art appreciation to the city attracted the curiosity of San Francisco's less-well-to-do. As word spread of the bounty at his Mission District estate, people started showing up at his house, especially on Sundays, just to peer through his gates, hoping to spy some of his marble statuary or one of his aviaries. Woodward seemed not to be disturbed by all this attention. In fact, being a generous sort, he rather reveled in it.

Only the most meager impetus was needed after that to convince him that he had a future in the entertainment industry. As Altrocchi related the story, "One day at the Sunday dinner table Mr. Woodward exclaimed: 'Did you ever see such a crowd of gapers and gazers? I might as well let the public have the run of the grounds.' To which one of his daughters responded, 'Well, why *don't* you, Father?' The philanthropist pondered this for a moment, then said, 'Well, that's a *thumping* good idea. I think I will.'"

CHEAP RECREATION WAS much in demand in San Francisco after the Civil War. Circuses, minstrel shows, sporting events (including marathon walking contests), club teas, and fairs all received enthusiastic attendance. Golden Gate Park didn't yet exist, but the first of several Cliff Houses did, and horse-drawn stages carried passengers 4 miles out there from the city, just so they could watch the ocean and listen to the sea lions bickering on the rocks offshore. Families that couldn't afford streetcar fares might be found on a holiday picnicking upon the tended grounds of a cemetery.

Woodward's Gardens wasn't the first of this city's amusement parks, but it was something quite apart from its predecessors. Opened in 1866, it was bigger. Bolder. *Gaudier.* "It is," wrote social historian B. E. Lloyd, "a spot of perennial beauty." Domes, minarets, and seemingly every other eye-catching architectural style sprouted above the park's many trees. Woodward turned his own two-story home into a museum. He built a dance hall, a theater, and a restaurant. An amphitheater hosted Gilbert and Sullivan's *HMS Pinafore* and Yankee Robinson's "Ballet of Parisian Beauties." Youthful swains and their dates found a chance to talk privately aboard one of several small boats for rent on a lake. A collection of rare stuffed animals—tigers, polar bears, kangaroos, rabbits, hyenas, and more—were scattered about the property, waiting to be touched or to serve as distinctive fixtures in family travel photos. Woodward offered a live menagerie on his acreage, too (*Step right up, folks, and feed peanuts to a bear!*), plus a sea lion pond, conservatories, ornamental waters coursed by black swans, and Sunday afternoon balloon rides. Parrots, tethered to stakes in front of the museum, would squawk as tourists promenaded by. An arena hosted Roman chariot races. The nation's first saltwater aquarium included a variety of colorful fish and sea anemones.

SLIP-SLIDING AWAY

In addition to large-scale amusement parks, San Francisco hosted three mammoth slides, down which patrons raced in boats toward a pond. The first of these opened in 1895 in the Haight and closed six years later. The two others were located just north of Golden Gate Park and to the south of Japantown.

Walter Morosco's Royal Russian Circus performed inside a huge canvas pavilion. Christal the Frenchman wrestled bears. Herman the Great was shot from a cannon. And just when patrons thought they'd seen everything there was to see, around the bend would saunter an 8-foot 3-inch Chinese Giant, robed in colorful silk and slowly flapping a paper fan.

This place drank up Woodward's most creative, most exotic ideas, and always demanded more, more, *more*. The owner was often spotted in his magic kingdom, observing how people related to the exhibits, tweaking anything that seemed not quite right. He kept a critic's finger on the pulse of entertainment trends. After a roller-skating rink opened at Union Square in 1870, only to be overrun by novelty-seeking San Franciscans, Woodward immediately built a second rink at his gardens. When he realized that some women were averse to riding alone all the way out to the park on conventional horse-drawn streetcars, he invested in his own elegantly appointed "palace car," which he advertised as "luxuriously fitted up with velvet carpet, and sofas extending the length of the car, upholstered in embroidered tapestry costing sixteen dollars per yard."

THERE WAS MORE THAN a wee bit of Barnum in Woodward. He couldn't pass up bizarre attractions that he thought would suck in the masses. A two-headed child, a man with no legs, a headless rooster, an allegedly haunted windowpane—all of these were on view at one time or another in Woodward's amusement gardens. As the *Examiner* put it, "any freak that did not make [Phineas T.] Barnum gasp Woodward seized on with avidity."

In part because of Woodward's willingness to change and adapt, his empire of genteel kitsch lasted until 1894—more than a quarter of a century—longer than most of its competitors.

The property on which it sat was eventually subdivided into building lots (much of

---

SEASIDE SILLINESS

Playland-at-the-Beach was San Francisco's last surviving amusement park, closing finally in 1972. It started out in the early 20th century as a combination of carnivalesque venues clustered around the western end of a streetcar line. Arthur Looff, son of a famous Coney Island carousel artist, operated the handsome merry-go-round; John Friedle ran the nearby shooting gallery. In the 1920s, the two entrepreneurs decided to create a single amusement park. Their venture soon boasted of rides ranging from the Eden Wonder Museum (featuring "the most

☞

it is now occupied by the grim-visaged old Armory). But not all reminders of Woodward's Gardens disappeared. In *Ark of Empire*, a study of bohemian San Francisco, historian Idwal Jones reported that Adolph Sutro bought up the "moth-eaten aviary and zoo" that once attracted crowds to the Gardens, along with that park's "collection of sea shells" and a "startling concourse of Japanese wax figures," and installed all these at his elaborate baths, on Point Lobos.

Because Woodward's Gardens lasted for so long, it was heavily photographed. In the frozen world of black and white, Woodward's art gallery is again a source of enchantment, his stuffed tiger poses once more in the arms of a dark-haired matron, and the Chinese Giant stands as big as his legend.

GETTING ON TRACK

Terror. That's what the young workman assigned to pilot Andrew S. Hallidie's cable car on its maiden journey must have felt on August 1, 1873, as he stood at the brow of Jones Street, peering down Clay Street on the east side of Nob Hill toward Portsmouth Square and Kearny Street. Terror, because despite all the careful testing that Hallidie and his minions had done, this was the moment of truth. Terror, because it was just after 5 a.m. and a dense fog had crawled in from the ocean to cuddle Clay Street. There was no way at all to see the bottom of the hill.

"Jimmie, are you ready?" shouted Hallidie, who was standing in the vehicle, flanked by his three business partners and several of his company's employees. Jimmie looked down again from his position at the front of the streetcar and studied the impenetrable fog. Pale with fright, he shook his head and stepped off the car.

The men around him were clearly agitated by this 11th-hour act of cravenness, and they thought to leave as well. But Hallidie acted quickly. Grabbing the levers of the car, he used them to pick up the wire cable that had been laid beneath the street, and together with his human cargo, the father of San Francisco's cable railways lurched for the misty edge.

INVENTORS LEARN TO TAKE risks, in hopes that the rewards will outweigh the sometimes high costs of daring. Hallidie's father, a Scottish-born engineer who spent many years developing and patenting techniques for the making of wire ropes, infected his second son and namesake with the discovery bug.

Young Andrew was born in London, England, in 1836. The boy took his early training in mechanical and scientific fields, and by the time he turned 13, he was already serving in a machine shop owned by his elder brother. It was rewarding work, but full days of labor and nights crammed with studying took their toll on his health. Andrew Sr. resolved that a change of atmosphere was called for, so in 1852, he and his son sailed for California.

They landed here after the Gold Rush had peaked but when it was still possible for minor men to make major names for themselves in San Francisco. Andrew Sr.'s fate appears lost in the pages of history. But his 16-year-old son survived by gold mining, blacksmithing, and surveying. On the side, he experimented with transportation technology. At age 19 he built a wire-suspension viaduct that stretched over 200 feet across the middle fork of the American River. This was his first large-scale application of cable technology, and it marked a turning point in the young man's life.

Back in San Francisco by 1856, Hallidie set himself up in the business of "metal rope" manufacturing, using his father's innovations as the basis for his own work. Eleven years passed before he secured his first patent—for a rigid suspension bridge. After that, though, his creations followed upon each other in fairly quick succession; one of them was the "Hallidie Ropeway or Tramway," which employed iron buckets hung from an endless elevated cable for the transport of ore and other items out of mountainous areas. And he spent many hours perfecting a woven steel cable that could be bent over and over again without breaking. A. S. Hallidie & Company soon became known in town for the superb quality of its products.

THE TALE OF JUST HOW Hallidie came by his idea for streetcars propelled by underground cables has been told so many times that it now sounds more apocryphal than real, yet historians swear by its veracity. It was the dismal winter of 1869 and the then-33-year-old Hallidie was out for an evening stroll in the rain. He stopped to watch a streetcar pulled by four horses begin the slow trudge up a steep hill. The car was overcrowded with men and women trying to get home out of the storm, and the steeds were having difficulty pulling it over the roadway's slick cobblestones. About halfway up the hill, one of the damp, panting horses slipped and fell. The driver's response was to apply the brake, but he did it with such speed and force that the brake chain snapped. As Hallidie watched, the weighty vehicle began slowly to slip back down the hill, picking up speed as it went and dragging the horses behind it, until it finally settled at a level crossroads. Hallidie rushed to help release the battered beasts, and in that moment, the concept for today's cable cars began to form in his head.

In the late 1860s, horse-drawn streetcars (carrying 10 or more riders) were the city's principal means of public transportation. Steam-powered street railways had been

---

NEIGH-SAYERS II

Horsecars came in all sizes and some odd styles, including an oval-shaped "balloon car." By 1870, they operated across the face of downtown, from as far south as the Mission District, all the way up to North Beach. You could even hop a scheduled car headed west to the cemeteries at Lone Mountain and transfer from there to a line that would take you out to the original Cliff House on the coast.

considered just after the Gold Rush began, but they'd given way to larger (and thus more profitable) horsecars. "By 1873," Edgar M. Kahn wrote in *Cable Car Days in San Francisco*, "there were eight horsecar systems operating. There were eighty miles of single track, and transportation facilities were increasing rapidly with the opening of additional streets and the development of new districts." The next evolutionary step was up to Andrew Hallidie.

The cable-car concept seems so elementary now: Hallidie proposed installing an endless and continuously moving loop of steel rope in a slot beneath a roadway. When the operator of a car running on street-level tracks wanted to move his vehicle forward, he'd mechanically grip the cable with what was essentially a giant pair of pliers. To stop the car, the cable would be released and the brakes applied. Tension would be adjusted to keep cables from slipping.

Yet, locals laughed at Hallidie when he first suggested that he could adapt his mountain ropeway technology to inner-city transit, dubbing his project "Hallidie's Folly."

Undaunted, the young inventor decided to mount a demonstration of his cable car on steep Clay Street. A survey of that thoroughfare was made, and a franchise was secured to allow him to operate his contraption. Subscriptions for stock purchases were invited, but the public's initial response was again less than favorable. To build support for his cause, Hallidie printed flyers describing his invention and even put a model on display that would help explain its function. Property owners along Clay Street were finally convinced to pledge money toward the project, but Hallidie still had to both put up his entire life savings ($20,000) and secure a bank loan to make his dream a reality.

According to the terms of his franchise, Hallidie had to have a cable car up and

PIECEMEAL PROVENANCE

It's not proper to say that Andrew Hallidie "invented" cable cars, since his San Francisco system relied so heavily on previous mechanical studies. "Cable traction was a highly derivative invention, not only in drawing on a combination of existing technology, but in having abundant precursors," explains George W. Hilton, in The Cable Car in America. *As early as 1812, W. Chapman and E. K. Chapman had suggested that vehicles could be pulled along roadways by means of fixed cables and winding devices on their wheels. There was discussion in the 1820s of moving public cars along highways by means of a chain buried*

☞

in a hollow rail. In fact, every component of cable street railways had been patented or used experimentally by 1873. Hallidie, however, was the first to pull the various puzzle pieces together and create a viable cable-car operation.

ALL THE NEWS THAT'S FIT TO IGNORE

Astoundingly, the cable car's 1873 San Francisco premiere wasn't given widespread attention by the local press. The top news story in the Chronicle *that day was a fire that had destroyed 20 downtown blocks in Portland, Oregon.*

running on Clay Street by August 1, 1873—or his rights would expire. It required vast expenditures of nervous sweat and tension for workmen to complete the cable road in the nick of time. But Hallidie had no choice. If he hadn't careened his wobbly metal experiment off the lip of Jones Street, down Clay Street, and into the fog on that morning of August 1, his project would have been a total loss.

As it was, the cable car's maiden voyage was a success. The tram went downhill just fine, Hallidie dropping and grabbing the cable several times. When the group reached Kearny Street, a turntable was used to reverse course, and the car traveled back up the hill through the fog, the inventive genius still in control.

By that afternoon, word of the cable car's journey had spread, and the line was mobbed by politicians, businessmen, and others wanting to be the first in line for a ride. Policemen were helpless against all the people elbowing their way to a seat. At one point, the crowd, trying to help, shoved the car onto the turntable too quickly and a bolt on the cable grip snapped. It took 20 minutes to fix—20 minutes during which pessimists renewed their charge that the project was a failure. But as soon as the necessary repairs had been completed, the waiting crowd abandoned the naysayers and climbed aboard for Mr. Hallidie's wild ride.

THREE CABLE RAILROADS were in operation by 1878. In that same year, railroad magnate Leland Stanford built a line up California Street, not so he and his fellow Nob Hill burghers could ride in the open-air cars, but in hopes that this improved access would drive up property values in the area. In the 1880s, at the height of the cable car's popularity, eight different lines crisscrossed the city over 112 miles of track, with some 600 cars in all running up Nob and Russian Hills, north to the Presidio, and out to Golden Gate Park and the Cliff House. They generated more than a few laudatory remarks. "They take no count of rise or fall," wrote Rudyard Kipling during a visit here. "They turn corners almost at right angles, cross other lines, and, for aught I know, may run up the sides of houses."

By the 1890s, cable cars were giving way to electric trolleys. Some cable-car lines were destroyed in the 1906 earthquake and fire, and many were never rebuilt. In time the city decided that it was cheaper and easier to run electric trolleys and, later, gasoline-powered buses.

In 1947, only three cable lines remained. Mayor Roger Lapham finally urged the Board of Supervisors to "get rid of our cable car system as promptly as possible. . . . They are old, outmoded, expensive and inefficient, and do not belong in any modern transit system." The outcry was slow to boil but loud when it arrived. San Franciscans were sentimental about their cable cars. Petitions were signed and the campaign to save the cable cars was picked up by *Time*, *Life*, and other national publications.

The deciding moment carried all the drama of Andrew Hallidie's first descent on Clay Street. Mayor Lapham told the Twin Coach Company to prove once and for all that buses could fare better than cable cars in this city of hills. It was proposed that a dual-engine motorcoach give a public demonstration of its power with a climb up Powell Street to the crest of Nob Hill. City officials loaded onto the designated bus at Sutter Street and waited for a sign to begin the demonstration. As they waited, off in the distance could be heard the clanging of an approaching Powell Street cable car.

The bus driver finally put his growling behemoth into gear and the ascent began. Clouds of diesel smoke poured from the coach as it crept upwards, the civic dignitaries smiling. But long before the summit was reached, the bus's engine started to complain loudly, its putrid belchings increased, and the mighty coach stopped dead in its tracks.

⚜

SAVED!

In 1955, San Francisco voters elected overwhelmingly to preserve their cable-car heritage. Nine years later those vehicles earned distinction as the first National Historic Landmark on wheels. Forty-four cars still operate on over 19 miles of track, carrying some 13 million passengers every year. San Francisco boasts the world's only surviving cable-car system.

⚜

Then it began to lose ground, and as crowds were cleared away, it reversed down the hill to its starting point.

Meanwhile, the Powell Street cable car, which had been steadily scaling the same roadway from Market Street, reached Sutter and, with the gripman ringing its bell in triumph, conquered the last stretch of Nob Hill in classic style.

THE BENEFACTOR

Adolph Joseph Heinrich Sutro was only 68 when he died in 1898, yet his life had been fuller than that of most men half-again his age. Against the objections of powerful bankers, he had built a mammoth drainage tunnel through Nevada's Comstock Lode. He had created opulent baths, built a baronial new Cliff House at Point Lobos, and collected rare books for the largest private library of his time. When other capitalists might have retired from public life, he had served as mayor of San Francisco. A magneto of energy, Sutro had filled his days spinning off new challenges.

Sutro was one of 11 children born to prosperous German-Jewish parents in what was then Prussia. The studious young Adolph was fascinated with books, mechanical things, science. He had almost blown himself to smithereens in an early chemical experiment and would stay up well into the wee hours of a morning, just gazing through his telescope at constellations. He imagined himself becoming a great scientist. Then his father was injured in a carriage accident, and Adolph had to quit school to help his elder brother run the family woolen-cloth mill. This change of course frustrated Sutro. However, it also

HAIR APPARENT

Sutro was recognized not only for his entrepreneurial escapades, but also for his prominent muttonchop whiskers. It is said that he grew his cottony features after a shocking attack in 1855, during which a stockbroker — infuriated at Sutro's cousin Charles — lashed out instead at Adolph, slashing him "from the ear to the mouth" with a knife. Whiskers hid the scar and in the bargain gave Sutro's face some mature dignity.

left him with a lifelong respect for labor and laborers, along with a belief that if you treat your workers well, they will do well for you. Though his prospects for advancement in Europe seemed good, brewing revolution in Prussia, imminent war against Austria, and the death of his father finally drove Sutro and his family to America, where he headed for Nevada's new silver find in 1859.

Sutro's first success in Nevada mining country was the development (with a German chemist named John Randohr) of a highly efficient chemical technique for extracting residual silver and gold from already processed Comstock ore. This process made Sutro rich, but it didn't satisfy his entrepreneurial desires. That's when his mind fastened on the idea of carving a tunnel into Nevada's prime mining area.

It sounded like a crazy idea. But it had a most practical purpose. As excavators of the Comstock Lode drilled their mines deeper into the earth, they had encountered enormous pockets of superheated underground water and deadly gases. Both made mining more hazardous. And more expensive. The solution, Sutro reasoned, was to bore into the Lode's heart and bleed out those natural dangers.

He began to survey the course of his proposed underpass in 1864. In that same year, Sutro persuaded the first Nevada legislature to grant him a tunnel franchise—despite the fact that mining experts assured lawmakers that the whole venture was laughable. What those experts didn't know, of course, was that Adolph Sutro had little capacity for humor. (Mark Twain, who'd met him during his Virginia City days, once quipped that "I don't think Sutro minds a joke of mild character any more than a dead man would.") And he *never* joked when it came to making money.

In 1865, Sutro approached William Chapman Ralston, the bullish engine behind the Bank of California and a major player in the Comstock silver-mining district.

EGALITARIAN VALUES

Adolph Sutro's appreciation for workingmen led him, in his later years, to act as patriarch to his employees, providing Comstock tunnel diggers with an early form of health insurance and sharing his dinner table with his servants. "Why should they not eat with me?" Sutro asked ingenuously. "They are as good as I, and while they work for me they must eat as well as I do."

By this time, Sutro had done much to refine his plans. Yet he still lacked credibility. What he needed was for someone of Ralston's caliber to endorse the construction of his tunnel—four miles long and at least 1,650 feet deep, beginning in the foothills of Nevada's Carson River Valley, running beneath booming Virginia City, and cutting into the Lode's most central mine at Mount Davidson. Lateral tunnels would cover the entire mining area. This excavation, Sutro explained, would not only drain off hot water and gases, it would also provide easier access for men and ore-wagons going to and from the mines, and might even reveal some hidden silver pockets. Stamp milling could resume its once-vigorous pace, and the new income would inevitably flow into the Bank of Califor-nia, which held loans for so many of the Comstock's mining operations.

Intrigued, Ralston studied his office guest more closely.

At the time of his meeting with Ralston, Sutro was in his mid-30s, "tall, dark-haired, massive physically, with the look of a dreamer, and the burning eyes of a seer," according to historian George Lyman. He exuded self-confidence. Ralston knew that Sutro's resumé of endeavors since coming to the Bay Area hardly seemed to recommend him for the Nevada tunnel project—the most significant engineering effort in America. Yet Ralston understood Sutro's tunnel vision. He'd gambled on many a long shot himself—and won big. So he wrote Sutro an enthusiastic letter of introduction. It was an act of generosity he would soon come to regret.

BEARING RALSTON'S ENDORSEMENT, Sutro immediately set about winning support from the mine owners who would be affected by his tunnel and would have to pay royalties for its use.

In May 1866, he went much further. He said goodbye to his family in San Francisco and steamed east to Washington, D.C., where he convinced Congress to give him a right-of-way for his excavating. Then he made the rounds of New York financiers, drumming up enthusiasm for his plans, as well as promises of funds. There would be no hard cash, however, until Sutro had first approached California investors for a fraction of the $1.5 million he needed to begin construction. This was an unanticipated setback, but Sutro could be very persuasive.

Sutro turned to Ralston and the Bank of California for funding. As long as Ralston had thought the tunnel scheme would be paid for mostly out of deep East Coast pockets, he had championed it. But now that Sutro had come begging to Californians *first* . . . well, suddenly Ralston—whose finances were habitually overextended, anyway—couldn't seem to get his wallet open. He and his more avaricious partner, William Sharon, convinced themselves that the Comstock didn't really need this expensive "sewer," after all.

When the Bank of California turned down Sutro, so did most of the influential Nevada mine owners. Once a star in Virginia City, he almost instantly became a pariah. "Old friends crossed the streets rather than shake my hand," Sutro recalled later. He was forced to seek primarily European backing for his enterprise.

The turnaround for Sutro came in 1869, with a fire at Virginia City's Yellow Jacket Mine. This hellish blaze lit up the sky, and for days, poisonous vapors belched out of the earth's Dantean depths. By the time rescuers could get into the pit, there were only bodies to recover—45 of them. Disgust spread like a plague among the miners. If Sutro's tunnel had existed, they charged, those gases would have leaked out long ago and the 45 miners would have had a back door through which to escape the conflagration. The miners had no doubt that the greed of mammonists like Ralston and Sharon had caused those men to perish.

SUTRO TURNED THIS ANGER to his advantage. He attacked the Comstock

Sutro replaced it with a Bavarian castle. Five stories tall, bristling with turrets, spires, and slim chimneys, and decorated inside with fine woods, Sutro's Cliff House was the ultimate locale for a respectable rendezvous. Locals went there to dine, to dance, and to look out over the moonlit sea from the tremendous bay window on the west side. By 1901, the Cliff House had become so well regarded that the Palace Hotel scheduled daily horse-drawn coach excursions between downtown and Seal Rocks. Sadly, that Cliff House was destroyed by a suspicious fire on September 8, 1907.

capitalists and beseeched laborers to help pay for the tunnel project that their bosses thought frivolous. It was, he said, "a cause which will make you the power of this land, make powerless your oppressors, and break up your archenemy, the California Bank. . . ."

Within a week, the Miners' Union had subscribed $50,000 toward tunnel construction, with pledges of more to come. Meanwhile, Ralston, Sharon, and their fellow moneychangers were lucky not to be shot on sight.

Nine more years passed before the Sutro Tunnel could be dug as far as Mount Davidson. The task was fraught with hazards. Workers suffocated, almost drowned in tunnel mud, and grew frustrated with the German entrepreneur as he sought to manage construction from afar (mostly from the nation's capital, where Sutro kept up such a steady campaign for his tunnel that opposition congressmen labeled him "the Great Bore").

Those nine years brought new developments on the Comstock. Ralston died, the Silver Kings grabbed control, and even before the Sutro Tunnel was fully operational, the district's largest ore bodies had been pretty much tapped out. Though his passageway was used for another half-century, it never did pay off as Sutro had expected. He sold his tunnel stock in 1881 (much of it at a loss) and returned with his millions to San Francisco.

IT'S SAID THAT SUTRO'S interest in the Point Lobos area originated from a buggy ride he took to the coast in March 1881, accompanied by his oldest daughter, Emma. There they discovered a small but idyllic white cottage poised on the bluff overlooking the Cliff House and Seal Rocks. Sutro quickly purchased this cottage and converted it into his own retreat, complete with an observatory tower, from which he could gaze out over the ocean and up toward the constellations. He spent more money on the surrounding gardens, filling them not only with plants and fountains, but with an abundant clutter of statuary, many of the pieces duplicating European works. Though some critics derided Sutro's taste for topless plaster goddesses and marble elk, many other San Franciscans delighted in weekend outings to Sutro's parklike grounds.

His residence became the center of his coastal barony. Sutro eventually bought the Cliff House and much of the surrounding property, as well as thousands of sandy acres stitched between downtown and the Pacific. (At one point, Sutro owned a full one-twelfth of San Francisco's buildable land, including several blocks in the financial district.) People thought him crazy for purchasing all that seemingly useless real estate, but as San Francisco expanded westward over the peninsula, Sutro sold his lots at considerable profit. He held onto the Cliff House, however, converting it from a seedy hangout for drunks, political bosses, and prostitutes into a respectable family resort, and finally rebuilding it entirely. Just north of it, he constructed the world's largest indoor swimming complex, the renowned Sutro Baths.

Sutro believed in spending his money. An avid reader and collector of books, he snapped up whole libraries as they went on the auction block, instructing his agents in London and Germany to spend $2,000 a month on new acquisitions. By the time he died, Sutro had accumulated the world's largest private library, with nearly 250,000 items, including 3,000 to 4,000 rare incunabula (books printed before the year 1500). He had the vague idea of erecting a spectacular athenaeum for use by all Californians, but could never identify an ideal site. He'd originally wanted to build at Sutro Heights, but experts told him the climate there was too damp. Instead, he stored his volumes in 24 suites at the Montgomery Block and in a loft on Battery Street. (They were still there in 1906, when half the collection—including all but 42 of Sutro's incunabula—was destroyed by the earthquake and fire. The remainder now rests with the San Francisco Public Library.)

And still, his energies were not fully exploited. So he planted thousands of euca-

Water-shy visitors could listen to band concerts, check out educational exhibits of mummies and such curiosities as Tom Thumb's bed, or partake of carnival rides.

The baths, built between 1891 and 1894, hung on for seven decades, although half of the biggest tank was covered with a skating rink in the 1930s. Swimming was finally discontinued after World War II, although the skating rink and some exhibit facilities remained open till 1966. In that same year, a suspicious blaze consumed what remained of the swimming pavilions. Only ruins remain on the site, now supervised by the National Park Service.

Among Adolph Sutro's various bat-
tles for the workingman was his late-
19th-century campaign against
Collis P. Huntington, whose
Southern Pacific Railroad gained
control of the trolley line to Sutro
Heights—and promptly increased its
fare from 5 cents to a dime. Sutro
told Huntington that if he did not
reduce the fare, Sutro would build his
own street railway to the coast. In
the meantime, he fenced off his prop-
erty and charged 25 cents admission
to visitors who came via the Southern
Pacific cars; others got in free. With
his usual arrogance, Huntington
refused to bargain, and so gained a
powerful rival in the streetcar biz.

lyptus and other trees to beautify barren Mount Parnassus (now Mount Sutro), and then gave part of that property away to the University of California for a medical school. Falling in love with the furry inhabitants of Seal Rocks, in 1887 he pushed Congress to guarantee their protection. During the devastating Panic of 1893, when banks were shutting their doors nationwide and thousands of San Franciscans lost their jobs, Sutro purchased some 10,000 meal and bed tickets from the Salvation Army and handed them out freely to men who crowded his Montgomery Street offices from morning till night.

WITH HIS POPULIST SYMPATHIES and his avuncular magnetism, Sutro seemed an ideal candidate for political office. Yet on two previous occasions (in 1874 and 1880), he'd campaigned for a U.S. Senate seat from Nevada—and lost. Only the ego-arousing support of the new People's Party induced him back into the ring in 1894, this time as a contender for the San Francisco mayor's office. To even Sutro's surprise, he won by a large margin. It didn't take long, however, for onlookers to realize that he was no politician. He wanted to run city government the way he ran a tunnel-drilling company, and failed to understand why elected officials didn't hop immediately to his every command. As the *Examiner* put it, "He passed his term in a state of exasperation."

It was with barely restrained glee that Sutro handed the mayor's seat over to James Phelan in 1897 and returned to Sutro Heights. He had a long list of projects in mind for the near future, including construction of his library and an oceanfront hotel, and improvements to his gardens.

Within a year of leaving the mayor's office, however, he had disappeared from the public spotlight. It was rumored that he had become incompetent to manage his own affairs, that he was dying. News of Sutro's death came in August 1898. His obituary lists the cause of death as diabetes, but Alzheimer's disease would be consistent with many of his symptoms. How sad, if that was the case, that a man who had triumphed over such indomitable adversaries as Ralston should find his most vicious adversary not in the halls of government or business, but in the tiny gray cells of his own fragile brain.

THE MONSTER OF MARKET STREET

When William C. Ralston proposed in 1872 to build a new hotel on a sandlot he owned at the corner of Market and New Montgomery Streets, everybody knew it would be a monumental undertaking. The archon of the Bank of California never did anything on a small scale, whether extracting silver or wrestling for the fur trade in Alaska. But none of his dreams was bigger than the one he had for San Francisco. He wanted this city to be one of the finest on the planet.

So rather than just build a respectable hotel (which he'd already done right across the street: the three-story, multidomed Grand), he determined to raise on this lot a certifiable palace—"a symbol of San Francisco's coming of age," as Oscar Lewis and Carroll D. Hall put it in *Bonanza Inn*. The building would fill 2½ acres, stand 7 stories tall, and contain 800 rooms. It would be a permanent grin of brick and glass on the city's maturing face, a show of confidence in the future. Ralston would make his hotel a marvel of luxury and convenience, even if it was the last thing he did. And it was.

HOTELS WERE ABUNDANT in early San Francisco. Credit this to the fact that so many people arrived here so quickly. Hotels, boardinghouses, and apartment buildings

NO ROOM AT THE INLET
Some of San Francisco's earliest hostelries were slapdash affairs, filled almost to bursting with shelves of bunk beds. When the forty-niners started pouring in, lodging space was at such a premium that one ship abandoned in the harbor by anxious argonauts, the Niantic, *was tethered permanently among dockside buildings and converted into an inn.*

PEARLY GATES
Mark Twain tended to eschew other San Francisco hotels in favor of the Occidental on Montgomery Street. He once called that Greek-porticoed establishment not only "Heaven on the half shell" but "Heaven on the entire shell."

were erected to house the influx of gold seekers. The city grew up catering to the transient lifestyle, with an abundance of both elegant and disreputable places to eat out and no shortage of rentable lodgings.

By the time more solid community foundations had been sunk, San Franciscans were already wedded to a social, commercial, and political life that revolved around service institutions such as hotels and restaurants. It was common practice until at least the 1890s for wealthy citizens to live in or at least maintain suites permanently in hotels, to hold meetings in hotels, to dine and gamble in hotels, and to concoct business deals and consummate love affairs in hotels.

Five pretentious hotels had risen on the local skyline by 1875. None of these, however, measured up to Ralston's dream for his new Palace. The Bonanza King instructed his architect, John P. Gaynor, to visit the country's leading hotels—including the Palmer House in Chicago and New York's Sturdevant House—before he even sat down to design the Bay Area's latest symbol of prosperity. The true dimensions of Ralston's dream became clear to William Sharon, the silver millionaire and former Nevada senator who was a partner in the project, when he realized that the $1,750,000 he'd been told would suffice to complete the new hotel had been exhausted merely in the construction of its 12-foot-thick masonry foundations. A million dollars more, the thriftier Sharon calculated, would be consumed by the first floor—and six more had to be built on top of that!

Ralston had no intention of scrimping. He purchased an oak tree–covered ranch in the Sierra foothills, just to provide the wood he wanted for his hotel's floors. (Only later was it learned that those oaks weren't even the sort used for flooring.) He bought a foundry to forge nails for Palace carpenters. He established a factory to turn California

HEAVY PUBLICITY

The weekly News Letter *estimated that the Palace Hotel's weight, "when full," was "eighty-six billion, nine hundred and forty million, six hundred and four thousand, two hundred and one tons, and eleven pounds." This astounding heft, quipped the paper, "accounts for the recent singular bulge noticed in the earth near Shanghai, China, within a few months past."*

laurel into appropriate guest-room furniture. He created a lock-and-key business that would produce the hardware needed on all the hotel's doors.

Although exasperated by the mounting bills, Sharon didn't withdraw his support from the Palace scheme. Nor did he seek to control its administration. Like the rest of San Francisco, he wanted to see the final result of Ralston's monument-making. If it cost millions of Comstock dollars to find out . . . well, Sharon had those, and Ralston had made even more in his time.

A FEW NUMBERS GIVE a sense of the original Palace's overwhelming nature. The hotel took a rectangular shape, with its long sides (350 feet) fronting on New Montgomery and Annie Streets, and its shorter ends (275 feet) rising above Market and Jessie. To protect against earthquake damage, the outer walls were 2 feet thick, and double strips of iron reinforced them at 4-foot intervals. Fourteen hundred men worked on the building, including 300 bricklayers who placed about 300,000 bricks every day. Contracts had to be signed with 15 separate marble firms to manufacture the structure's 804 mantels, 900 washbasins, and 40,000 square feet of marble paving stones. There were 435 cast-iron bathtubs in the building, 20 miles of gas pipe, and 755 toilets, each one endowed with "an arrangement by which the water is carried off without producing the horrid noise one usually hears," according to promotions of the time. Nine thousand cuspidors were placed strategically about the floors. The hotel's main dining room was the largest in the West: 155 feet long, covered with carpets woven in France. Even the billiards room and barber shop were guilty of ormolu overstatement.

Three courtyards were arranged to allow the passage of air and light to interior rooms. The central and largest one of these, the quadrangular Grand Court, measured 84 feet by 144 feet and held a circular carriage drive (52 feet in diameter), entered through

<hr>

❧

KEEP IT DOWN OUT THERE!

The Palace's Grand Court, originally open to carriages and horses entering from the street, later had to be closed. It seems that guests complained about hooves making too great a racket on the court's marble turnaround. The space was turned into a mammoth lounge dotted with couches and chairs.

❧

WHAT DO THEY DO FOR AN ENCORE?

Nary a week went by during the Palace Hotel's construction that some fresh and amazing fact about the place wasn't revealed by the press in reverent detail. So overwhelmed were San Franciscans by the enormity of Ralston's vision, and so hungry were they to know more, that wild rumors had to be circulated just to keep pace. Nothing seemed impossible, not even the story about piano players entertaining guests in the elevators or the one about a flume being erected from Yosemite, so that Bridal Veil Falls could be redirected to spill over the hotel's eastern front.

huge archways off New Montgomery Street. Guests arriving in broughams or on horseback were protected from the elements as they stepped down onto a marble-tiled floor dotted with palm trees. If they looked up before entering the reception area, they'd see six levels of colonnaded balconies, topped by a tremendous dome of amber-hued glass and a magnificent seventh-level roof garden. "It was a magnificent, ethereal tower of space," George D. Lyman said of the Grand Court in *Ralston's Ring*, "surrounded by illusive white columns and delicately turned balustrades. About it there was something unreal, dreamlike. . . . With its physical properties robbed of all sense of weight, the court had the tenuous fragility of one of those hymeneal towers so dear to the confectioner's heart."

Tucked into the sub-basement beneath the main court was a reservoir able to hold 630,000 gallons of water. Fed by a series of artesian wells, the Palace's reservoir guaranteed that guests would have water even if the city's ample supplies went dry. It was also meant to ensure a water supply in the event of a fire at the hotel. A trio of pumps in the basement kept water pressure high, and there were 350 outlets around the building where hoses could be attached. Seven tanks on the roof contained an additional 130,000 gallons of water. Ralston even installed rudimentary electric fire detectors in every room and scheduled hallway patrols at 30-minute intervals day and night. The supposition was that, even if the rest of San Francisco burned to a crisp, the Palace would survive.

INNOVATIONS WEREN'T RESTRICTED to fire protection. Individual guest chambers were connected to an early air-conditioning system. Though electric lights were still a thing of the future, engineers installed electric room-service call buttons in the rooms, along with a major innovation: electric clocks. Pneumatic tubes carried incoming letters and even small packages to various parts of the building, while a central mail system conveyed outgoing mail to an appropriate box. Four large hydraulic passenger elevators (or, as they were known at the time, "rising rooms") anchored the building's corners.

Although one itinerant Scotsman of the time derided Ralston's Palace as "more monstrous than elegant," few people in the 1870s could fail to have been impressed by its streetside presentation. The upper six stories were lined with parallel banks of bay windows, designed to allow a maximum of light into the rooms, but giving the edifice "the air of a mammoth bird-cage," according to one magazine report. Brick facades were painted white and trimmed subtly in gold; even the bolts that secured reinforcing beams in the exterior walls had their ends gilded, and they sparkled in the sunlight. Unfortunately, soot released from the cheap coal burned in most of the city's buildings quickly dulled much of this brilliance. (In the late 19th century, *Harper's Magazine* referred to the hotel as "a vast drab-colored building.")

But that seemed to have no discernible effect on the Palace's reception. It opened for business on October 2, 1875, and was an immediate hit, outshining every competitor in town.

"For three decades merely to register at the Palace was a hallmark of social and financial standing," noted historians Lucius Beebe and Charles Clegg. A Who's Who of the international upper crust trooped through the original Palace, everyone from former President Ulysses S. Grant and robber baron J. P. Morgan to playwright Oscar Wilde and heavyweight boxing champ James J. Jeffries. Lillie Langtry drew a crowd as she danced in the ballroom. Actress Sarah Bernhardt booked an eight-room suite, where her entourage—including a parrot and a baby tiger—could be comfortable. Emperor Dom Pedro II of Brazil arrived in town only a few months after the hotel's opening and, before returning home (where he was overthrown), proclaimed, "Nothing makes me so ashamed of Brazil as the Palace Hotel."

Not to miss out on any of this excitement, many of San Francisco's older well-to-do

IMITATION IS THE SINCEREST FORM OF FLATTERY

Commenting on the Palace Hotel, Harper's Magazine observed that "The devoted San Franciscan, wherever met with, never fails to boast of this hotel as the most stupendous thing of its kind in the world." Ralston's dream so impressed Richard D'Oyly Carte that, after returning home to London, he determined to build lodgings in the same grandiose style—and thus was born the Savoy Hotel, which welcomed its first guests in 1889.

residents leased suites at the Palace. They filled the top story, spilled down to the floor below, and were much in evidence at the restaurants and the roof garden. Younger notables came to join them, creating a compact colony of the elite that was as much "above it all" as anybody living atop Nob Hill.

Ralston would have appreciated the acclaim received by his giant gift to the city. Sadly, he died just five weeks before his caravansary had its gala inauguration. William Sharon, who had objected volubly to his partner's indulgence in architectural ostentation, was left to reign as prince of the Palace.

THE EARTHQUAKE STRUCK just after 5 a.m. on the morning of April 18, 1906, stripping the City Hall dome of its masonry shawl and toppling many lesser buildings. Fires broke out all over downtown, stunning the sky with their heat, joining together in a wave of destruction. For hours, it seemed that the Palace Hotel would be all right, despite cracks in its marble and burst windowpanes. Flames licked their way up from the neighborhoods south of Market Street, but spectators outside the Palace were heartened to see jets of water showering its 2-acre roof. While firemen in other parts of the city found hydrants inoperable, hose-wielding Palace employees fended off the hot ashes that rained down.

Ralston and his engineers had planned well against conflagrations. But they hadn't figured on such a prolonged battle. By early afternoon, the reservoir beneath the hotel and its rooftop tanks had been bled dry, while flames rose on all sides of the Palace, consuming the Grand Hotel on the east and the new Monadnock Building to the west. By half past three o'clock, the now abandoned Palace "presented the appearance of being afire in every part . . .," recalled *Chronicle* editor John P. Young. "The spectacle was one calculated to inspire awe despite the fact that all around it were structures which had already succumbed to the destroyer. . . ." As their city's symbol was ravished, crowds

---

HE DIDN'T GIVE A SPIT

Rudyard Kipling, passing through town in the late 1880s on his way back from India, was less generous in his estimation of the Palace Hotel than previous observers had been. He even dared to poke fun at the Grand Court. "In a vast marble-paved hall under the glare of an electric light," Kipling related, "sat forty to fifty men, and for their use and amusement were provided spittoons of infinite and generous gape. Most of the men wore frock coats and top hats—but they all spat. They spat on principle."

cheered to see a single American flag still fluttering atop a pole on the hotel's Market Street side. Not until that banner disappeared in the smoke and angry candescence of the fire was the San Francisco That Had Been finally deemed dead.

The Palace (now called the Sheraton Palace) was rebuilt and reopened in 1909. But to many people in this city, the true Palace has never been replaced.

OUR GREAT GREEN "LUNGS"

San Francisco wasn't even a decade old before residents started lobbying planners for more parkland. "Over all these square miles of contemplated thoroughfares," newspaper editor Frank Soulé wrote in 1855, in *The Annals of San Francisco*, "there seems no provision made by the projectors for a public park—the true 'lungs' of a large city. The existing plaza, or Portsmouth Square, and [an]other two or three diminutive squares, delineated in the plan, seem the only breathing-holes intended for the future population of hundreds of thousands. This is a strange mistake, and can only be attributed to the jealous avarice of the city projectors in turning every square vara of the site to an available building lot."

Looking for land on which to establish a park, as early as 1852 the city petitioned land commissioners for use of acreage on the opposite (western) side of the peninsula from the growing city, in an area then referred to dismissively as the Outside Lands. However, squatters there refused to vacate their rudimentary abodes and backed up their property claims with both court petitions and cocked rifles. Not until 1868 did the Board of Supervisors finally manage in federal court to wrest free a strip filled with blowing, shifting sand

PISTOLS IN THE PARK
No matter how hard William Hammond Hall endeavored to beautify Golden Gate Park's Panhandle during the 1870s, there were people who would not visit that part of town. "That district was inhabited by many undesirable characters who had been evicted from San Francisco by the Vigilance Committee," wrote Raymond H. Clary in The Making of Golden Gate Park. *"A walk through the area was sure to subject any lady to cheers, jeers, and insults. . . . Indeed, the area was so disreputable that the sheriff authorized early park workers to carry guns on their way to and from the new park."*

dunes, 3 miles long and a half-mile wide, that abutted the city's Pacific edge—the area familiar now as Golden Gate Park. And even then, City Hall had to pony up almost a million bucks to buy off the dunes' spurious owners.

TO MANY PEOPLE, this whole affair smacked of utopian folly. In *Bay Window Bohemia*, author Oscar Lewis quotes a typical 1870s newspaper editorial on the subject: "Of all the elephants . . . San Franciscans ever owned, they now have the largest and heaviest in the shape of 'Golden Gate Park.'" No less cynical was Frederick Law Olmsted, the supervisor of New York's Central Park and 19th-century America's premier landscape architect. Visiting San Francisco at the behest of its Board of Supervisors, Olmsted walked the Outside Lands, listened to the plans for the area's Edenic rebirth—and then recommended that a completely different park site be selected. There was no way, he declared, that this "great sand bank" could be made hospitable to a complexity of flora.

Fortunately, the new park's first superintendent, William Hammond Hall, was more optimistic. A surveyor who had mapped the Outside Lands for the U.S. Army, Hall won a bid in 1870 to design the mammoth greensward. He started planting the Panhandle section of the future park with barley and sand grass, and then worked up the botanical chain to tempest-resistant trees such as Monterey cypress and flowering eucalyptus. Blue gum and live oaks took root where gentler breezes blew.

By 1878, Golden Gate Park could claim 2 miles of roads and bridal paths, with another half-mile under construction. More than 135,000 shrubs and trees had already gone into the ground, with 32,000 more being nurtured for placement.

People who had looked askance at the project early on were amazed at its success. According to one news report, more than 50,000 people a day (a full fifth of San Francisco's population at the time) visited the city's growing greensward in 1886, most of them arriving by streetcar. They came to picnic or to wander around the lakes and artificial waterfalls. Many others came to see the domed Conservatory, which was modeled after one in London's Kew Gardens.

WHILE HALL WAS MAKING his mark on the Outside Lands, John McLaren—another visionary landscaper—was planting tens of thousands of trees around the Bay Area. Born in 1846 in central Scotland, McLaren had studied horticulture at the Royal Botanical Gardens in Edinburgh and gone on to land beautification and reclamation projects along the North Sea coast. In 1870, he left Europe to explore—and, perhaps, enhance—the storied golden mountains of California.

According to history writer Samuel Dickson, McLaren's father had instilled in him a love of trees. "Me boy," Dickson quoted McLaren's father as saying, "if ye have nothing better to do, go plant a tree and it'll grow while ye sleep." With that admonition and his gardening bona fides behind him, McLaren set about installing trees on the estate of millionaire George H. Howard, in the San Mateo foothills. He created botanical gardens on the 8,000-acre Palo Alto stock farm owned by Leland Stanford (now the site of Stanford University), and labored over the grounds of millionaire-miser James Lick's estate near San Jose. As his trees grew, so did McLaren's reputation.

In 1886, William Hall hired McLaren to succeed him as superintendent of Golden Gate Park. By 1890 Hall had turned the reins completely over to the Scotsman.

With his North Sea coast experience, McLaren seemed the ideal steward. Hall had been expanding Golden Gate Park to the west, but the closer it got to the ocean, the more difficult it was to keep the sand from blowing away. McLaren had just the trick. From his native Scotland, he began importing a plant called *Ammophila arenaria*, a hardy grass that pushed its shoots up every time sand tried to engulf it. The higher the grass

THE ENDS JUSTIFIED THE MEANS

McLaren would stop at almost no deception to protect the sanctity of his park. One wonderful story concerns his battle against a streetcar line that was supposed to cross over one corner of the property. McLaren denounced the project, saying it would uproot some of his trees. Engineers protested that their tracks would go only through unplanted areas, but Uncle John told city supervisors that this was patently untrue, and he invited them out to see for themselves. Sure enough, when the gents from City Hall visited Golden Gate Park the next morning, they found shrubs, grew, the more sand was banked up around it. Eventually, the winds buffeting San Francisco's coast could no longer push sand as high as the bank's crest, and McLaren's *Ammophila arenaria* were free to grow and spread unhindered, anchoring the ground with their roots.

After that, the landscaper ordered thousands of bundles of wood laths, which were laid down along the beach. Regular prunings from the park's myriad trees were dumped in front of those, and the ocean and wind were allowed to pile sand in and around the fragile bulwark. When the first barricade was covered, McLaren mounted a new one, and another on top of that, and still another and another, until man and nature had built a natural seawall more than 20 feet high and 300 yards wide. The process took four decades, but McLaren—who'd come to measure time by life cycles of trees—was willing to wait. Today's Esplanade, severed only slightly from the body of Golden Gate Park by the so-called Great Highway, is the result of his patience.

MCLAREN WAS STRONG-WILLED, with a talent for making enemies among the municipal bureaucracy. He also claimed more than his fair share of eccentricities. It was said that he drank heavily of Scotch, that he would fire a worker for protecting his hands from the rich earth with gloves, and that he swore at his employees inventively and continuously—and expected them to return his expletives with energy.

But even San Franciscans who had initially pooh-poohed the prospect of Golden Gate Park and McLaren's salary demands ("Thirty thousand dollars a year? *Outrageous!*") were amazed by the energy and innovation that he brought to his post. They learned not to doubt McLaren's actions, even when he talked city street sweepers into depositing their wagonloads of manure around his 1,107 acres of parkland. Yes, it was a malodorous business, but who could object to the results that McLaren got from all this natural fertilizer?

---

rhododendrons, and trees all over the proposed streetcar path, leading them to veto the transit company's plans. What they weren't told, of course, was that all this plant life was brand-new, and that McLaren had had 300 of his employees out the night before with picks and shovels, landscaping the entire area.

NATURAL ACTS

Convinced that parks should be used, not treated as untouchable museum pieces, John McLaren prohibited "Keep Off the Grass" signs at Golden Gate Park during his tenure there as superintendent.

❦

And it didn't cost taxpayers a dime! 'Twas sad indeed when, in the 1890s, horse-drawn vehicles started giving way to automobiles, for suddenly fertilizer became an essential line item in the park's budget.

By then, McLaren was known to the city as "Uncle John." He lived in the park (at McLaren Lodge) and, without question, the park lived in him. He was its feisty guiding spirit, its chief advocate. What he wanted, he pretty much got, whether it was fertilizer or Dutch windmills, two of which he erected near the ocean in 1902 to help pump up fresh groundwater for his thirsty gardens. McLaren even overruled city fathers who'd envisioned formal settings for the park in favor of a plan that hued to natural principles. What few roadways Uncle John incorporated in his designs were contoured around the land's many dips and hillocks, in order to take advantage of the best growing sites and to prevent drivers from traveling too fast through this arboreal reserve. He kept the number of park buildings to a minimum and mandated that purely functional structures such as bridges should look "rustic" and blend in with the natural surroundings.

Uncle John wasn't always able to prevent infringements on his suzerainty, however, especially when it came to statues. McLaren despised these marble or bronze "stookies," as he called them, and when he was compelled to accept one into Golden Gate Park, he'd surround it with enough trees and shrubbery that passersby were barely aware of its existence.

MCLAREN TRIED ALSO TO FOIL plans for the 1894 Midwinter Fair, scheduled to be held in Golden Gate Park. That he was not successful was due to the man who'd conceived of the West Coast's first world's fair, Michael Harry de Young, publisher and co-founder (with his brother Charles) of the *San Francisco Chronicle*. De Young had taken charge of California's exhibits at the magnificent 1893 World's Columbian Exposition in Chicago. He returned to San Francisco full of ideas for a somewhat smaller spectacle here,

---

MIDWAY MARVEL I

Little Egypt (a.k.a. Fahreda Mahzar, a.k.a. Catherine Devine) was allegedly a slender young daughter of the Nile who had come to America with a troupe of Syrian dancers. Dancing in a semitransparent skirt, her performances at the 1893 Chicago World's Fair won her coast-to-coast fame. Her appearance at San Francisco's Midwinter Fair spawned a whole new form of entertainment. Suddenly, "harem dancers" were all the rage. A score of Little Egypts were bumping and grinding long after the original had left.

MIDWAY MARVEL II

In 1896, the original Little Egypt was arrested by New York police during a raid on the famous Sherry's restaurant, where she had been dancing her specialty at a stag party for showman P. T. Barnum's grandson. This time, she really was writhing in the nude. Later, she decided that stag parties were her key to riches. Men of the time were often treated to paintings of unclad ladies in bars, but the rarity of seeing a real, live naked woman who was not their wife provoked men to pay $10 apiece to attend her party performances. When she died in 1908, Little Egypt left behind an estate worth a quarter of a million dollars.

ॐॐॐ

intended to publicize the city's man-made virtues and its temperate winter climate, as well as invigorate the local economy, which had ground to a virtual standstill during the Panic of 1893. De Young's enthusiasm for the fair and the *Chronicle*'s campaign to hold it in Golden Gate Park surpassed even McLaren's obduracy, and so on January 1, 1894, the Midwinter Fair opened on 200 acres at the park's eastern end.

Most of the major buildings were designed with Egyptian or Indian flair, and were grouped around a central Grand Plaza. All of California's counties, most of the states, and 37 foreign nations were represented. A giant Tower of Electricity, celebrating man's latest technological mastery, rose from the middle of the fairgrounds and at night cast a beam of light over the surrounding city. But the biggest attractions were the exotic entertainments, everything from a re-creation of a Moorish townsite to a Japanese Tea Garden to an Eskimo village (complete with a pond where native Alaskans paddled around in skin-covered kayaks). A Ferris wheel and trained animals kept children giddy, while adult males tended to gravitate toward afternoon performances by Little Egypt, the provocatively clad dancer who had shocked and thrilled audiences at the Chicago exposition a year before.

The fair proved to be a memorable event. When its gates closed on July 9, total attendance was recorded as 2,255,551, about seven times the city's population.

But McLaren could hardly wait to get rid of de Young's exhibition. Fair buildings were quickly demolished, save for the Egyptian-styled Art Museum (which survived until the 1920s), the sunken Music Concourse, and the Japanese Tea Garden complex. Never again did the Emperor of Golden Gate Park permit such extravagant misuse of his verdant domain.

UNCLE JOHN'S RULE lasted for 56 years. He refused to leave the superintendent's office when he became eligible for retirement at age 60, and again when he passed 70, the compulsory retirement age for city employees. The Board of Supervisors finally exempted McLaren from the retirement regulations altogether.

He still had so much to do. Following the earthquake and fire of 1906, the park demanded intense refurbishment, since many frightened refugees had gone there to wait out the aftershocks, leaving their shabby tent cities behind. And then there were McLaren's schemes to expand his gardens. He maintained communication with botanists all over the globe, constantly seeking to enhance Golden Gate Park's bounty. (It's said that, in 1931 alone, McLaren introduced some 700 horticultural species into California.) To exhaust some of his high energy and make the most of his many ideas, McLaren took on design projects elsewhere (he created woodsy Lithia Park in Ashland, Oregon, and planned the landscaping for the Panama-Pacific Exposition of 1915). But his attention always swung back to the park that Frederick Olmsted had said couldn't be built. Asked on his 90th birthday what he most wanted for a present, Uncle John answered "10,000 yards of good manure"—for his beloved gardens.

When he died on January 14, 1943, at the age of 97, McLaren's coffin was given à final ride through his huge public creation, while 400 gardeners and foremen stood by, many weeping. As an additional tribute, Rhododendron Dell was planted with more than 500 species of McLaren's favorite flower. It's easy to imagine the old Scot enjoying this vale, peaceful and fragrant as it is.

But all of Uncle John's enjoyment of those rhodies would be quickly overcome by ire if he could only see what City Hall decided was necessary to mount at the entrance to Rhododendron Dell. For there stands a dark bronze "stookie" of none other than John McLaren himself.

CONFUCIAN CONFUSION

Golden Gate Park's Japanese Tea Garden was maintained from 1895 until World War II by the Hagiwara family. A member of that Japanese clan, Makato Hagiwara, is credited with inventing the clearly misnamed Chinese fortune cookie.

THE CITY THAT NEVER WAS

"Burnham was the chief architect at San Francisco during the rebuilding of the city following the earthquake, and his plans for reconstructing the business district were carried out by the city."
—Obituary for Daniel H. Burnham, *Pittsburgh Dispatch*, June 2, 1912

If only this statement were true, San Francisco might be a very different—and, some critics would argue, much more interesting—place than it is at present. But architect Burnham's 1905 proposals for the city's evolution, visionary as they were in suggesting broad and landscaped avenues, an ambitious park system, subways, and one-way streets to relieve traffic congestion, fell victim to the oldest civic stumbling blocks in the book: greed and expediency.

Famous in New York City and his adopted home of Chicago, where he had served as chief of construction at the famed World's Columbian Exposition of 1893, Daniel Hudson Burnham possessed an expertise in urban planning that, for his time, was unrivaled in the United States. He had chaired the 1901 commission supervising modifications to Pierre L'Enfant's Washington, D.C., plan, had helped create Cleveland's civic center, and in 1909 would develop the design blueprint for Chicago's future. To a significant extent, it was Burnham who showed American cities the real value of "comprehensive plans," outlining development strategies for entire urban or geographical regions.

Who could have done a better job of turning raw-edged San Francisco into a place that St. Francis Hotel manager Allan Pollok imagined as the American equivalent of "what Paris is to Europeans—the great city of pleasure"?

Indeed, Burnham seemed to understand innately this city's desire for greatness, and he delivered to it a growth prospectus that, in his words, would "combine convenience and beauty in the greatest possible degree." His was a hopeful plan, and its reception here was duly enthusiastic. The beautification commission that had recruited Burnham reported, "All classes are pledged to see that [the plan's] principal features are carried out as soon as possible." Local newspapers generally endorsed Burnham's call for sweeping changes, with the *Chronicle* reminding its readers how much more difficult and expensive the same modifications would become if they were put off until a later date. *The Overland Monthly* was more blunt in challenging city fathers to act quickly on the foundations of Burnham's program. "Do not let it be simply—a dream, and a forgetting," the magazine wrote.

Yet only months after Burnham gave his plan to the city, it was abandoned—ironically, at the very time when it would seem to have been most easily executed: right after the 1906 disaster. Today the architect's legacy can be seen only in a few scattered fragments about town, vague hints of the "San Francisco Beautiful" that might have been if citizens had acted with less desperation and more deliberation.

AS WITH MANY OTHER Western boomtowns, San Francisco was a patchwork of architectural vernaculars—some Victorian here, a little Queen Anne there, and lots of storefronts that defied categorization. Campaigns to give the city a more cohesive appearance or one that took greater advantage of its exceptional location surfaced periodically between 1870 and 1900.

Perhaps the most significant of those early efforts came during the four years of Mayor James D. Phelan's tenure, beginning in 1897. Young and reform-minded, Phelan appointed a committee to solicit and review various face-lifting options for the local skyline. That committee produced few results, but it did offer San Franciscans something of

ROOT SOURCES
For the 20 years preceding his invitation to reinvent San Francisco, Daniel Burnham worked with his architectural partner, John Wellborn Root—a man who'd garnered considerable attention with his exquisite Rookery Building (1888) in Chicago, as well as other edifices that contributed to the evolution of American skyscrapers. After Root died of pneumonia in 1891, in the midst of helping to design the

☞

an education in the "City Beautiful" movement, a popular design philosophy of the time that promoted metropolises as cooperative art projects, combining monumental architecture with formal courts, sculptural works, and plentiful greenery.

This movement owed a tremendous debt to the design of fairgrounds, and specifically to the well-attended 1893 Chicago World's Fair, which celebrated the 400th anniversary of Christopher Columbus's arrival in the New World. Providing sights "not paralleled since the Rome of the emperors stood intact," as the critic Mrs. Schuyler Van Rensselaer gushed in her 1893 book, *A Week at the Fair*, the expo was an awesome amalgam of domes, colonnaded walkways, and towering monoliths, all sprouting with figures of oxen, cascades of grapes and vines, and water creatures in bas-relief. Newspapermen referred to those fairgrounds as the "Great White City," partly because of all the pale-painted plaster facades, but also because of the resolute cleanliness and wholesomeness that predominated there. Deliberately distinct from the grubbier blocks of surrounding Chicago, its soaring architecture meant to lift American spirits after the recent economic depression. The fair was an idealized, Beaux-Arts definition of what a city should be. It was a broad expression of faith in urban grandness and permanence, in the ability of public-spirited reformers to manage municipal growth, in the education that Europe's old cities had to offer the builders of a new America. As supervisor of the fair's overall design, Daniel Burnham was consciously prophesying an Olympian Age for America's urban centers.

Some architects positively bristled at the Columbian Exposition's obeisance to a traditional European idiom over a less-adorned American one. But many fair-goers, as well as scores of mayors and town councilmen from around the country, hoped that Burnham's ordered, well-scrubbed, and festive conception for cities could eventually drive out the cluttered ugliness of their own industrialized hometowns.

That wish was shared by James Phelan and his fellow Progressives in San Francisco, and they continued to pursue it even after Phelan was driven out of City Hall in 1901. Sensing that their town was losing out to upstart Los Angeles in terms of stature, tourist popularity, and business attractions, Phelan's bunch made radical civic surgery their cause celebré. San Francisco must adopt a thoughtful city plan "before it is too late . . .," Phelan contended, "prepared by a competent person or commission, as has been done recently for the city of Washington, D.C., and for Cleveland, Ohio. . . ." The former mayor's references to those two other places—both of which had enjoyed Burnham's aesthetic massaging—strongly suggested Phelan's interest in producing for San Francisco not just a Burnham-like plan, but one that sprang straight from the magic pen of Burnham himself.

Phelan and Burnham were already familiar with one another. The Chicago planner had, for several years, operated a branch office in San Francisco, overseen by designer Willis Polk, and he'd produced a handful of local towers, including the distinguished 1891 Mills Building at 220 Montgomery Street (the city's oldest example of Chicago School skyscraper design) and the 1890 Chronicle Building at 690 Market Street (now all but unrecognizable behind "modernizing" metal panels). As early as 1903, the architect and the ex-mayor were actually engaged in a continuing discussion, through Polk, about crafting a comprehensive plan for this city.

Burnham was excited by such a prospect, especially since he saw San Francisco as a hill town just waiting to benefit from what he'd learned after years of studying aged European hill towns. But he was also concerned that Phelan and company should allow him "a completely free hand. It would have to be a labor of love or I could not touch it," he wrote to Polk.

This was consistent with Burnham's personality: he never had been one to do things halfway. Not tall but portly, with a gentleman's carriage and lips that were almost completely obscured behind a walrus-style mustache, Burnham had graduated from Paris's L'École des Beaux-Arts, the supreme architectural finishing school of his day. Maybe it was that specific training, or perhaps it was simply that he'd studied in a city where design had been given such exquisite rein for so long, but in any case, he developed expansive ambitions. "Make no little plans," the designer had once written. "They have no magic to stir men's blood and probably will not be realized. Make big plans. . . ."

Big plans were just what Phelan had in mind when he and his new Association for the Improvement and Adornment of San Francisco formally invited Burnham in 1904 to come and re-create their city as a "Paris on the Bay."

IT TOOK ALMOST a year and a half before Burnham completed his plans. During most of his time in the Bay Area, he lived like an Olympian overlord, camping out with his planning assistant from Chicago, Edward H. Bennett, in a wind-caressed cottage atop Twin Peaks. "Being up there," Burnham explained in a letter to Polk, "we can constantly see the city and everything else and this will be of great value to us." Indeed, he hoped the panoramic view from Twin Peaks would "stimulate Golden Gate Thoughts."

Stimulating would certainly describe the well-illustrated, 184-page report that he finally submitted to the Improvement Association on September 15, 1905. But *over-whelming* might be a better term, considering the breadth (and cost) of the alterations Burnham had in mind.

He explained right up front that his plan was a blueprint for at least half a century's gradual development. Stage one, Burnham wrote, should be the creation of a boulevard bordering the waterfront to which all other principal streets would lead. This "beautifully treated" thoroughfare must provide "enough space to allow a foot or two of earth for planting," the architect specified. "It will then be an ideal place for a ride or a walk, the passer-by looking down on the shipping below, and when he tires of watching the activities and listening to the voices of the men engaged in the work of the port, he may note the changing aspects of the sea and study the effects of sunshine and shadow on islands and mountains seen through the masts of the ships."

Burnham proposed new diagonal streets that would break up San Francisco's militant grid pattern and create connections with some outlying neighborhoods. The most important of these new arteries was to radiate from the intersection of Market Street and Van Ness Avenue downtown, where a semicircular plaza would carry traffic around an appropriate monument (much as Paris's Place Charles de Gaulle channels cars around the Arc de Triomphe). This plaza would also serve as the core of a landscaped government and cultural district, which linked City Hall conveniently with an opera house and a new railroad terminal. And running west from the axis plaza to Golden Gate Park would be a wide, well-planted extension of the park's Panhandle section.

Parks played a major role in the Burnham plan. Telegraph Hill was slated to be topped with a huge recreational area, reachable by way of a level, contoured roadway that would spiral around the hill and be "accented at places of interest by terraces and approached gradually from the abutting streets." The Presidio was to be transformed into a giant landscaped park. And Burnham observed that some of the city's "less expensive and flatter sections" could be enlivened by substituting parks for streets and connecting backyards of homes into communal nature chains.

SHORTSIGHTEDNESS

Inspired by Daniel Burnham, the British-born Edward Bennett went on to create a "City Beautiful" plan for Portland, Oregon. Residents of that Willamette River town approved the principles of Bennett's plan in 1912, but critics complained that it would cost too much to widen and landscape streets and that land set aside for parks and plazas was too valuable not to be used for buildings and factories. The result, explained Portland historian E. Kimbark MacColl in his book Shaping of the City, *was that "the real estate and business interests successfully emasculated [Bennett's plan]." All that remains of his European vision for Portland are his exquisite illustrations.*

Architect Burnham wasn't the first man to find a warm place in his heart for Twin Peaks. Indeed, the Spanish called those two perfect green cones Los Pechos de la Coca, *meaning "the breasts of the Indian maiden." They apparently had a particular young girl in mind, too, though her name seems somehow to have escaped historians. N. P. Vallejo, son of the famed* Californio *and general Mariano Vallejo, reminisced once about this maiden's virtues: "Never have I seen a cultivated woman half so fair as this untaught, uninstructed daughter of the wilds."*

"But," Burnham enthused, "the Twin Peaks and the Lake of Merced beyond are to be made the occasion of the largest and probably the most beautiful park of all . . . and by the time San Francisco has a population of several millions, it may well be the most convenient spot for the great popular festivities . . . for public fêtes and entertainment on a very considerable scale, so that this park will contribute more than any other single feature of the city to the fulfillment of San Francisco's obvious opportunity to become a great pleasure resort." A Roman-style amphitheater would fill up a natural hollow just to the north of Twin Peaks.

While Burnham emphasized landscaping in the city's improvement, he encouraged the use of new technologies as well. He suggested, for instance, that subways be dug beneath Market Street and other main diagonals. (It would take another 60 years before the city realized Burnham's wisdom and built BART—the Bay Area Rapid Transit system.)

Copies of Burnham's completed *Report on a Plan for San Francisco* were carefully printed and bound, and while newspapers rhapsodized over his labors, in early 1906 the urban prophet left for Europe with his wife Margaret, his head spinning with other dramatic design opportunities for the Bay Area.

ONLY WEEKS LATER, the earthquake struck. In addition to its other damage, "Fire destroyed all of the original drawings and models and most of the copies of the newly printed plan," recalled biographer Thomas B. Hines in *Burnham of Chicago.*

Hearing of the catastrophe, Burnham rushed back from Paris to lobby for his ideas. He surveyed the city's remains and recommended which parts of his proposal— including widening old streets and creating new diagonal ones—should be instituted first. With 4 square miles of its landscape covered in rubble and twisted steel skeletons, San

Francisco's broken landscape was just waiting for an aesthetic reawakening on the scale suggested by Burnham. The Board of Supervisors quickly approved a modified first stage of Burnham's plan, and the architect left for Chicago, satisfied that his Paris on the Bay was taking shape.

Just then, however, backbones began to weaken among the burghers most responsible for making Burnham's scheme a reality. Assaulted by the demands of anxious merchants and worried by the cost of relocating some core-area streets to fit Burnham's specifications, those pragmatic chieftains decided that it was more important to rebuild downtown *quickly* than *well*.

"The crying need of San Francisco today," the *Chronicle* opined after the earthquake and fire, "is not more parks and boulevards; it is business." Even Fremont Older's *Bulletin*, which had once so warmly welcomed both Burnham and his planning concepts, completely forsook its architectural idealism after the disaster, remarking cavalierly that "visions of the beautiful must not blind us to the real needs of the city [and] the indispensable conditions of industry." Civic enhancement, the paper declared, would have to be left to "a future and more opulent generation."

And so the cataclysm that buried the San Francisco of old also buried Daniel Burnham's magnificent vision for its rebirth. The final insult came when voters refused to approve financing for even a scaled-down version of Burnham's civic center—the very core of his program.

BURNHAM WENT TO HIS grave in 1912 thinking that he had had little impact on California's most vibrant town.

In fact, fragments of Burnham's plan do survive, among them the stepped terraces and circular drive on Telegraph Hill, the BART system, and downtown's one-way streets.

Today's Civic Center, though less ambitious than the one proposed by Burnham, also owes much to his concepts. Unfortunately, in the absence of Daniel Burnham's personal, prophetic, and poetic ministrations, that combination of buildings and plazas has turned out to be rather cold and boring. And Mayor "Sunny Jim" Rolph, Jr., even stole most of the credit for getting City Hall built there in the first place.

THE CHARACTER QUESTION

"San Francisco is a mad city, inhabited for the most part by perfectly insane people whose women are of remarkable beauty."

—Rudyard Kipling

MAN OF DESTINY

Colonel Oliver North, who helped scandalize the Reagan administration by selling arms to Iran to fund the Contra rebels in Nicaragua, may be the best-remembered American ever to manipulate Nicaraguan politics. But he was not the first. More than a century before North, a daring San Franciscan named William Walker stormed the Nicaraguan capital, then at Granada, and declared himself that country's first dictator-president.

Descriptions of Walker inevitably bring to mind comparisons with Napoleon Bonaparte. Both men were small (Walker stood just under 5½ feet tall and weighed 130 pounds), they shared a contempt for authority, and they both envisioned themselves as empire builders. Yet Walker was a squeaky-voiced soldier of fortune, not a career commander in chief. And unlike Napoleon, who at least had the chance to see out his old age in exile, Walker's days ended abruptly—on the wrong side of a firing squad.

BORN IN NASHVILLE, Tennessee, in 1824, Walker was trained in medicine and the law, but had practiced journalism in New Orleans before drifting to San Francisco in 1850, where he became editor of the *Daily Herald*.

Walker was not timid about voicing his opinions on life and politics in this Gold Rush capital. But not everyone appreciated his opinions—particularly not Judge Levi Parsons, a cantankerous magistrate who first had Walker arrested for his contumelious portrayals of the local court system, and then tossed the editor into a cell for contempt when Walker refused to pay his fine. Special action by the territorial legislature at Monterey was required for Walker to regain his freedom. Shortly thereafter, he left San

Francisco and opened a quiet law office in Marysville, to the north of Sacramento. He was incapable, though, of remaining quiet for long.

Following the Mexican War and the weakening of President Santa Anna's government, a number of schemes were hatched whereby soldiers of fortune ("filibusters") in California might capture parts of Mexico and topple other weak Central American governments. One of these intrigues was the brainchild of William Walker, who proposed raising an army and seizing Baja California and the northern Mexican state of Sonora. The government in Washington (which presumed that Walker would append his mini-empire to the Union, even if it was as a slave-holding territory) mounted only perfunctory opposition to his escapade, and so on October 16, 1853, Walker sailed out through the Golden Gate with a guerilla force of about 50 men. They landed at the town of La Paz in southern Baja, kidnapped the local governor, and declared Walker president of the new Republic of Lower California. San Franciscans were astounded at Walker's audacity and called him "the Gray-Eyed Man of Destiny," a firebrand who could triumph where men of greater caution would meet defeat.

However, his moment of glory was brief. His troops had trouble getting food, since federal authorities in San Francisco had decided to sever his supply line and hold back reinforcements. Mass desertions from his own ranks finally broke Walker's hold over the peninsula. To save their necks, he and his most loyal filibusters surrendered to the U.S. military at the border. Some of his compadres were remanded to prison for violating international neutrality laws, but Walker pled his own case before a court-martial at San Francisco and won acquittal.

AGAIN HE TRIED TO settle down, this time as an attorney in Stockton. And again, he was summoned to change the politics of his hemisphere. In 1855, with Nicaragua embroiled in political upheaval, Walker and 56 of his men joined with revolutionaries to capture the Nicaraguan capital of Granada, on the shores of Lake Nicaragua. This time, the California Napoleon had lots of local support. The nation's former ruling party, the Legitimists, were not popular. Walker was hailed by Granadans as a liberator and someone who could make Nicaragua a true power on the world stage. All this hope, however, couldn't guarantee him success. Inaugurated as president of Nicaragua in July 1856, he had very little money at his disposal—about $20,000 in mostly ill-gotten gold—and no assurances that his new Liberal Democratic government would win recognition from either of the two largest international powers, the United States and Great Britain.

Turning up the heat on Walker, too, was "Commodore" Cornelius Vanderbilt, the piratical New Yorker who had made his family fortune in transportation services. Some years earlier, the Legitimists had given Vanderbilt control of charter-boat transport across Lake Nicaragua. This was significant, since many people traveling between the Atlantic and Pacific Oceans preferred to go by way of Nicaragua—and across Lake Nicaragua—rather than brave a hike through Panama's humid, virus-infested jungle or sail all the way around Cape Horn. The Commodore suspected that President Walker might rescind his cozy franchise. He was right to worry, for at the time financier William Ralston, along with his mentor (and former Panama banking partner), Cornelius K. Garrison, and another transportation magnate from New York, Charles Morgan, had proposed that Walker help them take over the cross-lake route. Enjoying an opportunity to play David against a Goliath of Vanderbilt's stature, Walker agreed, seizing the Commodore's charter boats and setting off another round of hosannas from Nicaraguans, who had long felt that Vanderbilt was underpaying their country for his lake franchise.

But the Commodore didn't take kindly to William Walker's actions and struck back in the way he knew best: with money. Over the next two years, the multimillionaire financed efforts by the armies of Honduras, Costa Rica, Guatemala, and El Salvador to crush Walker's fragile government and win back Vanderbilt's precious franchise. There was no way the Nicaraguans could repulse such an onslaught. Although his cause was lost, Walker again refused to surrender to the opposing Central American forces. Instead, in May 1857 he found a convenient U.S. warship that would take him into custody and escort him safely back to the States.

THOUGH REBUKED OFFICIALLY by President James Buchanan for his Central American adventures, Walker never stopped dreaming of a return to Nicaragua. His mind and heart were there, even if his body had wound up back in San Francisco. Dressed in his big, floppy hat and his long black coat, he became a familiar sight at Abe Warner's Cobweb Palace in North Beach. It was there that his fate was foretold. On one occasion, as he watched Walker flail with his cane at an offending web inside the bar, Warner chided: "That cobweb will be growing long after you've been cut down from the gibbet." He may not have been correct about the specific method of execution, but he was right that Walker's days were numbered.

By 1860, the California Napoleon was right back in the thick of a war, fighting for Nicaragua against Costa Rica. He was commanding the largest and most valiant contingent he'd ever had behind him in Central America. Still, the odds defied their optimism, slowly wearing them down with disease and hunger. For the third time in his paramilitary career, Walker realized that surrender was necessary, and that his life depended on giving himself up to a neutral third party. He chose the captain of a British warship anchored in the Bay of Trujillo. Unfortunately, the British weren't as willing as the Americans to brave the censure that might come from harboring a man as prone to defying international law

MEDICINE MAN

A century before the British rocker Sting sang about the "King of Pain," the real King of Pain traveled San Francisco in a shiny black coach pulled by six white horses. He'd made a fortune as a medicine man, peddling aconite liniment (a crude painkiller) at the corner of Third and Mission Streets. "King of Pain" was his promotional nickname; his real moniker has been forgotten. But nobody forgot his public raiments. He wore bright red long johns and a thick velour robe, and on his head sat a high top hat plumed with ostrich feathers. A heavy sword swung at his side. It was a great loss to the sidewalk menagerie when gambling debts drove the King to suicide.

as William Walker. Rather than ship him off to a safe haven, they turned him over to the commander of the Honduran army.

He was only in his mid-30s. Had he lived, he might have made a splendid showing during the Civil War. But his life was cut short when a Honduran court-martial declared that Walker should forfeit his future for spreading insurrection.

And so William Walker was marched out into a Honduran palace yard and positioned with his back against a wall. He was offered a blindfold, but turned it down, preferring to stare death—this time in the form of a firing squad—in the face one last time.

VOODOO QUEEN

She could be seen abroad in San Francisco's late 19th-century financial district, a silent apparition clad in an expensive black silk dress and tight black bonnet, with a white muslin kerchief snugged at her neck and a shawl to bind her shoulders against frigid winds blowing in off the Bay. She always seemed intent upon her errand—whether she was bound for a consultation with her financial advisor, a meeting with one of the many spies she'd placed in service positions around town, or a confrontation with some powerful man who'd become the target of her latest extortion scheme.

Whatever this woman's mission, people looked upon her curiously. It was said that her mother and grandmother were both voodoo queens from Santo Domingo, in the Caribbean, and that she kept tight control over San Francisco's black community with spells and potions and the hypnotic influence of her strangely mismatched eyes (one brown, one blue). It had also been widely rumored that Mary Ellen Pleasant—or "Mammy" Pleasant, as she was called—was responsible for the murder of several men and an unrecorded number of unwanted babies at her landmark "House of Mystery" on Octavia Street.

Even unsuperstitious San Franciscans treated Mammy Pleasant with cautious respect. There was just no sense, they figured, in courting danger.

MARY ELLEN PLEASANT landed in San Francisco in 1852. A slender, rather tall and handsome woman with dusky skin, a straight nose on an oval face, and long black hair parted down the middle, she presented herself as a fine cook from one of the plantations outside of New Orleans. Since there were few cooks or housekeepers available then in San Francisco, she had no trouble finding employment.

Although she passed for white and had, in fact, once been married under the guise of *being* white, Mary Ellen Pleasant had been born a slave on a plantation near Augusta, Georgia. In her early teens, she was purchased for $650 by a Missouri planter who decided that she was too attractive for field labor, and so instead sponsored her education at a New Orleans convent. Passing herself off as white, she subsequently moved to Boston, where she was wooed and wed by a wealthy widower named James W. Smith, who took her with him to his tobacco plantation in West Virginia. There Mary Ellen became enamored of Smith's plantation overseer, John James Plaissance, a light-skinned black man from Richmond. Her fear that her infidelity might be discovered vanished when her husband suddenly perished, leaving her his estate.

The widow Smith left her lover in charge of the plantation and returned to Boston, where she secretly gave birth to the product of her liaison with Plaissance. Mary

Ellen decided the child could have no place in her life, however, and abandoned her to the care of an accommodating matron.

During the years leading up to the Civil War, Mary Ellen became active in New England's abolitionist movement. She shuttled escaping black slaves along the Underground Railroad into Canada, until suspicions of her double life endangered her freedom. The resourceful Mary Ellen then fled New England, in company with Plaissance, for New Orleans.

During that voyage, the lovers were married, and Mary Ellen convinced Plaissance (now calling himself John Pleasant) to continue on alone to San Francisco, which she hoped would provide a safe haven for ex-slaves. She stayed in Louisiana; by day, she served as a plantation cook, but many a night would find her "stealing" slaves from Louisiana planters and sending them north to liberation. Again, however, when rumors of her activities got about, Mary Ellen was forced to flee. This time, she sneaked aboard a ship bound around Cape Horn to the Pacific Ocean.

EVEN PRIOR TO REACHING the Golden Gate, she was busy making plans. Some of these included a man she'd met on her voyage, a cocksure Scotsman and former banker named Thomas Frederick Bell, who longed to put his investment ideas to work in gold-rich California. If Plaissance/Pleasant fulfilled her sexual needs, Bell would help fulfill her desire to be rich.

In San Francisco, Mary Ellen spent her first few years cooking and cleaning for a living, eventually squirreling away enough money to buy a "supper club" (boardinghouse) on Washington Street. With income from that enterprise, she bought a saloon, a livery stable, and a laundry business. She began investing in expansion property on the Barbary Coast and even built one or more parlor houses. She kept her hand in the national abolitionist

REUNITED

Mary Ellen Pleasant's abandoned daughter, Elizabeth, reportedly tracked her mother down and joined her in San Francisco during the 1880s. The daughter was a testy and unhappy young woman, however, who finally drank herself to death. Mary Ellen didn't display much grief upon her daughter's demise. In fact, according to one observer, she seemed uncommonly gay.

movement as well, and started helping out less fortunate San Francisco blacks, getting them jobs and money. At one point, she employed 50 or more African-Americans in her own businesses. Her efforts were not wholly altruistic, though: every ex-slave she helped, she also filled with fear of her voodoo powers. She arranged eerie orgies for ex-slaves outside of town and obscene dances for wealthy white men at her country home—all designed to reinforce the idea that she wielded extraordinary and evil powers. She wanted a hold over the white men for their money and influence; she wanted the blacks as spies.

In 1863, she reacquainted herself with Thomas Bell. He was courting the support of men like William Ralston, whose money he hoped to use in a variety of enterprises, and she wanted to ride the wave of his success. Together they made more than a tidy profit from shrewd and sometimes unethical stock market speculations.

However, Mary Ellen had still bigger plans. For some while, she'd engaged in the lucrative business of blackmailing wealthy but less than scrupulous members of San Francisco society. (The Voodoo Queen liked to brag that she "held the key to every closet in town with a skeleton in it.") But sometimes she had to create her opportunities. On several occasions, it's said, she taught young prostitutes just enough refinements to pass in upper-crust society, and then turned them loose on bachelors of means. Once a relationship was consummated, Mary Ellen would threaten the man with scandal if he didn't wed his paramour or fork over large sums of "hush money." Anyone who balked was sure to be presented, after nine months, with a baby—supposedly his own—and told again to pay up or face the consequences.

Most of these marriage intrigues bilked men Mary Ellen knew only by reputation. But then her sights turned on none other than her "investment advisor," Thomas Bell.

THE PLOT BEGAN in 1868, when she met Teresa Marie Percy, a bonny blonde

THE HOUSE OF MYSTERY

*Wild tales were told about Mary
Ellen Pleasant's residence at 1661
Octavia Street—and some of them
may have even been true. But since it
was impossible to separate fact from
fiction, people simply took to calling
her home the House of Mystery. Its
walls were said to be riddled with
secret passageways, and its rooms
reportedly hosted orgies on a semireg-
ular basis. Passersby often reported
hearing peculiar sounds from inside
the mansion, and nearby real estate
was often hard to peddle. Desperate
unwed mothers who went inside supposedly exited without their children,
the young ones having either been*

☞

in her early 20s who would become Mammy Pleasant's private Pygmalion project. The Voodoo Queen moved Teresa into her boardinghouse at 920 Washington Street, provided the girl with a fine new wardrobe, had her tutored in the arts, and showed her off on carriage rides through the city. She also coerced Teresa into signing over her power of attorney. And then she waited for Bell to step into her trap.

In 1878, Mary Ellen finished building a labyrinthine 30-room home at 1661 Octavia Street. Two stories tall, with a spacious attic and red mansard roof, the house cost about $100,000. Mary Ellen built her own apartment on a corner of the second floor, another one across the hall for Teresa Percy, and a third suite at the rear of that floor which, though he didn't yet know it, was intended for occupation by Thomas Bell.

How Mary Ellen convinced Bell to move into her house is a mystery. The pair still maintained a business relationship; he'd named her executor of his will and loaned her money on occasion. However, Bell was a wealthy man who already had his own lavish digs. Yet he finally agreed to move under Mary Ellen's roof.

One morning shortly after taking up residence in the Octavia Street house, he rose with a hangover to find Teresa Percy sharing his bed. Right on schedule, Mary Ellen showed up to talk terms of marriage, but Bell wasn't interested. The Voodoo Queen initiated her usual Plan B, presenting Bell over the next couple of years with not just one but *two* babies—named Frederick and Marie—who she claimed were produced by his intimacies with the lovely Teresa. And still, Bell was recalcitrant. Worse, he was starting to withhold his confidences from Mary Ellen, sharing them instead with the coquettish Teresa.

A split between the two women was inevitable, and it came after Teresa finally convinced Bell to marry her. Mary Ellen, away at the time of the marriage, was furious with both of her pawns. But she wasn't worried. After all, she still held Teresa's power of attorney and, with that, control over her protégé's share of Bell's estate. But one day in 1892, Teresa, acting out of increasing fear of Mary Ellen, stole into her patron's bedroom and found the secret compartment in which the Voodoo Queen kept that signed paper. Teresa burned it immediately.

Mary Ellen Pleasant wasn't privy to this deception. If she had been, the events of October 15, 1892, might not have occurred. On that chill evening, Teresa and most of the mansion's 10 servants were away. Mary Ellen, swaddled in a fringed red blanket, appeared in her kitchen and warmed some wine, which she said she was taking up to a "very badly run down" Thomas Bell. About an hour later, a scream was heard, followed by the snapping of a balustrade and the thump of a body smacking the tiled floor below the circular stairway. Servants found Bell twitching in death and Mammy kneeling over him—pulling at brains that had leaked through a hole in his head. There was nothing doctors could do to save the millionaire's life.

AMAZINGLY, THE VOODOO QUEEN escaped prosecution. The coroner ruled Bell's fall an accident. Teresa Bell knew better, and she determined to keep Mary Ellen from benefiting from Thomas's untimely end. In this cause, Theresa was abetted posthumously by her husband, who at some point in the past had replaced Mary Ellen with Teresa as his executor. Unfortunately for Teresa, Bell had also cut his wife off from the main body of his fortune, dividing it between his two alleged children. Only after Teresa's headline-grabbing revelation (and Mary Ellen's confirmation) that Frederick and Marie Bell were not, in fact, Thomas Bell's biological children was Teresa declared her husband's sole beneficiary. By then, of course, the case had gone on for years and most of his money had been gobbled up by lawyers.

One of Teresa's first acts after the resolution of her case was to boot Mary Ellen

suffocated or adopted into Mary Ellen's bizarre household. Four of her servants met tragic ends, probably because they knew something they shouldn't have. There seems little question that Mary Ellen even committed murder when she lured one of her servants to the mansion's roof and then pushed him to his death onto the sidewalk 60 feet below.

ALL THAT'S LEFT

Mary Ellen Pleasant's House of Mystery burned down in the 1920s, though its six eucalyptus trees out front still stand. There's now a plaque nearby, installed by the African-American Cultural Society to commemorate the Voodoo Queen's life.

out of the Octavia Street house. It seems the Voodoo Queen had put her mansard-roofed abode up as security against some of Thomas Bell's loans, and now Teresa owned it. Until she died in early 1904, at the age of 88, Mary Ellen lived in a tiny abode on Fillmore Street. After her death, she was said to haunt the Octavia residence. She certainly haunted Teresa Bell. Until her own death in 1922, Teresa remained in that gray mansion, endlessly searching for Mary Ellen's secret closets and passages.

GENEROUS, DESPITE HIMSELF

He appeared to be the grimiest of beggars, a gaunt, morose man who trudged the back alleys of San Francisco, a gunnysack slung over one shoulder. Calling at the rear entrances to the city's many restaurants and hotel kitchens, he'd ask quietly for the scraped bones left over from that day's meal preparations. Cooks were happy to oblige. What good were bones, after all? And so the beggar collected this detritus and reentered the shadows from which he had come.

Never in their wildest dreams would those kitchen helpers have guessed that the whiskery pauper upon whom they'd just unloaded their trash would one day be the richest man in San Francisco.

JAMES LICK WAS HIS NAME. He was born in Fredericksburg, Pennsylvania, in 1796. And almost as soon as he understood something about the world, James Lick knew what he wanted most from it: money.

Not many people really understood Lick—certainly not the organ maker with whom he apprenticed, or the piano manufacturer who subsequently employed him. They were craftsmen who balanced their pursuit of money with their appreciation for the art that their efforts supported. Lick saw only that people wanted pianos; popular music was a favorite entertainment of the 1800s, and every household in the East with the slimmest grasp on social refinements desired a piano prominently displayed in the parlor. So he made pianos, and made money in the process.

In 1820, when Pennsylvania had become crowded with his keyboards, Lick lit out for newly independent Argentina, where he spent some 10 years enhancing the musical resources of Buenos Aires and the dusty Pampas. On the side, he made a handsome profit trading in animal hides—enough money so that he could move on from the piano business to more profitable ventures.

Lick's pockets were sewn tightly shut around savings of some $40,000 when, in 1847, he reached San Francisco Bay and the sleepy village of Yerba Buena. To make the trip, he'd signed on as the supercargo aboard a ship, the *Lady Adams*, which was carrying coffee, cowhides, and mahogany from South America. No sooner was he off the ship than Lick began peddling his own valuable commodity to Californians: "600 pounds of chocolate made by a man in Lima, Peru, named Domenico Ghiradelli," according to David Siefkin's *The City at the End of the Rainbow*. The chocolate sold quickly, as Lick knew it would, and he added that money to his growing grubstake.

HE ROAMED THE STREETS of Yerba Buena, looking for his place in this roughshod pueblo's future. A misanthrope, locals called him if they were of generous mind. A madman, said others. But Lick didn't care what people thought of him. There was literally no profit in such concerns.

SWEET SUCCESS

The chocolate that James Lick brought from South America was made, of course, by the same Domenico Ghiradelli who arrived in San Francisco from Peru in 1850 to open a chocolate and spice factory on Jackson Street. In 1897, the Ghiradelli family relocated its operation to North Point Street, taking over and enlarging brick buildings that had been abandoned by the Columbia Woolen Mills. That factory complex has since been transformed into the warren of boutiques that is familiar to tourists today as Ghiradelli Square.

He went ahead and did what he wanted . . . which was to plunk down a handsome portion of his savings on a bunch of windblown sandlots along a cattle trail to the east of Portsmouth Square. His gamble paid off, for that cow path became Montgomery Street. Only a couple of years later, gold was discovered at Sutter's Mill, and men by the tens of thousands poured into what was by then known as San Francisco, some of them staying to exercise their entrepreneurial talents and in need of property. By the 1860s, Montgomery Street had become *the* main business thoroughfare, and Lick could ask top dollar for his sand dunes.

San Franciscans were no longer so quick to call this man nuts. Knowing what he had already accomplished, they nodded sagely when Lick purchased sand dunes elsewhere in town. But they could find no explanation for why he'd snap up a huge chunk of sere acreage surrounding the Mission San José, a 1797 structure located 50 miles south of the Golden Gate. Nor could they get used to the disheveled, almost skeletal appearance of this illiterate pragmatist who held on so tightly to his money that he even denied himself proper nutrition. What kind of behavior was this for a man who, in 1851, was supposed to have assets totaling $750,000, making him the wealthiest individual in town?

Then, of course, came the matter of Lick's nighttime foragings for bones. There was simply no way to reckon that behavior, either. Even the explanation, when it came, smacked of too much alcohol and not enough acuity: Lick was building a $250,000 flour mill at San Jose, finished in mahogany and as impressive "as a palace," according to *Harper's Magazine*. And part of what he would be grinding in the machinery were the many pounds of free bones he had accumulated. The resulting dust was to be carefully worked into the parched soil of the Santa Clara Valley, and then fruit trees would be planted. Fruit trees in California? Preposterous! cried San Francisco's clerisy, only to

NOW, WHICH WAY DID THAT GO AGAIN?

It's said that the eccentric James Lick once fired a gardener because he refused to obey orders. It seems the millionaire had handed the nursery-man a rare shrub and then insisted that it be planted upside down.

witness that valley reborn over the next decades in a sea of orchards, fragrant with plum blossoms and moist loam.

AFTER ALL OF THESE peculiar endeavors, it was with a sense of relief that San Francisco greeted Lick's next vision: a hotel to outshine all others in town. Finally, a *normal* idea.

Opened in 1863, more than a decade before William Ralston raised his Palace, the Lick House, bordering the west side of Montgomery Street from Sutter to Post, was the city's "first palatial hotel." Although he was a miser in most respects, when it came to realizing his dreams Lick didn't scrimp. This hotel, 3½ stories tall, was no exception. Its dining room was an imitation of the dining hall at the Palace of Versailles, with mirrors and murals of California landscapes lining the walls. Its lobby was brightened with gold and marble. Amelia Neville, in *The Fantastic City*, explained, "It soon became the fashion to dine at the Lick on Sunday evenings. The dining-room and lobby were beautiful rooms, with their flagged marble floors and fine woodwork. James Lick had been a cabinetmaker in his youth, and for his hotel . . . he imported rare woods from South America and the Orient, doing much of the finishing and polishing with his own hands, reveling in the work."

Reveling? It was hard to tell when Lick was happy. Neville called him "a sad-looking man." Intent upon gleaning treasure, he had no time for frivolities nor any apparent concern for his personal environment. He moved into a private room at the Lick House, which he quickly reduced to squalor. He seemed to have no family, no friends. He was content to be by himself, in the company of his money and his eccentricities.

OR AT LEAST HE was content until the early 1870s, when the facts of his mortality suddenly made themselves clear to him. Then this Scrooge did two things that were even more unexpected from him than begging for chicken bones in the twilight. First he decided

MONEYCHANGING

To understand just how much business in California boomed after the Gold Rush, consider that Lick, who had been the richest man in San Francisco with $750,000 in 1851, was only the sixth richest in 1871, with his $3 million in assets.

MISSING SON

Contrary to popular assumptions of his time, millionaire James Lick had a son, John Henry Lick. John Lick doesn't appear in San Francisco city directories of the 1870s, but his name is featured among those designated as trustees of James Lick's estate. Lick fils *received $150,000 from his father's will, which also set aside $20,000 for the erection of granite monuments to four other "near relations." Yet the elder Lick's affairs weren't completely in order when he passed away. As a result, John Lick faced what* Harper's Magazine *described as "a course of litigation between the different beneficiaries and his son and heir, which was not finally settled until 1880."*

to give away his vast fortune. Then he actually asked another human being for help in carrying out that important assignment.

The assistance came from George Davidson, a cultured gent who served as president of the California Academy of Sciences. Lick told Davidson that he was tired, sick, probably running the last stretch of life. Before he wound up in the ground, Lick said, he wanted Davidson's direction in giving away his riches. Davidson was flabbergasted. According to estimates, Lick had banked $3 million. It might take months, years even, to disperse that much among worthy causes. If that's the case, Lick retorted, shouldn't they begin the task right away?

It was indeed a Scroogelike transformation that James Lick underwent. He had spent his whole life concentrating on himself, and now all he wanted to do was put his fortune to use for the common good. To paraphrase Dickens, Lick was better than his word—he did it all and infinitely more. He began by setting aside some prime property on Market Street for the benefit of Davidson's science academy. Then, having been seduced by either reports of astronomical wonders or actual sights that Davidson had pointed out to him through his own telescope, Lick decided that he should give everybody the gift of heavenly study. He proposed building a stellar observatory with "the most powerful glass in the world." With Davidson's help, this structure would be erected atop Mount Hamilton, 18 miles east of San Jose. In his will, the penurious millionaire set aside $700,000 for this project. The now-famous Lick Observatory was completed in 1888.

As Samuel Dickson explained in *San Francisco Is Your Home*, Lick then told his new partner to take the rest of his money and "Give it to the poor. Tell them to wash and be clean." He had been a dirty, ill-kept man, but that became his favorite phrase—"Wash and be clean." Davidson followed through by creating a free bathhouse on Sansome Street. He also doled out money to orphan asylums, to a home for old women, and to the Society for the Prevention of Cruelty to Animals. In a last gasp of largess, the late-blooming philanthropist approved the creation of a school to teach the manual arts and sciences: San Francisco's still-extant Lick-Wilmerding Polytechnic School.

James Lick died in his 80th year, in 1876. Men and women who'd criticized Lick in years past were more generous after his death, singing his praises. Yes, he'd been a miser, a skinflint, the most selfish of the selfish. But fate hadn't locked his fingers permanently around his purse. He had proved to be the area's greatest benefactor.

LUCKY STRIKES

The legends about Elias Jackson Baldwin—the 19th-century Comstock millionaire, hotelier, and race track–lover who came to be known as "Lucky"—are so colorful, so representative of his wild times, it's regrettable to think that some might not actually be true.

Take, for instance, the story about a paternity suit being lodged against him when he was 60 years old. Baldwin, a skinny, walnut-hard man with a sharp nose and a thick, silvery mustache, argued convincingly that he couldn't possibly have fathered a child by the plaintiff, a woman only half his age: she was far too old and ugly to ever have attracted his attention.

Or consider the tale of how Baldwin acquired his nickname. During the 1870s,

For a man who didn't put much faith in luck, E. J. Baldwin certainly enjoyed it in spades. Three days after he sold his Ophir Mine stocks to Billy Ralston in 1875, Baldwin lost his wallet—including an IOU from Ralston for $3,600,000. Had it been anybody other than Lucky, this story would have had an unhappy ending. But it happened that later that same day, Baldwin's brother-in-law was walking down the street, minding his own business, when what should appear before him but the missing pocketbook.

after he'd become obscenely rich through canny purchases of real estate and mining-stock speculations, he decided to see the world. So he set sail for India and the Orient, and just before he left, he told his broker to sell off some of his Comstock investments. Only after the millionaire's departure did the broker discover that Baldwin had forgotten to leave behind the key to his safe. The mining stocks were locked inside! By the time Baldwin finally returned to San Francisco, the broker was absolutely beside himself—not because the investments had lost value over the weeks Baldwin was away, but because their price had skyrocketed and they were now worth four to five million dollars. Baldwin had been lucky . . . and Lucky is just how he'd be known for the rest of his days.

BALDWIN WAS 25 YEARS OLD in 1853, when he arrived in San Francisco from Ohio. Having had some success with buying and selling horses, he carried with him a vague notion about setting up livery stables. But the first thing he did here was spend his savings on a hotel called the Pacific Temperance House. The owner wanted $6,000 for the property; Baldwin offered $5,000. According to Samuel Dickson, writing in *San Francisco Is Your Home*, the two men dickered for three days over the sale price of the Temperance House, before its owner agreed to Baldwin's price. After shaking hands on the agreement, the former Ohioan asked that his check and the boniface's receipt be dated three days previous. This, Baldwin said, would convince his friends back East that he was one hell of a fast dealmaker. The seller appreciated this joke and signed his receipt accordingly.

Their transaction concluded, Baldwin reminded the now ex–hotel man that three days of lodging and boarding costs were still due. Oh, right, said the innkeeper, impressed with Baldwin's willingness to pay his debts.

"On the contrary," Dickson quotes Baldwin as saying. "*You* owe *me*. According to this check and agreement, I have owned the hotel for three days."

Lucky wasn't a con man—he just did his shrewd utmost to engineer financial negotiations in his own favor. He was ever on the scent of new opportunities. A month after winning control of the Temperance House, he sold it again—at double the price he'd paid. With that money, he set up a private brick-making operation, making a phenomenal (for the time) $1,000 to $1,400 a month. Eventually, he had enough money to fulfill his dream: he built the first of several stables to be associated with his name in California.

But all of this was low-level capitalism. It wasn't until Baldwin bought into Nevada's Comstock Lode that he really demonstrated his money-making skill . . . and his luck.

HE'D MADE HIS FIRST forays into silver stocks during the 1860s, when bankers William Ralston and William Sharon still controlled that "hole in the ground with silver and gold in it," as Ralston described Nevada's lucrative Comstock diggings. Baldwin bought low, sold high, and, by being cautious about his level of investments, managed to avoid being hurt by the *Sturm und Drang* of the silver game.

Ralston was less conservative, spending heavily on any and all active claims he could find. For a while, it looked as if Ralston and Sharon held unassailable dominance over the Comstock. But then, in 1869, a shrewd stock-market raid deprived Ralston of his control over the Comstock's old Hale & Norcross Mine. A year later, that mine—assumed to be pretty much tapped out—suddenly revealed a new, rich ore body. Within another three years, the mine's owners—the Consolidated Virginia—struck a deep vein of silver ore that San Francisco's *Mining and Scientific Press* called "absolutely immense, and beyond all comparison superior in every respect to anything ever seen on the Comstock Lode." This find was Nevada's "Big Bonanza," and would ultimately yield up a third of a billion dollars worth of silver.

Not surprisingly, Ralston was incensed. The earth was hemorrhaging a fortune in

GILBERT & SULLIVAN & BALDWIN

Besides a knack for money-making, Baldwin also had an eye for artistic talent. Following his fight with Ralston for control of Nevada's Ophir Mine, Lucky decided he needed some relaxation. So he set sail for Asia, intending to experience a big-game hunt in India and then tour royal monuments in the Orient. While he was there, he came upon a troupe of Japanese acrobats who amazed him with their juggling and ☞

wrestling performances. Nothing like it had ever been seen in America, Baldwin knew, so he commissioned the troupe to return with him. Baldwin and his visiting vaudevillians toured the United States, making the millionaire yet another fortune at the box office, before he sold the act to a struggling English playwright by the name of William S. Gilbert. The playwright took the Japanese troupe to London, where they wowed the crowds at Piccadilly and inspired Gilbert, with his partner Arthur Sullivan, to write an opera: The Mikado.

silver, from a mine that he had once owned, and he couldn't lay his hands on a single ounce of it. To remain a major player on the Comstock, he needed a really big strike—fast. Sharon advised him to acquire a controlling interest in the Ophir Mine, located immediately north of the Consolidated Virginia. It was Sharon's contention that deep development there would disgorge a rich silver vein that began on Consolidated Virginia land but ended under the Ophir Mine. The trouble was, most of the Ophir's stock was owned by Elias J. "Lucky" Baldwin.

Lucky had already conjectured that the Consolidated Virginia ore body might bleed north, under the Ophir shafts. That was why he had bought so heavily into the mine in the first place. And he wasn't about to sell out to Ralston and Sharon. So in the winter of 1874–75, Ralston decided to seek revenge against Baldwin and win the Ophir in the bargain. First, he dumped all of the Ophir stocks he owned, thus depressing the value of the remaining shares. Then, as additional shares of the mine came onto the market—sold off by more timid investors who hewed to Ralston's lead—Ralston's confederates tried to quickly and quietly buy them up. However, rumors soon hit the San Francisco Mining Exchange that Ralston was trying to corner Ophir stock. Prices immediately shot up. Ophir shares that Baldwin had secured for $2 in 1870 were now worth over $300 apiece. Only then did Lucky decide to sell, taking a couple of million dollars in profits from Ralston for his trouble. When the Ophir failed to produce a second bonanza, Baldwin could only thank his lucky stars that he no longer owned a piece of it.

BALDWIN HAD ENOUGH CAPITAL, an estimated $7 million, after the Ophir affair to buy or build or do just about anything his heart desired. Like so many wealthy men, he erected a mansion on Nob Hill, with a stable that one source said "overshadowed his house." What he really wanted, though, was to own another hotel, one that would rival even Ralston's Palace, which was still under construction.

The $2 million–plus Baldwin Hotel, opened not long before the Palace and wrapped in French Renaissance–style splendor around the northeast corner of Market and Powell Streets, didn't suffer tremendously by comparison with its larger competitor. Rhomboidal in shape, it rose six stories, contained 400 plushly decorated guest rooms, and was capped with a mansard roof, out of which sprouted elaborately crafted turrets and a spectacular dome. Patrons took in a rooftop conservatory, a high-ceilinged billiards hall for men (and a smaller ladies' version), and a giant marble-filled barber shop. Carpets had come from Europe at $30 a yard, twin mechanical birds from Paris kept up a twittering chorus in the hotel's lounge, and the lobby was filled with paintings on glass that depicted notable events from Lucky's life. Also in the lobby was a $25,000 Tiffany clock; Mark Twain quipped that it told "not only the hours, minutes and seconds but the turn of the tides, the phases of the moon, the price of eggs and who's got your umbrella."

What really set the Baldwin Hotel apart from other lodgings, though, was its built-in luxury playhouse—the first on Market Street. Originally called the Academy of Music (and later just Baldwin's Theater), it outshone even Ralston's giant California Theater. "It is not large; its seating capacity accommodating seven hundred persons," B. E. Lloyd wrote of the Baldwin Theater in *Lights and Shades in San Francisco*. "But for elegance and style of finish, for comfort and cheer, it doubtless has no superiors, even in art-loving Europe." Performances in the theater had to be outstanding just to draw people's attention from the opulent surroundings. They usually were, thanks to Baldwin's partner in this venture, impresario Tom Maguire (proprietor of the popular Maguire's Opera House) and a stock troupe that included such luminaries as child star Maude Adams, James O'Neill,

❧

A RICH RAKE

The Baldwin Hotel's blasphemous, cigar-smoking owner could be seen about the property at all hours of the day or night, but especially when he was anticipating a little money sport. He frequently hosted high-stakes poker games, generously accompanied by food and Kentucky bourbon, in his personal suite. It was just outside that suite, where Lucky was shot by a woman claiming that he'd "ruined her body and soul." "Baldwin never bothered to deny the charge," according to *San Francisco's* Golden Era, *and the woman "shortly showed up as one of the foremost madams in Denver where her armed skirmish with the aging millionaire was an asset and advertisement."*

❧

and David Belasco, who served as stage manager at the Baldwin before becoming a national producer and theater owner himself.

EVEN WITH ALL OF THIS, E. J. Baldwin wasn't content. In 1875, he helped found the Pacific Stock Exchange and was its first president. While touring southern California, he became enchanted with the San Gabriel Valley just north of Los Angeles. He bought tens of thousands of acres there and developed a ranch. Then, because he'd never lost interest in the beauty of horseflesh, he erected a racetrack at the heart of his claim and called it Santa Anita, after his favorite daughter. From there, he moved on to Lake Tahoe, was again swept away by natural wonders, purchased more land, and built the grand Tallac Hotel.

Lucky should have known better than to take on so much at once. He had lots of assets but almost no cash. The bottom was falling out of the Comstock market, dragging the San Francisco economy down with it, and everyone who had spent heavily was suffering. Both of Lucky's hotels were in financial straits. He resisted paying his debts and ignored lawsuits. Eventually his near-impregnable Herring Brothers safe and all of its contents were attached by suppliers trying to force payment of their bills.

In desperation, Lucky began selling off some of his southern California land holdings. Los Angeles was still a sleepy village, but Baldwin never gave up easily. In a statement that would become a cliché in the next century, Lucky told one potential buyer who complained in 1881 about paying high prices for undeveloped property in the San Gabriel Valley, "Hell, we're giving away the land. We're *selling* the climate."

What he wouldn't let go of, however, were his ranch, his racetrack, and his San Francisco hotel and theater. He had a sentimental spot in his heart for all of these investments, but especially for his ranch, La Merced. Just to keep people from bothering him

SPIRITED PERFORMER

The legend is that Lucky Baldwin befriended David Belasco when the former was still a livery stable operator and the latter was a hooky-playing schoolboy in San Francisco. Even then, Belasco knew that he wanted to make a life on the stage. Baldwin wasn't sure what his days would offer, but he knew that he wanted to make money. He vowed that when he finally did grow rich, he'd build Belasco his own theater — but only if Belasco would let him watch performances for free. Belasco later acted in 175 different roles at the Baldwin Theater, and Baldwin never once had to fork out the cost of a ticket.

with offers, Lucky made up an outlandish story about the property: he said there was oil beneath its surface.

Then real disaster struck. In November 1898, fire engulfed the Baldwin Hotel, killing five people. Baldwin's luck seemed to have finally run out. The hotel/theater had been assessed at $3 million—and it was completely uninsured. The former Comstock millionaire could be seen wandering the smoldering wreckage, picking up anything that might be valuable. He sold the property as soon as he could to James L. Flood, son of the Silver King, who built the now-familiar Flood Building on the site. And soon afterward, Baldwin embarked for Nome, Alaska, hoping to tap veins of gold that had recently been discovered in the Last Frontier.

BALDWIN WAS STILL TRYING to make a comeback when he died in San Francisco in 1909 at the age of 81. He'd made some money in Alaska, but lost it again. People said he'd been defeated by his own sentimentality, that he should have dumped his worthless San Gabriel Valley ranch and used the money to rebuild his empire.

Only after Lucky was gone did geologists discover that his little fantasy about oil beneath the La Merced Ranch was no fantasy at all. Baldwin thought he'd died broke. Instead, thanks to those crude liquid riches, his heirs realized an estate valued at $35 million. If that wasn't luck, nothing is.

LUCKY'S LEGACY

The Los Angeles subdivision of Arcadia (meaning "a place of rural simplicity") was carved out of E. J. Baldwin's huge La Merced Ranch in the early 20th century. Today the Los Angeles Arboretum occupies another portion of Lucky's former property and includes the central lake where Gabrieleno Indians once drew water. Visitors to the arboretum should note the delicately detailed Lucky Baldwin Queen Anne Guest Cottage, which was built in 1881, as well as the Queen Anne–style doghouse, stables, and 1890 railroad station.

THE UNITED STATES OF NORTON

MYSTERIES OF THE MIND

Just how mad was Joshua Norton? San Francisco wanted to know. After his death, Norton's brain was autopsied, but "no traces of insanity were found," according to the local press.

G oing quietly but very publicly insane may have been the wisest thing Joshua Abraham Norton ever did. The 30-year-old son of a Jewish merchant in the British colony of Cape Town, South Africa, Norton was said to have arrived at San Francisco along with the gold-hungry hordes in November 1849. But he was no gold seeker himself. Like many a wily soul, Norton waited in the Bay Area's scrawny boomtown for the hills to come to him, borne in the pockets and knapsacks of scrappy miners. Over three years of savvy real estate investing and commodities trading, he parlayed a grubstake of $40,000 into $250,000. "Men called him the merchant with the Midas touch," Samuel Dickson wrote in *San Francisco Is Your Home*. "They called him a genius; they said he was destined for great things; they said he had the potentialities of an empire builder, the qualities of an emperor." Honest and gentlemanly, yet pugnacious when necessary, Norton became a valuable resource for bankers, brokers, and speculators who trusted his advice on how and when to spend their money.

But in 1852, Joshua Norton made the mistake of trying to corner the international rice market. He figured that he could buy up shiploads of this staple as they entered port at San Francisco, hold onto them until the price of rice skyrocketed, and then release his monopoly supply onto a hungry market. He convinced fellow merchants to invest in his scheme, drumming up at least $300,000 in operating capital.

Norton had expected that rice shipments would arrive at San Francisco at a slow pace. As it happened, however, several unanticipated shiploads sailed through the Golden

Gate, and Norton's combine couldn't buy them all. Then rice prices suddenly plummeted. Norton couldn't sell the shipments he'd bought at the same price he'd paid for them, much less at the inflated rates he had envisioned. He was ruined, and some of the men who'd put their faith in his financial prescience took a bath with him.

Years of legal suits followed, most of which were decided against the ambitious merchant. He tried several other enterprises, but was unable to bounce back. In the fall of 1856, the former empire builder filed for insolvency, listing debts totaling $55,811.73, losses of $45,000, and assets of $15,000, which were quickly sold off by the local sheriff to satisfy at least some of Norton's creditors.

It wasn't long after the last of his money had disappeared that Joshua Norton vanished, too.

WHERE HE WENT and why may forever remain mysteries. But by the spring of 1860, he was back, now strutting through San Francisco thoroughfares in a florid, blue-and-red, militarylike uniform with high epaulets and gold tunic buttons cascading down under his thick, curly beard. On his head he sported a high beaver hat with a brass rosette in front that held a plume of brightly colored feathers. He carried a grapevine-wood cane and an umbrella, or hung a long curved sword off his belt, depending on his mood. And no longer was he the mere scion of a Cape Town shipping agent and chandler; in tune with a most extraordinary transformation, he now claimed to be "a Crown Prince of the French throne" who had only been "sent to South Africa to be safe from assassination." He further announced, through the *Bulletin*, that he should thereafter be addressed as "Norton I, Emperor of the United States and Protector of Mexico."

People said that Norton's business failure had unbalanced his mind. That may have been true. Or it may have been that he was just an uncanny actor and con man. In

THE EMPEROR'S NEW CLOTHES

San Francisco's Board of Supervisors was as responsive to Norton's wishes as was everybody else. Appealing to that august body for a new uniform—his original one having become too threadbare for a man of his station—the Emperor not only received the cost of new togs, but the supervisors wrote an act into the city charter calling for an annual expenditure of $30 to cover his uniforms. In return, His Highness sent each man a note of thanks and a patent of nobility.

DOG DAYS

Emperor Norton's two dogs, Bummer and Lazarus, were no less well-loved in this city than was their master. Even as citizens campaigned to rid the streets of abundant canines, they made exceptions for this pair of mutts. And when Lazarus was run over by a fire truck in 1863, he was given a long funeral procession, and was then stuffed and put on public display by a hard-liquor purveyor. Bummer passed away soon after Lazarus; he was also stuffed, and together they were displayed in a museum in Golden Gate Park, until people forgot why they were supposed to honor that pair of mongrels.

either event, he was rewarded with 20 years of the most bizarre respect. On afternoons he would leave his "imperial palace" (really a boardinghouse on Commercial Street) and promenade through town, greeting people as if they were his loyal subjects. Some people saluted him, others asked after his health and his possible courtship of various royal ladies. The frequent manifestos he submitted to the newspapers came to be valued for their unique and often blunt perspectives, rather than dismissed as the rantings of a crazy man.

He was allowed to eat for free at lunch counters, saloons, and the city's many restaurants. He took a shine to bicycles, and could sometimes be seen weaving along in a very undignified state atop a creaky metal contraption. On weekends, he was found in the central library's reading room, brushing up on his knowledge of world affairs, or else at church. Theaters would loyally reserve three seats in the first row of their front balconies for use by the self-appointed monarch and his two constant companions, a part-Newfoundland hound named Bummer and a cur that Bummer had befriended named Lazarus.

ON THOSE RARE OCCASIONS when the addlepated Emperor actually needed money, he simply went to an accommodating printer in Leidesdorff Street and ordered up promissory notes in denominations of 10, 25, and 50 cents. Perhaps people felt sorry for the short, thickset man, or perhaps he touched them with an outlandish ingenuity that they wished they had possessed; for whatever reason, San Franciscans actually took Norton's bills seriously. For the rest of his life, all merchants in the city accepted this "royal scrip" in trade for the paltry goods he required.

On only one notable occasion, as Dickson recalled, was Norton's money questioned. Taking the train to Sacramento, where the benevolent despot regularly attended legislative sessions and did his best to counsel lawmakers, he was confronted by a waiter in the dining car who refused to accept the Emperor's bogus bills. Norton fairly burst with anger. "He pounded the table and shouted for all to hear," Dickson explained, "declaring that he would revoke the railroad's franchise. The commotion spread the length of the train. The conductor rushed in, recognized Norton, apologized to the Emperor in the name of the Central Railroad and the Empire in general. And the next day the Central Pacific sent Emperor Norton a pass good on all trains, with free service in its dining cars for life."

Being a leader of the free world, Norton had an opinion about anything and everything that went on within his empire. In 1862, he "ordered" that the offices of U.S. president, vice president, and speaker of the house all be abolished, and that the U.S. Senate appoint a single presiding officer who, he hoped, could do better than Abraham Lincoln at ending the Civil War. He also dispatched a telegram to President Lincoln, ordering him to marry the widowed Queen Victoria in order to keep England on the side of the Union. Norton also penned telegrams to Kaiser Wilhelm I of Germany and Czar Alexander III, suggesting ways they might better run their own empires. He attended a meeting of the National Woman Suffrage Association and told the female speaker to go home, have babies, and attend to her housework.

Maybe he was crazy, but Norton had a habit of being right about some things. He insisted that the future of travel lay in airborne vehicles. And in 1869 he issued an edict calling for a bridge to be built across San Francisco Bay. He even pledged a "royal bank draft" of $3 million toward the project. Everybody said that no span could ever stretch across that great expanse of water, yet 57 years later, the Bay Bridge was completed and opened to traffic.

HAD HE REMAINED a boring, respectable businessman for all of his days, Joshua Norton would not have been allowed to live for free during the last two decades of his life. His words might never have received the broad hearing that they did. And most

MADMAN OF THE PEOPLE

"No citizen of San Francisco could have been taken away who would be more generally missed," the San Francisco Call *opined after Joshua Norton's death. The Bohemian Club held a memorial meeting in his honor, and some 30,000 people showed up for his obsequies at Lone Mountain Cemetery. It took a while for the city to accept that Norton's careful ruling hand had been lifted — he may have been a madman, but hell, he was San Francisco's very own madman.*

certainly, the city would never have lowered all of its flags to half-mast the way it did when Emperor Norton perished during a walk on the night of January 8, 1880.

"In what other city," Robert Louis Stevenson mused in *The Wrecker*, "would a harmless madman who supposed himself emperor . . . have been so fostered and encouraged?" For that matter, in what other *time* would this former merchant have received such a regal reception? A few years earlier, and gold-hysterical San Francisco would have been too busy to suffer his eccentricities. Any later, and he'd not have enjoyed the generosity of spirit or whimsy that characterized the city during the Gilded Age. "More than likely," Allen Stanley Lane conceded in *Emperor Norton: Mad Monarch of America*, "he would have been arrested and shut up in a state home."

Even 54 years later, when Lone Mountain was being broken up and the Emperor's remains had to be removed to Woodlawn Cemetery, at Colma, the ceremony merited a military salute, a speech by the mayor, and taps played from a nearby hill. Norton would have been pleased, especially proud of the inscription etched onto his tombstone:

NORTON 1
EMPEROR
OF THE UNITED STATES
AND PROTECTOR OF
MEXICO

—

JOSHUA A. NORTON
1819–1880

❧

THE INDOMITABLE MISS SILVERHEELS

Devastating fires were so frequent in early San Francisco that the men who battled the blazes actually became the city's first heroes. They marched in parades and were idolized by children, who loved their colorful uniforms and sweeping patent-leather helmets. The fireman's tug-of-war was a featured entertainment at large public festivals. Cries of *Fire!* brought out not only the volunteer blaze-busters themselves, but also masses of rubberneckers who delighted in the sight of horse-drawn steam pumpers and hook-and-ladder wagons careening through the streets. The excitement was always heightened by the competitive nature of local fire-engine companies, every one of which wanted to be the first on the scene of any new holocaust.

Among the better tales surviving from that period is one dating back to the early 1850s. It seems that three companies of firemen were madly pulling their engines to the top of Telegraph Hill, where flames fingered out cruelly from the roof of a weathered shack. One of these parties of volunteers, Knickerbocker Engine Company No. 5, was unexpectedly short of men that day, so it soon fell behind its rivals. Observing the Knickerbockers' plight, a slim schoolgirl at the side of the street suddenly dropped her books and rushed toward the engine. She grabbed an extra rope attached to the vehicle, and then, seeing a crowd of bystanders nearby, she yelled, "Come on, you men! Everybody pull, and we'll beat 'em!" Five or six healthy gents rushed to help, and between them and the regular volunteers, Knickerbocker 5 had its hoses out and the fire in retreat before the other two companies had even reached the fire scene.

From then on, that daring schoolgirl was the Knickerbockers' mascot. And even though she eventually became one of San Francisco's richest women, Eliza Wychie Hitchcock—Lillie, for short—never lost her taste for fire chasing.

THE DAUGHTER of Southern aristocrats, Lillie arrived at San Francisco in 1851, when she was nine or ten years old. Her earliest experience with fire came that same year, when she and some friends went to explore the unfinished skeleton of a hotel. While they were inside, the building caught fire and the children found themselves trapped. Two of Lillie's companions perished, but she herself was rescued by a volunteer with Knickerbocker Engine Company No. 5. The girl was so grateful for this act of heroism that afterward, whenever she saw the Knickerbockers charging through town

LIGHT MY FIRE

Lillie Hitchcock's first experience with fire may have come in the company of her mother, a Southern belle named Martha, who clung to her Dixie roots so tightly and with such pride that she bought and burned her childhood mansion in North Carolina rather than see it fall into decline or be violated by squatters.

on urgent business, she would cheer them on or run to keep up with their wagons.

Lillie's parents were not pleased by this dangerous, unladylike behavior. They sent her off to school in the Napa Valley, hoping to turn her mind toward more refined occupations. But Lillie's health declined so precipitously that she was allowed to rejoin her family. Firemen checked up on her and brought gifts during her convalescence, and by the time she was well again, even Lillie's parents had developed something of a warm spot in their hearts for San Francisco's blaze-runners. They no longer minded when she went off to visit the Knickerbockers at their Sacramento Street firehouse or when she rode in street parades atop the No. 5 engine, surrounded by flowers and dressed in the uniform that the company had given her: a red blouse, a black skirt, and a gold pin in the shape of a fireman's helmet.

HER DEBUTANTE-AND-TOMBOY personality became more pronounced as she moved through her teens. Dark-haired and attractively proportioned, with brown eyes full of barely restrained merriment, Lillie looked at home in the finest frilleries from Paris designers. She never worried about filling her dance card at formal affairs. Men nicknamed her "Silverheels," for the heels of silver that always decorated her dancing slippers. In *Personal Recollections of Lillie Hitchcock*, her friend Floride Green recalled that a contemporary of Lillie's once "told me that she had never seen her enter a ballroom. In amazement I asked her: 'Why not?' And she said: 'I would see a crowd of men walking into the room, another following, and then you knew Lillie Hitchcock was in the center!'" By the time she turned 20, Lillie had already been engaged 15 times.

At the same time, Lillie was not one to be controlled by Victorian expectations of her sex. She became a crack shot with a rifle and a sharp-tongued raconteur. She learned to ride horses like a cavalryman, and would often race her masculine admirers out to the

LEGWORK

As a young woman, Lillie Hitchcock could play the proper deb. But there was also a broad streak of the coquette in her. In Bonanza Inn, *Oscar Lewis and Carroll D. Hall wrote that she once lived near a medical school, where she did her best to charm and torment passing male students. On one occasion, she dangled a pretty foot and calf from an upper-story window and recited a line that was familiar from one of the day's popular music-hall ballads: "Doctor, doctor, come saw off my leg!"*

Cliff House, where she'd lead them on climbs up near-perpendicular rock faces. She reportedly disguised herself in male attire and went out on the town to bet on horse races, play poker, smoke cigars, and help empty capacious bottles of bourbon.

Lillie didn't hide her Southern sympathies, either. Not long after the Civil War's opening volleys, she helped a suspected Confederate to escape the Bay Area, disguising him in a red wig and finding him employment as a stoker aboard a ship bound for the Far East. Her father feared that such partisan escapades might not only hurt his own local business but also endanger the family's property holdings in the South, should the rebels lose the war. So he packed Lillie and her mother off to Europe, where they became regulars on the party-and-concert circuit and translated Confederate newspapers for Napoléon III and the Empress Eugénie. Only after Lillie agreed to behave herself did her father allow the women to return home. He didn't know that, on their way back, the not-quite-chastened Lillie planned to drop off some secret documents for delivery to Jefferson Davis's government.

ENGINE COMPANY NO. 5 was thrilled to have their Lillie back. But even more excited was one Benjamin Howard Coit, a mine owner from Buffalo, New York, and chairman of the San Francisco Stock Exchange. Lillie's parents objected to her marrying a Yankee, so the two eloped and were wed on November 19, 1868, when Miss Silverheels was about 26. After a honeymoon swing around the world, they returned to take up residence at the Palace Hotel.

Anybody who thought married life would smooth Lillie's wild edges was badly mistaken. If anything, she became more eccentric. Tiring of her dark brown hair, she bleached it using a process that supposedly included several bottles of champagne. When Howard Coit complained, she shaved herself bald and wore wigs the color of her gowns

THE FAB FIVE

Lillie so delighted in her affiliation with the fire company that she even had the number 5 embroidered onto her undergarments. Much later in life, she still signed her married name "Lillie Hitchcock Coit — 5."

every time they visited the opera or the theater. Fitting her figure again into gentlemen's garb, she began attending cockfights as well as card games. And, of course, she kept up her ties with Knickerbocker Engine Company No. 5. Though the city had established a paid fire department in 1866, volunteer companies continued as social organizations, and Lillie was always sure to celebrate No. 5's birthday on October 17, usually with a banquet at the Palace, which she attended in her feminine version of a fireman's uniform: a red flannel shirt, a tall hat with her insignia, and a scandalously short skirt held up with a thick leather belt.

Lillie's odd and mercurial ways eventually got on her husband's nerves, and after several trial separations, the Coits agreed to split permanently. Lillie took up residence at a country house in Calistoga called Larkmead, where she made mischief with friends and gleefully entertained authors from Robert Louis Stevenson to Joaquin Miller. But Howard Coit's unexpected death in 1885, soon after her father's demise, sent Lillie into a tailspin. Desperate for diversion, she escaped to France and Hawaii, and once entertained a group of conservative guests at her Palace suite with a private middleweight prizefight. At middle age, her life was more of a manic whirl than ever before.

IN HER 60TH YEAR, this whirl suddenly went dangerously out of control. One night in November 1903, Lillie was in her apartment at the Palace, chatting with her financial adviser, Joseph W. Clung, when another man forced his way into her rooms. He was Alexander Garrett, a distant and unsuccessful relative of Lillie's whom she generously employed to manage some of her properties. Garrett resented having to take such handouts and had apparently decided to kill Mrs. Coit, as a token of his "gratitude." But McClung stepped in front of Garrett when he raised his pistol against Lillie, and took a ball in his chest. McClung died the next afternoon, and Garrett—who had escaped the

❧❧❧

A SALUBRIOUS SALUTE

Lillie Coit never failed to celebrate Engine Company No. 5's birthday on October 17. It's said that in 1905, while on a horse trip in the Lebanon Mountains of what was then Palestine, she reined up her horse and drew a bottle of champagne from her saddlebags. The guides were sent higher up the peaks for some snow, and when the bubbly was sufficiently chilled, Lillie and other members of her party drank a toast to the Knickerbockers.

❧❧❧

night of the murder—was tracked down in an Oakland boardinghouse. During his trial, Garrett asked Lillie to give him a false alibi. When she refused, her relative swore that, upon his release from San Quentin prison, he would track her down wherever she was and put a bullet in her as he had in McClung.

Lillie appeared unshaken by this episode. After scanning a newspaper account of the shooting the next day, she reportedly flung the broadsheet angrily to the ground, complaining, "It says the shooting occurred in the apartment of 'a Mrs. Coit.' A Mrs. Coit, indeed!"

But Garrett's threat did in fact scare her, and she left San Francisco to tour the world, finally settling down for some years in Paris. Not until after 1923, when Garrett died in the Virginia mental institution to which he'd been remanded after serving only part of his term in California, did Lillie Coit move back to San Francisco, taking up residence at the St. Francis Hotel. Six years later, when she was 86, the wealthy former fire-chaser was placed in a sanitarium. She passed away there on July 22, 1929. Her funeral procession at Grace Cathedral two days later included 22 men from the San Francisco Fire Department, led by a troika of white-haired firemen from Lillie's heyday.

Even in the end, the former fire-company mascot showed her appreciation of San Francisco blaze-busters. Among her will's bequests were $50,000 for a monument to the city's gallant firefighters (the bronze statue of three firemen now prominent in Washington Square) and $100,000 that went to build Coit Memorial Tower, dedicated in 1932 atop Telegraph Hill. Lillie's most telling tribute, however, may have been the fact that when she was cremated, she was wearing the gold fire-helmet pin that had been given to her so many years ago by the brave men of Knickerbocker Engine Company No. 5.

ONCE MORE, WITH GUSTO

Lillie Coit died three years before the dedication of her Art Deco concrete column atop Telegraph Hill. But knowing how much "Firebelle Lil" would have liked to be part of that dedication ceremony, the city retrieved Knickerbocker Company No. 5's old engine, placed her black fire helmet atop it, and pulled the whole shebang up the hill in her honor.

CREATIVE TENSIONS

"It is an odd thing, but anyone who disappears is said to be seen in San Francisco. It must be a delightful city and possess all the attractions of the next world."

—Oscar Wilde

If Lola Montez's suggestive dancing flabbergasted some critics in Victorian-age San Francisco, it was nothing compared with the public shock over Adah Isaac Menken's simulated nudity in the 1864 production of Mazeppa, *or* The Wild Horse of the Tartary. *Adapted from a Byron poem, the play had a paper-thin plot concerning efforts by freedom-loving Tartars to escape the Poles who'd invaded their homeland. It had been performed periodically in San Francisco over the years, but always with a male lead. Menken— the Madonna of her time, famous nationally for her sex appeal and scandals—chose to play both*

☞

"ALWAYS NOTORIOUS, NEVER FAMOUS"

The concept of the dance was simple: a maiden blunders into a massive spiderweb and is soon covered by the furious, dangling creatures. But as executed by "Lola Montez, the Premier Spanish Ballerina," the infamous "Spider Dance" could send a houseful of lonely San Francisco miners into a dither. To the mounting rhythms of *La Tarantella*, Montez would pirouette and flail in an artful attempt to ward off the "spiders" (creations of cork and whalebone suspended by rubber) that sought to scurry down her arms and over her body. Finally breaking free of the web, she would begin extracting the imaginary arachnids from the folds of her costume, flattening each new capture beneath her heel. The extent of her searching depended on the enthusiasm of her viewers. As she hiked her skirts to locate a few spiders that had apparently scaled her legs, a unifying incantation would rumble its way forward from the back of the theater: "Higher! Higher!"

Lola Montez's Spider Dance was called "suggestive, lewd, and immoral." Not that this was of terrible concern to Lola. She'd made a career of being rebellious, promiscuous, and even violent. "A tigress," one newspaperman described her, "the very comet of her sex." "Wild and wayward, though never wicked," said Lola of her own life.

Her reputation preceded her to northern California, where she arrived in the summer of 1853 and caused an immediate sensation. "Her name," recorded *The Golden Era*, "has attracted . . . the most brilliant and overflowing audiences ever witnessed in this city. . . ." Stories were circulated about Montez's tragic marriages and frequent *affaires d'amour*. It was rumored that she had horsewhipped reviewers for their less-than-flattering assessments of her work and that she'd once rained fists down upon a manager who dared to leave her employ. Most of these tales were fabricated to enhance her box-office appeal, but some had a footing in truth. Even without benefit of hype, though, Lola's striking appearance and eccentricities were guaranteed to inspire curiosity. Men would rush out of San Francisco saloons just to see her sashay down the street, a cigar hugged in her teeth, a pair of greyhounds leashed at her side, and a large white cockatoo preening atop one shoulder.

SHE WAS SAID to be the illegitimate daughter of Lord Byron and to have spent a glorious girlhood among royalty in Seville, Spain. Actually, she was born around 1818 to English parents living in Ireland. Her real name was Marie Dolores Eliza Rosanna Gilbert, but she'd always been called Dolores, or Lola for short. "Montez" was a stage moniker meant to capitalize on her sultry Castilian features. The name also altered her character forever: as she grew more flamboyant and more Latin in temperament, she never wanted to be reminded that she had started life as Dolores Gilbert.

Lola began to shed her true identity in her early 20s. She was briefly married to a British army officer, Captain Thomas James, who abandoned her for a friend's wife. After this unfortunate experience, Lola turned her attention to the stages of London.

There was no reason, really, that she should have expected to succeed in the theater; Lola never was much of a dancer, and she demonstrated even less natural talent as an actress. Yet her beauty, combined with her spirit and audacity, opened doors that would have been closed to another woman. Eventually, she played the English capital, charmed Berlin, caused a mighty row in Warsaw, and was received at the glittering court of Czar Nicholas I in St. Petersburg.

Her touring introduced her to a rarefied cast of luminaries, everyone from Victor

principal roles, that of Mazeppa, an embittered Tartar girl, and Cassimir, the patriotic Tartar leader. As the tale concludes, Cassimir is captured, stripped, and tied to the back of a wild horse, then sent thundering off to his death in the mountains. What made Menken's version a hit was that, in this final scene, she wore a revealing flesh-colored body suit. "Her exhibitions," shrilled one California newspaper editor, "are immodest and overdrawn caricatures unfit for the public eye...." Yet, according to Samuel Dickson, when Mazeppa opened at Maguire's Opera House, "the enthusiasm of the audience was a mad frenzy never to be forgotten."

You can forgive San Franciscans of the late 19th century for their some-times limited grasp of the arts. After all, they were so busy trying to impress the rest of the world with what their money could buy, that they didn't always have time to learn what it was they were actually pay-ing for. A fine example of this came in the 1870s, when the Chamber of Commerce successfully sued the Wells Fargo express company for damaging a replica of the famous Venus de Milo. *It seems that the statue, shipped from France, had arrived at the San Francisco Art Institute* without arms.

Hugo to George Sand to Honoré de Balzac. For a time Lola shared her bed with the Hungarian composer Franz Liszt. In Paris, she fell hopelessly in love with a politically lib-eral editor of *La Presse*, Henri Dujarier, and determined to marry again. But before the nuptials could be arranged, Dujarier was killed in a duel (either over his politics or her honor—accounts differ). A distraught Mademoiselle Montez then quit France for Munich, in bucolic Bavaria, where she came to the attention of King Ludwig I. Though almost 30 years her senior, Ludwig was drawn to Lola's beauty and he proceeded to estab-lish her in a castle with twin royal titles: Countess of Landsfeld and Baroness of the Order of St. Theresa. He also made the mistake of accepting her political counsel. "Acting under her advice," said an 1858 account of her life that Lola adopted as her autobiography, "the king pledged himself to a course of steady improvement in the political freedom of the peo-ple." This was too much for the Bavarian aristocracy and the Jesuit clergy, who limned the new countess as "a fiend, a devil, a she-dragon." Even the poorer classes held her in contempt, and in 1848 they took to the streets, shouting, "Down with the whore! Down with the whore!" Lola had to flee to Switzerland disguised as a peasant girl. And not long after that, Ludwig, unrepentant but bowing to public pressure, abdicated in favor of his son, Maximilian II.

WHEN EUROPEAN NEWSPAPERS started vending tales about the riches of California's Mother Lode, the fugitive countess was living in Paris again—acting, beguil-ing sophisticates, and otherwise making the most of her status as the woman who'd helped bring down a king. She'd recently suffered the death of her second husband, a hand-some 20-year-old London heir named George Trafford Heald, whose meddlesome aunt had campaigned to have their marriage annulled on the basis that Lola had never properly divorced Captain James. The scandal blew over when it was discovered that

James had previously died in India. But Heald's spirits were down. He retreated to drink and to Portugal—not necessarily in that order—and though proof was inconclusive, suspicions ran rampant that his subsequent drowning in Lisbon harbor was a suicide rather than an accident.

Lola took this as her cue to move on, and in late 1851 she embarked on a lengthy theatrical tour of the United States, where she found she could complete the character transformation that she'd begun by changing her name. Americans didn't care whether she was really Irish or Spanish or even Lilliputian, as long as she remained a celebrity. Lola was enchanted, in turn, with her audiences, and by the time she reached her final scheduled stop at New Orleans, she was determined not to return to Europe. Instead, she sailed for the Golden Gate.

Montez knew next to nothing about San Francisco—except that it happened to be located not too far from Grass Valley, a town in the Sierra Nevadas where the Eureka Mine was located. At the height of the Gold Rush, when often-unscrupulous stock salesmen were plying the streets of Paris, Lola had been talked into taking a flier on the Eureka. Much to her surprise, it had paid off, and now she wanted to see the source of her rich dividends.

The "Spanish Ballerina" debuted at San Francisco's American Theater, on Sansome Street, in 1853, collecting mixed reviews for her acting but raves for her Spider Dance. As an added attraction, Lola would peel one silken garter down from her slender leg and toss it into the audience, causing a near-riot.

She soon left the Bay Area for the theaters of the Mother Lode, where she received praise from just about everyone. The most memorable dissenting opinion came from a reviewer for the Sacramento *Californian*, who charged that people attended

Montez's shows only because they held free tickets. Lola struck back in a letter filled with characteristic venom, denouncing the paper's editor for lying "in such a barefaced manner" and challenging him to a duel. "You may choose between my dueling pistols or take your choice of a pill-box. One [pill] shall be poison and the other not, and the chances are even." The editor chose (probably wisely) to ignore the challenge.

The last engagement on her mining-district itinerary that summer was at Grass Valley. It wasn't really much of a place, yet before long, Lola had decided it should be her new home. This came as quite a shock to her latest husband, Patrick Purdy Hull, a tall, witty, hard-drinking editor at the San Francisco *Whig*. Lola had met him during her ocean voyage to California, and they had been married at Mission Dolores only a few days after arriving in the Bay Area. Hull thought at first that she was kidding about settling in a frontier backwater like Grass Valley. But Montez was nothing if not mercurial, and so after a brief return to San Francisco, she and Hull took up residence in a newly furnished cottage on the town's Mill Road.

Lola naturally became the center of attention in Grass Valley. Local miners were so delighted with her presence that they named a high Sierra peak Mount Lola in her honor. Other male admirers came around with presents, including a grizzly-bear cub, which she received from an expatriate German baron and geologist, Dr. Karl Adler. Although most wives and preachers shunned her, they had little effect on her behavior.

In the end, the person most opposed to Lola's residency in the Sierras may have been Patrick Hull. The couple's fighting became a fertile source of gossip, and only two months after the newlyweds had settled in Grass Valley, the *Nevada Journal* noted that Montez had "applied to be divorced from the bonds of Hully wedlock." The application went uncontested.

RECOVERING FROM MATRIMONY and no longer performing, Lola stepped up her socializing in both San Francisco and Grass Valley. She was a gracious hostess, though her repartee was described by one listener as "scarcely above the level of pothouse [tavern] wit." To compensate for the applause that was now missing from her days, Lola surrounded herself with other comforts: a growing menagerie that at one point included her grizzly bear, four dogs, a monkey, a sheep, and parrots; a garden that she tended carefully; and, it's said, the earnest affections of Baron Adler. She even took up charity work, caring for wounded miners, carrying food to indigents, and arranging Christmas fêtes for the children of Grass Valley.

Approaching her fourth decade of life, however, Lola started to regret her retirement from the stage, fearing that her popularity in San Francisco and elsewhere was too ephemeral to last. As she later conceded, "I was always notorious; never famous." After Adler succumbed—as so many of her lovers did—to tragedy (he died in a hunting accident), Lola wondered how she could recapture the world's attention.

She never did. She arranged a long and costly series of engagements in southeastern Australia and tried to make comeback appearances in San Francisco, but failed to grab the headlines as she once had. People said she was a has-been. "Her dancing days are over," pronounced the *Daily Evening Bulletin*. "Though yet graceful in her posturing she does not display, nor is it to be expected at her age, that degree of elasticity and life which is required to maintain a high position as a danseuse." Hurt and angry, the impetuous Lola sold her Grass Valley property, auctioned off her jewels, and said goodbye to San Francisco in November 1856.

Although she lived more than four years longer, dying finally in January 1861, a victim of stroke and poverty in New York City, she never again set foot in the Bay Area.

PRIVATE PERFORMANCE

A persistent legend has it that Lola, upset by the castigations of a Grass Valley minister who had never even bothered to see her perform, showed up one evening on his doorstep in full costume. She then proceeded to give the pastor and his wife an energetic private dance, one that convinced them not only to cease their attacks but to strike up a friendship with this supposed "she-devil."

Perhaps as an acknowledgment of her despair or just to frustrate curiosity-seekers who might someday want to cast pity upon her grave (Lola hated pity), her headstone in Brooklyn's Green-Wood Cemetery gave her name not as Lola or even as Dolores, but obscurely as "Eliza Gilbert."

THE CALIFORNIA DIAMOND

Today, despite its prominent location (at the convergence of Market, Geary, and Kearny Streets), its height, and its age (the city accepted it as a gift way back in 1875), the rococo cast-iron landmark known as Lotta's Fountain rarely earns second glances from the many workers who pass it week in and week out. Discarded newspapers flap noisily at the pillar's base. Graffiti artists apply their signatures to the font's somewhat grim visage. Only on April 18, when the last survivors of San Francisco's 1906 earthquake and fire (some of them wearing period costumes) gather here annually in commemoration of the disaster, does this neglected street sculpture become the focus of anybody's attention.

Lotta Crabtree—after whom the monument is named—was a vivacious, red-headed comedienne who charmed the young San Francisco with her songs, her dancing, and her laugh. She went on to enchant other cities as well, but never forgot the place that had helped make her a child star right after the Gold Rush. When she became famous and wealthy, she had a fancy drinking fountain cast in Philadelphia and shipped all the way out to the Bay Area as a token of her enduring affection for this city.

It's that fountain that now squats at one of the busiest intersections along Market Street, dry and unappreciated—as forgotten, sadly, as Lotta herself.

THE FUTURE "California Diamond" or "California Pet," as she was variously called, was born Charlotte Mignon Crabtree in New York City in 1847. She came west with her mother, Mary Ann, in 1853. They were on the trail of Lotta's wayward father, John Ashworth Crabtree, who had been spectacularly unsuccessful in mining California gold but refused to leave the Mother Lode as long as he thought his luck might change.

Lotta and Mary Ann found San Francisco at the height of its first boomtown reverie. As a black-eyed moppet in a rough-edged town that claimed few women and still fewer cute little girls, Lotta was a welcome novelty and soon discovered she could draw a crowd. Samuel Dickson wrote that once, as Lotta and her mother rode in a carriage down the town's muddy avenues, "crude, rough-garbed, heavy-bearded, rum-soaked miners stopped and stared—and waved their hands to the child, and cheered. And Lotta played to her gallery. She reached out her tiny hands to the rough miners and laughed loud peals of childish laughter. . . ."

But San Francisco soon had to give up this precocious newcomer. Word came that John Crabtree had alighted in Grass Valley and planned to open a boardinghouse. Mary Ann was supposed to come immediately and run this enterprise while John pursued other get-rich-quick schemes. So Mary Ann and Lotta set off east on the final leg of their reunion journey.

As it happens, the Crabtrees moved in not far from the refurbished cabin on Mill Road where the infamous dancer Lola Montez, a.k.a. the Countess of Landsfeld, held court. It's said that one day, the curious Lotta wandered over to Montez's place, perhaps attracted by Lola's pet grizzly-bear cub, which lumbered about the cabin's front yard. There she found California's notorious Spider Dancer fluttering gaily through her garden. The two got along famously from the outset, and soon they were singing together, talking, and riding horseback. Grass Valley's sisterhood was shocked at this relationship, fearing for the child's very moral character. But after meeting Montez, Mary Ann Crabtree decided that Lotta was in good hands.

Debates have raged over whether the Countess actually taught Lotta to dance. One story says that Montez was not only responsible for Lotta's instruction but also for introducing her to the public stage . . . or rather, the public *anvil*, since it was a huge blacksmith's tool on which the aspiring artiste allegedly premiered, dancing a fandango for the enjoyment of some entertainment-starved miners, while Montez clapped out a rhythm. There are marked differences, however, between the Spanish choreography that characterized Lola's exhibitions and the Irish jigs for which Lotta became known. Regardless, Montez had ample opportunity to influence her young protégé.

It wasn't in Grass Valley, though, but in a remote mining village called Rabbit Creek, way up in Lassen County, that Lotta made her first significant bid for fame. John Crabtree had it on the best authority (naturally) that this remote gold-mining village was on the verge of greatness. He wanted in on the ground floor of that growth, and convinced Mary Ann once again to follow his lead.

Shortly after the Crabtrees moved to Rabbit Creek, 8-year-old Lotta was "discovered" by a man named Mart Taylor, a shoemaker, dancer, and musician who operated a log-cabin saloon-cum-theater for itinerant companies. This building doubled as a classroom for local children who, like Lotta, were interested in dance. But Lotta was no common student. She had an instinct for playing to an audience, and most important, she could do a neat jig. And she sang with a contagious delight.

One day, Lotta was invited to entertain the entire town of miners. Dressed in a long-tailed green coat and a tall green hat, Lotta gave her uneducated, unwashed audience a show such as they'd never seen. When Taylor's star pupil danced, the men clapped heartily. When she sang, and especially when she belted out her lachrymose closing number, they were transported by the quality of her maturing voice. And when she laughed, the towns-people all laughed with her. Lotta was a hit! She was also a budding financial success, as mother and daughter discovered when they collected the gold nuggets, silver Mexican coins, and $50 gold slug that had been tossed appreciatively at the girl's dainty feet.

NOW, MARY ANN CRABTREE was no fool. She knew that if Lotta could enchant one raw-edged mining burg, she might have the same good fortune at a string of similar places scattered up and down the Mother Lode. So in the spring of 1855, when John Crabtree suddenly decided to go off and investigate yet another pie-in-the-sky bonanza, she bundled up Lotta and they left town along with Taylor.

The prodigal performer sang and danced at every saloon, gambling den, and rude variety hall the troupers could reach by means of a buckboard. She jigged atop barrel heads, warbled on makeshift stages, and laughed every place she went. In time Lotta learned how to play the banjo, master steps from ballet, mimic voices, and engage in playful repartee. She became the darling of California. "The singing and dancing of little Lotta," one newspaper exclaimed, "was admirable and took our hearts by storm."

Twelve-year-old Lotta's San Francisco debut in 1859 lifted her to new heights of fame. Over the next five years, she kept up a rigorous schedule of appearances at her old Sierra haunts as well as on some newer stages closer to the Mexican border. But the Bay Area consumed more and more of her attention, and she accepted engagements at venues as diverse as the Barbary Coast's famous Bella Union, Robert Woodward's What Cheer

House, and The Willows amusement park. The town loved her ("Miss Lotta the Unapproachable," headlined one paper).

Lotta must have suffered a tremendous shock, then, when she made her first national tour. Gone was the comforting embrace of immediate recognition. In the South and Midwest, she was just one more traveling performer, struggling to make it. Not until 1867, when she finally rolled into Manhattan to star at Walleck's Theater in a trifle called *Little Nell and the Marchioness* (adapted from Charles Dickens' *The Old Curiosity Shop*), did the California Diamond finally regain her luster. And then there was no stopping her.

Having grown into a lovely woman with an extraordinary comic faculty, she wowed them in Boston and wooed them in Philadelphia. In San Francisco, which Lotta visited frequently even at the height of her East Coast success, her participation at the 1870 opening of William Ralston's giant new California Theater on Bush Street ensured that there wouldn't be a single empty seat. Although *Harper's Magazine* once called her a "minor actress," Lotta Crabtree proved herself to be much more than that, even in Shakespeare's London, where she appeared in a play called *Vitouche* in the early 1880s. "Wherever she went," explained popular historian Dickson, "she was the star, but a strange star, a generation ahead of her time. She ignored stage etiquette. She ad-libbed through her lines, rollicked through her lines, laughed and talked to the audience and, with every rule of the theater she broke, she made thousands of new friends."

BY HER RETIREMENT in 1891, Lotta had achieved a series of popular triumphs, including short vaudeville routines, blackface skits, and long-forgotten stage pieces such as *Heartsease*, a California play. Yet she had completely forsaken a private life for a public career. She had few close friends and despite a gallery of male admirers, she'd never married. She had become one of the richest and most famous actresses in the world, but the death of her mother and Lotta's departure from the limelight at the age of 44 left her a strangely solitary figure.

Although she lived for nine more years, San Francisco said its final goodbyes to the California Diamond in 1915. A celebration in her honor was held, appropriately, at Lotta's Fountain. Much of the town turned out to exalt the entertainer who had given them so much enjoyment. They thanked her with their speeches, with their cheers, and with their laughter, which had always been the chief coin of Lotta's realm. Longtime Lotta fans may have been clapping for a graying matron who stood beside the pillar she'd paid for on Market Street, but through the fog of fond memory, they could still see the red-haired young performer who had so charmed them in their youth.

Remember her the next time you stride by Lotta's Fountain, intent upon your daily business. Remember her and give that old cast-iron column a second glance. And a smile.

THE SAGEBRUSH SCRIBBLER

"I have always been rather better treated in San Francisco than I actually deserved."
—Mark Twain

San Franciscans knew of Mark Twain long before he set foot in town in the 1860s, for this city's *Daily Morning Call* often reprinted the prankish prose that Twain composed for Nevada's leading newspaper, the Virginia City *Territorial Enterprise*. He had also contributed some articles to that pioneering Bay Area literary weekly, *The Golden Era*. Yet Twain—the pseudonym, of course, for Samuel Clemens, the frowsy, loose-striding humorist from Hannibal, Missouri—wasn't at all sure that he cared to have fans in the Bear State. "These rotten, lop-eared, whopper-jawed, jack-legged . . . Californians," he grumbled in an early letter home from Nevada. "How I *hate* everything that looks, or tastes, or smells like California!" That, of course, was before he'd had the opportunity to explore the West Coast's largest city. Later, he would sing a distinctly different tune.

Clemens came west after the start of the Civil War, joining an older brother, Orion, whom President Lincoln had appointed as secretary to the governor of Nevada Territory. "I envied him the long, strange journey he was going to make," Clemens said later. "He would see buffaloes and Indians and deserts and have all kinds of adventure, and maybe get hanged or scalped and write home and tell us all about it."

Sam tried being his brother's private secretary for a while, but there was not much to do and he had little inclination to dock behind a desk, especially when all about him there were miners said to be striking it rich in silver. So for the next 2½ years, Clemens tried prospecting—an occupation at which he earned little. Finally coming to his senses in the summer of 1862, he forsook Nevada's desolate Washoe mining district to accept a $25-a-week job as a reporter for the *Territorial Enterprise*.

BY SOME ESTIMATES, Clemens penned as many as 3,000 pieces for the *Enterprise*—many of them pedestrian in nature, but some generously endowed with a brutal wit, guaranteed to anger pompous and church-going readers. Virginia City was a busy place, and he was one of only two reporters, covering everything from the Comstock silver diggings and stock values to theatrical performances, Indian affairs, and the large fire that blazed through the town in 1863. Additionally, he covered two sessions of the territorial legislature and was on hand for Nevada's constitutional convention.

Around this time, Clemens began writing under the pen name Mark Twain, the latest in a series of pseudonyms that he'd experimented with since the age of 16. It was as Twain that he first visited San Francisco in 1863, as a correspondent for the *Enterprise*. On three separate occasions that year, he traveled the more than 200 miles between Virginia City and San Francisco, and despite his initial reservations, in each instance he found the town more to his liking.

"I fell in love with the most cordial and sociable city in the Union," Twain remembered in *Roughing It*. "After the sage-brush and alkali deserts of Washoe, San Francisco was Paradise to me." Twain "lived like a lord" at the Lick House, from which he enjoyed convenient access to the town's half-dozen theaters, its numerous fine restaurants, and hundreds of saloons catering to all social calibers. There were nights when he didn't return to his hotel room till after midnight, there was so much to do, to view, to wonder over. He saw the actress Lotta Crabtree at Gilbert's Melodeon, side-tripped to Benicia and Oakland, and sat merrily through minstrel shows. In fact, he had so much fun that he was prone to neglect the dispatches he'd promised to the *Enterprise*, leading his editor to worry that his star writer would not return.

AT LEAST AS LATE as August 1863, Twain dismissed the idea that he might aspire to employment at some Bay Area daily. "No paper in the United States can afford to pay me what my place on the 'Enterprise' is worth," he explained in a letter to his family. "If I were not naturally a lazy, idle, good-for-nothing vagabond, I could make it pay me $20,000 a year. But I don't suppose I shall ever be any account. I lead an easy life, though. . . . Everybody knows me, and I fare like a prince whereever I go, be it on this side of the mountains or the other. And I am proud to say I am the most conceited ass in the Territory."

Yet Twain was getting spoiled by San Francisco, losing his appetite for the more austere pleasures of Virginia City. Few among his friends were surprised when, in May 1864, the author up and moved to the Golden Gate. Even the *Enterprise* took his departure with grace. Calling him the "Prince of Platitudes" and the "Profaner of Divinity," it joked that Mark Twain "will not be likely to shock the sensibilities of San Francisco long. The ordinances against nuisances are stringently enforced in that city."

Twain's first interest, though, wasn't in making trouble, but in making money. During his Nevada days, he'd socked away dollars in silver stocks, and he now expected to sell them at prices far in excess of what he'd paid. Unfortunately, the bottom fell out of the market even as he watched it closely from the sumptuous luxury of the Lick House and the Occidental Hotel. "The wreck was complete," Twain lamented. "The bubble scarcely left a microscopic moisture behind it. I was an early beggar and a thorough one."

Suddenly needing a job again, Twain turned to the *Morning Call*. Cheaper than its local competitors and full of sensationalistic copy, the *Call* wasn't much of a publication in Twain's estimation ("the washerwoman's paper," he scoffed). But his employment options were few, and so he became a *Call* reporter.

Twain usually took to newspaper work with vivacity. "Reporting," he once said, "is the best school in the world to get a knowledge of human beings, human nature, and human ways. . . . No other occupation brings a man into such familiar sociable relations with all grades and classes of people." But the drudgery of the *Call* was more than he could bear ("It was an awful slavery for a lazy man"). The most important compensation may have been that the *Call*'s offices were located next door to the old U.S. Mint, where Bret Harte was secretary to the superintendent. Harte, while about the same age as Twain, was then better established as a litterateur and gave the *Call* man some advice on his writing.

"He trimmed and trained and schooled me patiently," Twain explained, "until he changed me from an awkward utterer of coarse grotesqueness to a writer of paragraphs and chapters that have found a certain favor in the eyes of even some of the very decentest people in the land." Harte also brought him into a congenial and growing circle of local writers that included Ambrose Bierce, Ina Coolbrith, and Charles Warren Stoddard.

TWAIN SHOULDN'T REALLY have been surprised when, in October 1864, only four months after he'd begun with the *Call*, the publisher fired him. Still, he was devastated. Recalling his dismissal 45 years later, Twain wrote, "It was the only time in my life that I have ever been discharged, and it hurts yet . . ."

For the next two months, the broke and rudderless Twain's "sole occupation was avoiding acquaintances . . . ," he confessed. "I became very adept at slinking." He finally slinked clean out of town, retreating in December to a friend's cabin on Jackass Hill, near the Stanislaus River in Tuolumne County. There he resurrected his dreams of easy riches and spent a miserable three months pocket-mining for gold. He didn't find his fortune in the ground, but he did happen upon something of a bonanza in the nearby town of Angel's Camp. Trying to warm his rain-soaked bones around a fire at the Angel's Hotel, Twain is said to have been told about a frog that had been trained to jump but lost out in a frog-jumping contest because the owner of a rival hopper craftily loaded it down with shot. This tale would become the basis for one of Twain's most famous yarns, "The Celebrated Jumping Frog of Calaveras County," published (as "Jim Smiley and His Jumping Frog") in New York's *Saturday Press* in November 1865.

"Jumping Frog" brought Twain a national reputation for the first time, but it was no immediate cure for his impecunious circumstances. By the time the short story appeared, Twain had returned to San Francisco and was busily submitting material to

EYE OF THE BEHOLDER

Some of Mark Twain's observations on mid-19th century San Francisco were priceless. Commenting impertinently on the fine style with which a woman attending a high-class ball blew her nose, he wrote that her manner "marked her as a cultivated and accomplished woman of the world; its exquisitely modulated tone excited the admiration of all who had the happiness to hear it." He offered an assessment of hoop skirts, in which he concluded that "To critically examine these hoops — to get the best effect — one should stand on the corner of Montgomery and look up a steep street like Clay or

☞

Washington....It reminds me of how I used to peep under circus tents when I was a boy and see a lot of mysterious legs tripping about with no visible bodies attached to them." And he attacked the San Francisco police, whom he cast as corrupt and stupid. One of his most merciless satires concerned a man who was arrested for stealing 75 cents worth of flour sacks and for it, was heaved into a cell, where he soon passed away. None of the coppers paid the slightest bit of attention to their prisoner, Twain observed; if they noticed him at all, they probably thought he was just "sleeping with that calm serenity which is peculiar to men whose heads have been caved in with a club."

journals as varied as *The Golden Era*, the *Sacramento Union*, and the *Daily Dramatic Chronicle* (precursor to the *San Francisco Chronicle*). He also agreed to contribute regular letters on San Francisco to the *Territorial Enterprise*. Released from daily deadlines, he could cast his jaundiced eye over everything from politicians and prizefighters to theater critics and spiritualists. He produced an oeuvre of parody, burlesque, humorous philosophizing, and comic fantasy that reveals 1860s San Francisco in all its earnest, anxious, and unctuous glory. He had a remarkable ear for the language of common folk, and in his exaggeration of the quirks of local culture, he focused on details that most people would have missed altogether.

If not for the humor he brought to his disquisitions, Twain might well have been elevated to a hangman's noose rather than an honored pundit's pedestal. But his fate in life, he commented with mock shame, was "to excite the laughter of God's creatures."

After 1866, however, he no longer restricted his observations to the printed page. Twain took to the lecture stage at San Francisco in October 1866, preceded by advertising fliers that promised: "Doors Open at 7 O'Clock. The Trouble Will Begin at 8." The house was sold out, and Twain thereafter took his Victorian stand-up routine on tour throughout northern California and Nevada.

This was the beginning of his second and parallel career, one for which he isn't as well known now, but one that saved him more than once from the black hole of poverty. Twain's style had always been more like storytelling than traditional journalism anyway, and so it translated well to oratory. Twain wasn't a comedian; he was a humorist with an edge of wisdom, who kept his listeners entertained through half-cynical remarks about the conventionalities of life ("Golf is a good walk, spoiled"), wry advice ("Write without pay until somebody offers pay; if nobody offers within three years, sawing wood is what you were intended for"), literary criticism ("War talk by men who have been in a war is interesting," he said about poetry, "but moon talk by a poet who has not been in the moon is dull"), and even the occasional barb directed at himself (after receiving a doctoral degree from Oxford University in 1907, he said, "I don't know why they should give me a degree like that. I never doctored any literature. I wouldn't know how"). Sharing these gifts with audiences, he became one of America's favorite characters.

IT WASN'T LONG AFTER that first lecture that Twain left San Francisco. It's interesting to note how little this city appears in any of his work; Twain drew delight from the metropolitan life, but most of his inspiration came from more rural sources. Yet his connections with San Francisco were never really broken. As critic Bernard De Voto wrote, "All the rest of Mark Twain's books are embryonic in what he had written by December, 1866, when he went east. These casual pieces outline the future: the humorist, the social satirist, the pessimist, cynical, angry, and depressed, all are here. The rest is only development."

PROMISE UNKEPT

Bret Harte's witty, sometimes heart-rending tales of frontier California earned him acclaim during the 1860s as the "new prophet of American letters." Eastern magazines courted him for submissions, no less a critic than San Francisco's own Ambrose Bierce called his humor "incomparable," and the highlights of Harte's oeuvre—

from "The Luck of Roaring Camp" to "The Outcasts of Poker Flat" and "Mliss"—helped establish the foundations of Western American fiction.

Some of his San Francisco colleagues must have found it comical to hear this writer identified as "the voice of the West," for despite legends that have eddied up around Harte (it has been said that he once fought Indians and later battled bandits as an expressman—probably both untrue), he was really a dude, something of a snob, a city boy all the way down to his clean socks. He wrote about miners, yet his firsthand experience with mining was very limited. He described the travails of prostitutes and gamblers and other undesirables, yet he hankered after a life of genteel clubs and hansom cabs. Other San Francisco writers had experienced the hardships of a Western existence; Harte crafted his fiction from secondhand gleanings. He spent eight years in the Bay Area listening to men who'd journeyed to and from gold diggings, worked riverboats or stagecoaches—always trying to catch the tenor of their speech and the atmosphere of their lives so that when he finally sat down to pen a Western narrative, he wouldn't have to depend exclusively on his imagination.

But to most of his readers it didn't matter that Bret Harte romanticized this part of the country. Americans were anxious in his time to believe stories about miners with deep-seated soft spots and whores with hearts of gold. Harte was in the business of making legends; he was an aspiring Homer of the gold camps. And for the 17 years of his San Francisco residency, there were few others to rival him.

HE FOLLOWED HIS mother from New York to Oakland in 1854. He was known as Francis Brett Harte at birth (only after he took up a career as a scribe did Harte become known by his middle name, dropping its second *t*). Harte had no clear idea of what he might accomplish in California. He tried working for an East Bay apothecary and doing some tutoring, but it wasn't until he moved with a married sister to Humboldt County, on the coast near Oregon's border, that he discovered his true calling.

He obtained his first writing job at a newspaper called the *Northern Californian*, in the town of Union (now Arcata), north of Eureka. The pay was paltry and the hours long. Harte would probably have made more money fishing off Humboldt Bay or mining in the Trinity River district. Yet he kept at it, free-lancing some poetry and romantic prose to East Coast magazines as well as to San Francisco's venerable *Golden Era*. At the close of 1857, when Harte was just 21 years old, he decided to devote his life to the printed page, no matter what the cost.

The cost became pretty clear three years later when he made the mistake of taking the Indians' side in his *Northern Californian* report on the notorious Gunther's Island Massacre, during which some 60 peaceable Native Americans living near Arcata were slaughtered by whites. In response, Harte's neighbors angrily ran the young journalist out of town. This wasn't exactly an auspicious start to the career of a man who wanted freedom in what he chose to write, but at least it forced him out of the backwoods and into the city, where his talents would be more sorely tested and his style would more quickly mature.

San Francisco took him in. He went to work as a typesetter at *The Golden Era*, but it wasn't long before he was also regularly contributing stories, signing himself "Bret" or "The Bohemian." More than a hundred of his tales, essays, and sketches were featured in the *Era* over the next three years, including his half-tongue-in-cheek proposals for a new California order of bohemianism, based on writers and artists becoming nature-worshipping apostates. (Crazy as it sounds, that later became the starting point for this city's still-extant Bohemian Club.)

The *Era* gig was valuable not only because that weekly happened to be well read by people who were well-read, but also because it gave Harte contacts among San Francisco's rapidly growing literati. Its downside was that it paid bread-and-water wages. So in 1861, when Jessie Benton Frémont, author (*Far West Sketches*, *A Year of American Travel*) and wife of explorer-turned-politician John C. Frémont, helped Harte secure an appointment as clerk with the local surveyor-general, he could hardly get out of the *Era*'s offices fast enough. Two years later, he moved up to the San Francisco branch of the U.S. Mint, where he served for six years as the superintendent's secretary.

WORKING AT THE MINT was ideal for Bret Harte, since his responsibilities were minimal and rote. It left him time to start a family, which he did with his marriage to a New York woman, Anna Griswold, in August 1862. It also allowed him many free hours with his pen, without the anxiety of trying to live off what he could publish. Harte became an avid supporter of Abraham Lincoln and the pro-Union cause, creating some poems that were intended to stir patriotic fervor among his California readership. After 1864 he submitted many more of his musings to *The Californian*, an eclectic but sophisticated competitor of the *Era* that serialized novels, featured satire and articles on fashion, and covered a broad spectrum of eyebrow-raising phenomena, from hauntings to vampires to Haitian voodoo. Harte's contributions were more earthbound than some in *The Californian*, mostly wry essays ("Neighborhoods I Have Moved From; by a Hypochondriac") and parodies.

Harte made a name for himself as an editor in 1865, when he assembled California's first poetry anthology. Unfortunately, the act practically destroyed his reputation as a critic of verse. The idea for *Outcroppings* came from Anton Roman, a shy, rather owlish Bavarian publisher and book dealer whose San Francisco shop was considered fashionable. Since the city was sprouting more and more bards and would-be rhymers, Roman proposed to Harte that he collect some of their work between book covers. It seemed an

⚜

WHEN EGOS COLLIDE

Mark Twain's recollections provide a not-always-complimentary portrait of Bret Harte. Initially impressed with the former New Yorker, and thankful for his help in polishing up his prose, it wasn't long before Twain came to describe him as "one of the pleasantest men I ever knew — as well as one of the unpleasantest." After another decade, Harte's sarcastic, cold, and impatient manner wore their friendship down to a mean nub. The final straw was his difficult association with Harte in

☞

innocent enough project, and resulted in a volume containing 42 selections by 19 authors, plus a rather skeptical introduction by Harte. But the response was immediate—and overwhelmingly negative. Virginia City's *Territorial Enterprise* labeled *Outcroppings* a "feeble collection of drivel," while the San Francisco *News Letter* reported that "the 'country poets' were in a state of fearful excitement. Yesterday it was rumored that three to four hundred of these were coming down on the Sacramento boat in a 'fine phrensy' and swearing dire vengeance upon Harte." While he was spared the indignity of being run out of town again, Harte was notably excluded from a second compilation of local poetry, published several months after *Outcroppings*.

Harte could slough off such slights, for he was indisputably now one of the old men of San Francisco letters—even though he was only 31 years old. He was sought out for advice by other writers, including a rangy newspaperman who went by the name "Mark Twain." Harte's power in literary circles was confirmed in 1868, when he was installed as editor of San Francisco's newest journal, *The Overland Monthly*. Again, this was a brainchild of Anton Roman, who envisioned a publication less high-toned than *The Californian* and more concerned with the 31st state than with the balance of the world. Partly through Roman's influence, partly because of Harte's contacts, the magazine had access to a wealth of excellent prose. It featured Bierce's first short story, "The Haunted Valley," Swiss naturalist Louis Agassiz's reports on the animal kingdom, and other submissions from John Muir, Joaquin Miller, and even General William T. Sherman.

"The Luck of Roaring Camp" appeared in the second issue of *The Overland Monthly* and earned Bret Harte an audience well beyond the Rocky Mountains. "Luck" is the heavily romanticized tale of an infant boy, the progeny of a mining-camp prostitute, and how he brings out the redemptive virtues in even the most grizzled of gold-seeking veterans.

writing the unsuccessful play Ah Sin. *In his memoirs, Twain described Harte as "incapable of emotion, for I think he had nothing to feel with. I think his heart was merely a pump and had no other function...." For Twain, whose emotions often helped define him as a character, Harte was enigmatic and something of a phony. "He said to me once with a cynical chuckle that he thought he had mastered the art of pumping up the tear of sensibility," Twain explained. "The idea conveyed was that the tear of sensibility was oil, and that by luck he had struck it."*

BARD OF THE SIERRAS

When penmeister Bret Harte
descended on merry old England, he
went dressed in gentleman's attire,
though his stories about life on the
Mother Lode had led many people to
expect someone much more rustic.
When Harte's contemporary, the
poet Joaquin Miller, made that same
pilgrimage, he affected flamboyant
frontier garb, complete with spurs
and a bearskin thrown casually over
one shoulder. This was somewhat
more than artifice alone, but less
than the truth. Miller accused Harte,
whom he never did like, of misleading
people with his romanticized portray-
als of mining camp life. Of the two of

☞

Harte's fictional formula here, combining sentiment, pathos, and ironic humor, carried the strong scent of his literary inspirator, Charles Dickens—but it was Dickens transported to the wildest of settings, unfamiliar and appealing especially to readers in the East. He duplicated this yarn-spinning formula over and over again, yet readers never tired of it. In fact, his work became so popular that many young writers sought to emulate its "local color" style, importing traditional characters and situations to their own novel settings. You can still find some of Harte's motifs in novels by contemporary Western writers.

IN 1870, BRET HARTE published a humorous poem called "Plain Language from Truthful James" (better known as "The Heathen Chinee"). While he didn't think much of the work, many Westerners embraced it for its implicit condemnation of cheap Chinese labor, and the rest of the English-speaking world loved it merely for its exoticism. It boosted sales for Harte's book *The Luck of Roaring Camp and Other Sketches*, and it convinced the author that he was finally ready to take on the New York publishing world. He left San Francisco for the East on February 2, 1871.

Manhattan writers who had expected to welcome into their ranks a sweaty frontiersman wearing red long-johns and carrying a saddle over his shoulder must have been disappointed to shake hands with the foppish, well-spoken Harte. But appearances aside, *Atlantic Monthly* magazine was confident that this Californian had the stuff of greatness, and its Boston editors wanted it all. They offered Harte a whopping $10,000 for a year's worth of writing, at least 12 contributions. It was enough to set up Harte, his wife, and their four children in high clover.

Unfortunately, while he satisfied his contract with the *Atlantic*, the quality of his work didn't satisfy the editors. There was no talk of renewing Harte's contract, and he was left to make do as best he could in the crowded East Coast free-lance market. He struggled through a mediocre novel, *Gabriel Conroy* (1876), and composed two plays, including *Ah Sin*, which he wrote in 1877 with Mark Twain (and which bombed at the box office). Careless about money, he and Anna frittered it away. He tried to recoup his fortune by embarking on extensive lecture tours, but didn't like the long hours or the lousy pay, and gave it up.

Desperate, he accepted a consulate position in Prussia and sailed for Europe in June 1878, leaving his wife and children behind. He never again set foot in America. But in the 1880s, he did return to California—at least in mind. Living in London, where his reputation was still good, he locked himself away in a flat and, crippled by neuralgia and a chronic painful throat, tried to revisit the themes and Western characters that had briefly made him a household name. "I grind out the old tunes on the old organ and gather up the coppers," he lamented. It was a depressing task and an unsuccessful one. Harte had used up his best ideas by his 40th birthday. He died of throat cancer 25 years later, in the spring of 1902, after writing only two paragraphs of what he claimed would be his best story yet.

THE TOWN CRIER

Of all the curmudgeons San Francisco has produced, perhaps none can rival journalist Ambrose Gwinett Bierce, a man who seemed to hold contempt for just about everything and everybody in his late 19th-century world. He didn't like money . . . or businesses that made money . . . or the literature of his day . . . or religion . . . or teetotalers . . . or the forty-niners . . . or dogs (which he considered the most lunatic of

them, Miller contended, he was certainly the truer child of the West. Hadn't he fought Modoc Indians in his youth and escaped stage robbers? Hadn't he lived with horse thieves and amongst miners? Miller contended that he was congenitally more able than Harte ever would be to tell about life on the Pacific Slope.

Harte refused to engage in a feud, but he did make one comment that probably reflected the cynicism of many California writers who had been treated to Miller's increasingly farfetched accounts of his life. "Joaquin Miller," intoned Harte, "is the greatest liar the world has ever known."

God's creatures). Bierce even frowned mightily upon himself at times, not being satisfied with the quality of his writing or his place in the local and national power structures.

He had a low opinion of war, of peace, of Wall Street, of politics ("The conduct of public affairs for private advantage"), and even of barometers ("An ingenious instrument which indicates what kind of weather we are having"). He harbored a special antipathy toward women. "Her babies and her visitors are about her only society," Bierce once wrote of the so-called fair sex. "And though the former are usually a source of delight, and the latter of annoyance, neither is particularly well calculated to give her broad views or mental culture." Fortunately for Bierce, women seemed to forgive him his misguided opinions, and because he was handsome and well read, they flocked to his side.

For some reason, newspaper editors were convinced that a man so liberally endowed with distrust, one who defined a cynic admiringly as "a blackguard whose faulty vision sees things as they are, not as they ought to be," would make an ideal social critic. At least in Bierce's case, they were right.

HIS SKEPTICISM WAS long-standing, born of a difficult youth. Ambrose Bierce was reared on an Ohio farm, the youngest among a brood of 10 children whose names all began with the letter A. He had to pull his own weight from the moment it was possible, and there wasn't time left over for proper schooling. When the Confederate Army started shelling Fort Sumter in 1861, Bierce—then 18 years old—was the second man in line to enlist for Union Army duty. The bloody horrors of the Civil War eventually made him sick and angry, and he came to doubt both the intelligence and honor of men. Yet he acquitted himself valiantly in battle and remained in the military until he no longer saw room for advancement. Then he lit out for San Francisco, where his brother Albert was working at the U.S. Mint.

Clerking at the mint provided secure employment, but of course Bierce lacked the single characteristic that might have kept him at that job—an interest in money. He was interested, however, in writing and, during his slow hours at the mint, he could be found penning caustic verse, some of which found its way into *The Californian*, *The Argonaut*, and *The Overland Monthly*.

His true flowering as a writer came when he was named editor of Frederick Marriott's *News Letter*, an exuberant weekly that specialized in exposing San Francisco quackery. There Bierce introduced "Prattle," his dustbin column of biases and blasphemies, gossip and satire, and attacks on grafters, the Big Four, and whatever other societal vermin he perceived. He specialized in wit—but wit of a much more poisonous variety than had dripped from Mark Twain's pen. It wasn't long before he had to defend himself against offended readers. Samuel Dickson tells of one gentleman whose mention in "Prattle" caused him to rebuke Bierce as a "drunken scoundrel" and threaten to kill him on sight. The columnist seemed unconcerned at charges of intemperance (it was said that no man could buy Ambrose Bierce the last drink), but he bridled at some intellectual pismire calling him a "scoundrel." Bierce announced in print that he would appear outside his challenger's business on a specified day, at a certain time—a convenient target, though probably not an unarmed one. The rattled reader never appeared. In fact, it's said he left town—permanently.

Bierce also felt the need to escape San Francisco. This self-proclaimed town crier had deliberately set himself apart and a little bit above the rabble; as a result, he eventually came to feel somewhat alienated. He had also developed a distinct abhorrence for journalism (a "low and rotten" livelihood) and for almost all local practitioners of the trade. (Bierce once proclaimed his intention to "purify journalism in this town by instructing such writers as it is worth while to instruct, and assassinating those that it is not.") On top of all that, his

❦

health was declining. Asthma had soured his lungs, and he claimed that San Francisco's dampness left him a near-invalid.

He left for London in 1872, shortly after publishing his first short story in *The Overland Monthly* and marrying a local woman, Mary Day. England provided a gay old time for Bierce, whose editorial barbs had received almost as much attention there as they had in California. He became the toast of the town, invited to all the right parties by all the right people, lionized as he never had been in San Francisco. This public attention finally became too much for Mary Bierce, and she fled with the couple's two young children. But her husband stayed four years on the other side of the Atlantic, honing his satirical style for the popular magazines *Fun* and *Figaro*, carousing with American expatriates and European bohemians, and publishing three collections of his bitterly humorous sketches under the odd pseudonym "Dod Grile." He also came to believe that all things British were superior to anything America could hope to produce.

It was with no minor displeasure then, that in 1876 he returned to San Francisco, where he commenced a decade of writing for and editing the *Argonaut* and then the satirical *Wasp*. Colleagues began calling him "Bitter Bierce."

THE CREST OF BOTH his creativity and arrogance came after William Randolph Hearst hired him to write "Prattle" for the Sunday *Examiner*. Bierce used the column as a private pulpit. His premiere philippic first insulted the rival *Bulletin*'s art critic ("a smirking idiot") and then went on to attack the annual Western Art Show. "While always detestable," Bierce wrote, the latest show represented "a shining pinnacle of badness. The pictures next year will necessarily be better than the pictures of this, but alas, there may be more of them." In later columns, he opened wide the floodgates of his bile to cover everything from Jack London's socialism to bureaucrats to nature poetry.

In 1896, Hearst sent Bierce to Washington, D.C., where he expected the San Franciscan would stir up a hornet's nest. He wasn't disappointed. Publisher and columnist shared an enmity for the monolithic Southern Pacific Railroad, and when Collis P. Huntington proposed that Congress should forgive his company's obligation to repay tens of millions of dollars in government loans, Bierce lunged like a pit bull. He called Huntington a liar and a cheat and more. The Southern Pacific's position was already under heavy assault from Adolph Sutro and other California populists; Huntington couldn't afford journalistic broadsides. So he tried to silence Bierce—but in the dumbest way imaginable: through bribery. "Well, name your price," Huntington is supposed to have said. "Every man has his price." Bierce retorted that his price was precisely the amount that the Southern Pacific owed to the government, and that Huntington should make his check payable directly to the Treasury.

Bierce was on a writing roll, composing not only scathing political commentary and satirical essays, but also poems, ghost stories, and tales of war. It was with his publication of *The Devil's Dictionary* in 1906, however, that he made his most lasting literary mark. Fine examples of his sardonic wit were found on every page, from his definition of destiny ("A tyrant's authority for crime and a fool's excuse for failure") to those of history ("An account mostly false, of events most unimportant, which are brought about by rulers mostly knaves, and soldiers mostly fools") and mayonnaise ("One of the sauces which serves the French in place of a state religion"). Other authors have since tried to build upon Bierce's efforts with this volume, but they have never duplicated the original's consistent drollery.

For his many detractors, *The Devil's Dictionary* only confirmed that Bierce was, as Upton Sinclair phrased it, "a great writer, a bitter black sinner, and a cruel, domineering bigot." However, his friends—what few Bierce allowed into his circle—saw another side of the author. His two sons had died tragically, his wife Mary finally left him, and he was thereafter consumed by depression and drink. At the height of his local notoriety, he was periodically found in the lowest of all places—the gutter. He became a caricature of his former self, railing against injustice from the oracle of a barstool. Trying to restore his reputation, he edited 12 volumes of his collected writings, but the venture proved unprofitable to both Bierce and his publisher.

And so, at age 71, Ambrose Bierce decided to leave San Francisco and ride south into the barrens of northern Mexico. Some people said he'd gone to enlist in the revolutionary army of Francisco "Pancho" Villa. More likely, he just couldn't stomach the idea of perishing in obscurity. "Goodbye," he wrote in one of his last letters home. "If you hear of my being stood up against a Mexican stone wall and shot to rags, please know that I think it a pretty good way to depart this life. It beats old age, disease, or falling down the cellar stairs. To be a Gringo in Mexico—ah, that is euthanasia."

Altrocchi, Julia Cooley. *The Spectacular San Franciscans*. E. P. Dutton and Company, New York, 1949.

Bean, Walton. *Boss Ruef's San Francisco: The Story of the Labor Union Party, Big Business, and Graft Prosecution*. University of California Press, Berkeley, 1952.

Bruce, J. Campbell. *Escape from Alcatraz*. Ballantine/Comstock, New York, 1974.

Dickensheet, Dean W., editor. *Great Crimes of San Francisco: True Tales of Intrigue by the Bay*. Comstock, Sausalito, 1981.

Dillon, Richard H. *Fool's Gold: The Decline and Fall of Captain John Sutter of California*. Coward-McCann, New York, 1967.

_____. *The Hatchet Men*. Comstock/Ballantine, New York, 1962.

Dickson, Samuel. *Tales of San Francisco* (combining *San Francisco Is Your Home, San Francisco Kaleidoscope*, and *The Streets of San Francisco*). Stanford University Press, Stanford, 1957.

Foley, Doris. *Lola Montez: The Divine Eccentric*. Ballantine/Comstock, New York, 1973.

Gentry, Curt. *The Madams of San Francisco*. Ballantine/Comstock, New York, 1971.

Holridge, Helen. *Mammy Pleasant*. Ballantine/Comstock, New York, 1972.

Jackson, Joseph Henry. *Bad Company*. University of Nebraska Press, Lincoln, 1977.

Lamott, Kenneth. *Who Killed Mr. Crittenden?* Ballantine/Comstock, New York, 1973.

Lane, Allen Stanley. *Emperor Norton: Mad Monarch of America*. Caxton Printers, Ltd., Caldwell, Idaho, 1939.

Lavender, David. *Nothing Seemed Impossible: William C. Ralston and Early San Francisco*. American West, Palo Alto, 1975.

Lewis, Oscar, and Hall, Carroll D. *Bonanza Inn*. Ballantine/Comstock, New York, 1971.

Lloyd, B. E. *Lights and Shades in San Francisco*. A.L. Bancroft Company, San Francisco, 1876.

O'Brien, Robert. *This Is San Francisco*. Nourse Publishing, San Carlos, 1948.

Reinhardt, Richard. "Inside Alcatraz." *San Francisco Focus*, December 1987, 74–80, 124–133.

Siefkin, David. *The City at the End of the Rainbow: San Francisco and Its Grand Hotels*. G. P. Putnam, New York, 1976.

Stewart, George R. *Committee of Vigilance: Revolution in San Francisco, 1851*. Ballantine/Comstock, New York, 1971.

Thomas, Gordon, and Witts, Max Morgan. *The San Francisco Earthquake*. Dell, New York, 1971.

Watkins, T. H., and Olmsted, R. R. *Mirror of the Dream: An Illustrated History of San Francisco*. Scrimshaw Press, San Francisco, 1976.

SELECTED REFERENCES

INDEX

E–G

T–Z

"[San Francisco] is a moral penal colony. It is the worst of all the Sodom and Gomorrahs in our modern world....It is the paradise of ignorance, anarchy, and general yellow-ness....It needs more than all else a steady trade wind of grape-shot."
—Ambrose Bierce

"By George, this is a wonderful city, and the air is wonderfully invigorating. By George, it's simply great!"—Theodore Roosevelt

"San Francisco is a money-rattling city of nouveaux riches, a panorama of swells who dress to show themselves, feeding their vulgar desire to be seen....These are the mediocre people who will sink into oblivion within a few years."—Martha Hitchcock, mother of Lillie Hitchcock Coit

"You wouldn't think that such a place as San Francisco could exist. The wonderful sunlight there, the hills, the great bridges, the Pacific at your shoes. Beautiful Chinatown. Every race in the world."
—Dylan Thomas

"This is every misfit's favorite city."
—Reg Murphy, former *San Francisco Examiner* editor

"San Francisco is the genius of American cities. It is the wild-eyed, all-fired, hard-boiled, tender-hearted, white-haired boy o f the American family of cities. It is the prodigal son....It seems delirious with energy, incoherent because of the many things it has to say, broken-hearted with sorrowful memories. You walk through the streets of the city and feel its loneliness, and you wonder what memory is troubling its heart."
—William Saroyan

"God took the beauty of the Bay of Naples, the Swiss Alps, the Hudson River Valley, rolled them into one and made San Francisco Bay."—Fiorello La Guardia, former mayor of New York City

"There is almost nothing to see in San Francisco that is worth seeing."
—Anthony Trollope

FAMOUS LAST WORDS

ABOUT THE AUTHOR

J. Kingston Pierce, a longtime magazine editor in the Pacific Northwest,
is now a contributing editor of San Francisco Focus *and* Seattle *magazines.*
He's also written for Travel & Leisure, People, Metropolitan Home,
the San Francisco Chronicle, *and many other publications.*
Pierce says that, if he could, he'd gladly trade his life
today for the chance to be a gambler
on the old Barbary Coast.